STICKY DOGS AND STARDUST

First published by Fairfield Books in 2023

fairfield books

Fairfield Books
Bedser Stand
Kia Oval
London
SE11 5SS

Typeset in Garamond and Proxima Nova
Typesetting by Rob Whitehouse

© 2023 Scott Oliver
ISBN 978-1-915237-26-2

A CIP catalogue record for is available from the British Library

Printed by CPI Group (UK) Ltd

STICKY DOGS AND STARDUST

SCOTT OLIVER

fairfield books

4

For everyone who had faith. Thank you.

Contents

PART 2

Introduction

No other sport offers up stories quite like the ones collected in these pages. Only cricket – and especially the club cricket of England and the British Isles – allows recreational players to rub shoulders with international stars and even superstars in a fully competitive context, providing them with some of the most cherished memories of their lives.

I suspect that the majority of readers understand the reasons for this. Primarily, the fact that the English summer does not (or perhaps, *did* not) coincide with the cricket seasons elsewhere in the sport's traditional lands, along with the rules barring overseas players from the county game until 1968. The northern hemisphere summer thus provided very good international players with an opportunity to top up their usually meagre earnings, while well-run clubs, particularly in the north of England, could sprinkle a little glamour on their weekend fayre. With leisure options relatively limited compared to today's Garden of Earthly Delights, the crowds turned up in droves, the takings helping fund the substantial salaries of ever more glamourous recruits. When Learie Constantine was pro at Nelson in the Lancashire League between 1929 and 1937, he is reputed to have been the world's highest paid athlete.

The golden age of this type of story has now passed. Again, the reasons are obvious. Chief among them is the earning power of top players, both from central contracts and on the franchise Twenty20 circuit, as well as the fact that international and franchise schedules increasingly impinge upon the UK summer.

These stories are not entirely obsolete, however, although they will invariably involve players taking their first steps on the road to superstardom, *future stars* before they became household names. There are several of these in the book. Other chapters concern players in the twilight of their careers, if not *former stars* then certainly with their highest peaks behind them – although these stories, too, given the retirement pot that aforementioned earning power provides, are approaching obsolescence (not entirely, of course, for some people just need to scratch the cricketing itch). And between the springtime babysteps and the autumnal last knockings, there are a clutch of chapters involving cricketers in their high-summer pomp, living legends treading the league cricket boards. Most of the stories in this volume are indisputable all-time greats of the game (five of the Wisden All-Time XI, six of ESPNcricinfo's). Those that fail to meet that lofty designation are nevertheless *bona fide* superstars, although perhaps only in the white-ball game. Either way, the stories merit inclusion. And the stories are king.

The seeds for my fascination with these tales of overseas pros were doubtless planted when I was a 10- or 11-year-old scorer for Little Stoke, my father's team, and after that a 12 to 14-year-old mooching spectator when he moved to Leycett, half-watching him play against the likes of Vanburn Holder, Dilip Doshi and Ravi Ratnayeke. I would also pop down to Stone, my hometown club, and marvel at the 46-year-old Sid Owen standing up to Joey Benjamin – Kittitian by birth, though Dudley raised. Thereafter, I would collect my own direct experiences, starting out in first-team cricket for Moddershall in 1989, the club's final year in the North Staffordshire and District League, and then on through the 1990s and 2000s as we became an established club in the North Staffordshire and South Cheshire League. I would estimate having played against at least 50 international cricketers (teammates would tell you that, in the early says they could always tell you who the opposing pro was because I'd have buttonholed them in the bar), and a couple of these experiences are in the pages that follow.

So, these magical stories are unique to cricket. Moreover, notwithstanding the odd essay here and there, and various morsels in books such as Harry Pearson's *Slipless in Settle*, as far as I am aware no one has endeavoured to collect them in one place. This has become something of a mission of mine, with this the first despatch.

How that mission came to be so probably originates with early encounters with the brilliant Lancashire League website – back when far too many weeks seemed to involve trying to find a serviceable sub-pro, only later as a cricket writer of sorts – on which there is more or less a full archive of scorecards dating back to the pre-WWI years. In the optimal scenario, scorecards constitute a sturdy scaffolding for the narrative, an opportunity to see whether, beyond the simple fact that it is a famous player, there is a natural storyline. The first one was Vivian Richards, for ESPNcricinfo, and thereafter – without much rhyme or reason, as a freelancer looking for a payday – I pulled together the stories of a few other famous one-time Lancashire League pros, perhaps the most storied of all the country's leagues in this regard.

Over the next few years, I went in search of others, from beyond the Lancashire League. It soon became apparent that I was heading deep into an online informational desert, with the odd notable exception. A couple of leagues – or often, just individual clubs – had uploaded old scorecards to the cricketarchive website, and a couple more had lovingly-built if slightly unwieldy old websites with a mine of interesting facts on them, but not an archive of scorecards. In the absence of this, two of the stories were enormously aided by the sterling efforts of Rob Kilvington at Greenmount CC and Bobby Cross at Heywood CC, who scanned entire scorebooks for me. Where this wasn't possible, either the stories became primarily based on reminiscences or I got on my bike and did some old-fashioned research, visiting various libraries up and down the land and poring over old newspaper archives on microfilm: one of life's secret pleasures.

On top of the factual skeleton come the flesh and blood of the anecdotes – from colleagues and opponents, in some cases the subjects themselves – and it is these, naturally, that bring the stories to life. My heartfelt thanks go out to everyone who provided their recollections and memories.

It should be said that these chapters are only *versions* of the stories, renditions of the underlying musical score. There are doubtless dozens of people out there who might have offered yarns, providing a little flute or tambor to the ensemble. Perhaps next time the band is in town.

To continue the musical analogy, the book is organised as 22 self-contained chapters and should be read as you might listen to a favourite LP, jumping in wherever the mood takes you. Nevertheless, this means that, in one or two cases, there is some brief duplication of relevant background information about a particular league, while a couple of stories also directly intersect, and thus necessarily duplicate some minor passages. We could call these refrains, if you like.

Incidentally, the fact that the 22 chapters can be organised as two serviceable XIs is a pure coincidence, and no pecking order or pre-eminence should be inferred about these sides therefrom. They are not first and second teams. I would say they are optimised for the limited-overs format, given the personnel (Gilchrist and Mark Waugh are unlikely red-ball openers), although you just never know any more!

Finally, a note on the length of the chapters. To a degree, this was dictated by the amount of available material and/or the inherent drama of the story. They range from two-minute ditties ('Please, Please, Please Let Me Get What I Want') to hefty mid-sized workouts ('Paranoid Android') to 17-minute Sun Ra Arkestra space-jazz experimentalism. Some of the pieces herein are entirely new tunes, while earlier versions of various chapters have here been remastered.

I am aware that there are dozens more of these stories out there. The mission continues. If you have some flute or tambor to add to the mix, come and find me on Twitter [@reverse_sweeper] or drop me an email: reversesweeper@yahoo.co.uk.

Let the songs be sung.

Acknowledgments

Chapters 2, 3, 7 and 8 in the first part, and 1, 3 and 7 in the second part appeared at ESPNcricinfo.com; 10 in the first part, and 5 and 8 in the second at Cricbuzz.com; 1 and 9 in the first part, and 2, 6, 9 and 10 in the second at Wisden.com; 4 in the second part in the *Nightwatchman* and 5 in the first part in the *Cricketer*. My thanks go to them for allowing me to re-produce them here.

PART I

1

Adam Gilchrist (wk)
at Richmond CC

When Adam Craig Gilchrist sat down in December 1989 for his A-level equivalent HSC exams at Kadina High School in Lismore, a small town of around 25,000 people in northern New South Wales, he might have considered himself at a disadvantage – undercooked, in the local idiom – having been absent for the whole of Year 12's middle two terms. Then again, given the vocation that had already by that stage started whispering softly in his ear, he may also have thought that spending five months in London playing for Richmond in the Middlesex County League (MCL) was the perfect education. A boy of 17 when he arrived, a man of 17 when he departed, it's fair to say the polite, unassuming kid that had left Australia five months earlier got straight A's for his summer's work, contributing immensely to a season the club and his teammates will never forget.

Initially, though, recalls first XI captain Chris Goldie, they didn't know what to expect, "to the extent that, after an underwhelming first weekend, I didn't pick him for our penultimate Saturday friendly prior to the start of the league season. Graham Roope [the former Surrey and England batter] had phoned me to say he was living in the area and looking to join a local club. It's the 17-year-old Australian who hasn't scored any runs or the bloke with 20-odd Test caps, you know?"

However, on the Thursday that week, too late for weekend selection to be changed, Richmond played the first round of the Bertie Joel Cup, a competition entered by most of the top clubs from London and the Home Counties. Goldie wasn't available for the game against Metropolitan Police of the Surrey Championship, but kept abreast of things from his office. "I remember ringing the bar phone at the club in mid-afternoon to see how we were getting on. I spoke to our second XI captain, Ricky Cameron, a West Indian, who was skippering on the day. His response was, 'We are doing

14

okay. The boy Gilchrist just got his ton and we're 200 for none.' Adam ended up with 159 not out that day." He was up and running.

"On the Saturday, playing for the twos at Finchley," Goldie continues, "he scored 113 not out – seven fours and five sixes – and finished the match before the last hour. On the Sunday, he scored 112 against a strong Wimbledon first team. By the end of May he had 996 runs for Richmond and had earned himself the nickname 'Boy Wonder'." Back home, Boy Wonder's local newspaper, the *Northern Star*, ran the headline: 'Adam Gilchrist Terrorising the Poms.' It wouldn't be the last time.

Those 384 runs for once out in four days suggest he went pretty well with the bat in those early May matches, but Gilchrist – he of the 416 Test victims, second only to Mark Boucher – didn't have the gloves. Not in the league, at least. Goldie had kept in the 1982 Benson & Hedges Cup for the Combined Universities side skippered by Derek Pringle, and later spent three years at Hampshire. Plus, he was skipper.

Nor was he the only player with pedigree in the Richmond dressing room. Sitting unbeaten on 90-odd against Met Police when Goldie rang was Michael Roseberry, who later scored over 10,000 first-class runs for Middlesex as an opener. Also in the top four were Trevor Brown – who represented England Schoolboys and was offered a professional deal by Leicestershire only to have it withdrawn when he told them he was going to university – and Rupert Cox, who would play 19 first-class games for Hampshire between 1990 and '94, scoring a Championship hundred against Worcestershire at New Road. There was Roope, too, albeit only for that pre-season friendly (in which he scored a ton) and the first league match (a duck), before he headed off to play for Preston in the Northern League.

The new ball was taken by Andrew 'Animal' Jones, who had appeared in three first-class matches for Somerset four years earlier and was the hard-partying wingman to the previous season's overseas, Dean Waugh (brother of), while the attack's key man was 55-year-old left-arm spinner Peter Ray. Known as 'The Penguin' thanks to an uncanny resemblance to the actor Burgess Meredith from the cult 1960s *Batman* TV series, Ray was rated by Goldie as better than Phil Edmonds and Phil Tufnell, both of whom he'd seen at close quarters in the Middlesex League. Not only that, the former

Times and *Telegraph* cricket correspondent Michael Henderson considered Ray the best after-dinner speaker he ever heard. He was as "cantankerous and miserable" on the field as he was gregarious off it, says Goldie, and he would finish, at 64, with a record number of top-flight MCL scalps and its all-time best figures of 10/57. In such company, Gilly's stripes would have to be earned.

The Middlesex League was young – the same age as Gilchrist when he arrived in London – having emerged, belatedly, from a longstanding and ongoing tradition of competitive friendlies in the south east. It may have lacked the seasoned superstar pros of some of the venerable leagues further north, but it was unquestionably tough cricket – along with the Birmingham League, arguably the best in the country at the time – the standard beefed up by a steady flow of graduates gravitating to London to join the professions. It was exactly the sort of challenge envisaged by Gilchrist's father when he paid Adam's way across.

Richmond had only managed one top-half finish in the previous seven MCL seasons, with fourth – in 1976 and '77 – their highest ever. Finchley had won six of those first 17 titles, with another five clubs bagging two each. Among those were Enfield – the reigning national knockout champions, having seen off Wolverhampton the previous August – and Teddington, who lost the national final in 1987 to an Old Hill side featuring Dean Headley and Mushtaq Mohammad, but would win it in both 1989 and 1991. This was no kindergarten.

When he wasn't churning out those hundreds, Gilchrist spent some of the pre-season doing manual work, clearing the ancient ditches that separate Richmond's Old Deer Park ground – located just south of the river; or east, given the Thames' longitudinal course at those coordinates – from the Royal Botanic Gardens in Kew, a World Heritage Site whose 163-feet pagoda peers at the cricket over tall trees and the adjacent London Welsh rugby pitch, Richmond CC's co-tenants since 1957 on a ground still owned by the Crown.

"It was called a ha-ha," says Goldie, "a dry moat around old country estates to keep the livestock in without having a fence spoil the view for the lord. Adam cleared it out with big Albert Helg, a New Zealander who played rugby league, although I suspect Adam mainly stood around holding rakes. I'm not sure whether he was paid, but if he was it would be the only money he got off Richmond. We didn't charge him subs or match fees, obviously, but that was about it."

The league campaign – one game each against the other 17 teams, an expansion of two from the previous year – finally got underway on May 13. It was timed cricket with no over limits, a continuation of the pre-league traditions, and clubs could decide whether they wanted to play all-day games (11:30am starts) or half-day (2pm). There were 10 points for a win, four for a winning draw, one for a losing draw, and none for a defeat. "As declaration matches," says Goldie, "there were no restrictions on first-innings overs so theoretically the side batting first could bat as long as they wanted. Losing the toss was not an advantage when playing a weaker side on a flat pitch!"

Richmond began with a draw at reigning champions South Hampstead, Gilchrist stumped off Sussex's rookie off-spinner Bradleigh Donelan for 32. This dismissal was no harbinger of the cavalier dasher of his later years, though, the first man to hit 100 sixes in Test cricket, a player who scored 260 runs (54, 57 and 149) in his three World Cup final wins off a combined 188 balls. "The thing that stood out was his maturity, both on the field and off," remarks Trevor Brown. "He wasn't then what he later became. He didn't go in and smash the ball all over the park, although there were moments in friendlies and other cricket where you could see he could do it. He just had a big appetite for scoring huge amounts of runs and once he got in, he didn't get out."

Gilchrist made 93 on the Sunday in a friendly against Met Police, which was followed by the first of three straight league wins – against new additions Cockfosters – in which, opening the batting with Roseberry, he fell for just 8. A day later, however, there was another Sunday ton against Beckenham, followed on Tuesday by 72 against Wimbledon in the Bertie Joel, setting up Gilchrist nicely for the visit of Brondesbury, alma mater of Mike Gatting, whose chief threat was the former Indian Test left-arm spinner Dilip Doshi.

"They made 197," recalls Goldie, "and we were without Roseberry, Cox and Brown. I told Adam, a lad of 17 who I hadn't picked three weeks earlier and who was about to face a still very, very good bowler: 'You're our senior player. If you bat through for a hundred, we'll win.'" Doshi bowled unchanged from one end (22-5-53-2), but the Boy Wonder was up to it, compiling a masterful unbeaten 110. He followed this with 150* on the Sunday against Surrey Championship side Old Emanuel. This wasn't, it seemed, a young cricketer minded to give it away to allow teammates a hit.

An eight-wicket win at Stanmore, Angus Fraser's club, consolidated Richmond's early momentum. Meanwhile, Gilchrist's run glut had slid his feet firmly under the table and the rest of him out of the shadow – on the field, at least – of Dean Waugh, whose run-making and carousing had left such an impression at Richmond the previous year. In his autobiography, *True Colours*, Gilchrist looks back in anguish at the 17-year-old country boy's attempts to adapt to an unfamiliar social environment as well as his 19-year-old city-boy predecessor had done. On the field, of course, there was plenty to write home about – as indeed there had to be while continuing his HSC studies by correspondence – but his early-season letters also expressed these teething troubles with the booze and bravado, second-guessing what he thought was expected of him: "I wrote to Mum and Dad: 'I really want to get some runs. I'd love to get 100 so that everyone might stop talking about Dean bloody Waugh. The big hero who drinks everyone in the club under the table. We'll see how I go, eh?' (My thoughts on Dean would change by the end of the trip... a fantastic bloke. My ability to drink a beer would also change.)"

Gilchrist was living in the Twickenham home of the somewhat bacchanalian chairman of Teddington CC, Michael Welch, along with a couple of other, older Australian cricketers: Tim MacMillan and Brad McNamara, the future head of Channel 9's cricket coverage. It was an experience his book describes with some angst, the teenager often retreating up a pull-down wooden staircase to his loft room, 'the Birdcage', after being teased about his inability to hold his drink.

"In those early weeks I particularly dreaded the social occasions," he goes on. "English cricket clubs set world's best practice in putting away pints of warm beer, and Dean Waugh had left a few records in that department. He'd have been pleased to know I was no threat. We'd be in a pub after a game and I'd stand there and think: 'Whatever they're doing, I'll do.' But those beer glasses were so wide and so deep, and I'd never get to the bottom of them because someone would come around and, 'Oops, it's full again!' I'd stand there all night and talk, then get home and throw up. I'd had alcohol before, but going to parties and skolling a drink or two was no kind of preparation for English-style socialising. I hated it. I'd come home, throw up and cry my eyes out. It wasn't just the alcohol – it was feeling so alien to their culture, feeling that I wasn't fitting in because I wasn't drinking and kicking on through the night, wondering if there was something wrong with me because I couldn't be one of the boys."

Fortunately, Gilchrist also had his older brother, Dean, living a half-hour bus ride away in Ealing and playing in the Middlesex second tier for Old Actonians, for whose under-17s Adam turned out in midweek 20-over matches (Richmond didn't yet have a Colts team), keeping the engine ticking. Unsurprisingly, given the presence of one of cricket's greatest ever ringers, OAs under-17s won a league and cup double.

The brothers would spend a lot of time together that Ashes summer – a thumping 4-0 win for the tourists, with Mark Taylor scoring 839 runs, Terry Alderman taking 41 wickets, and England getting through 29 players. Adam joined OAs on a tour of northern England, while the pair later headed off on a three-day road trip of the country, taking in Edinburgh, Loch Ness, Glasgow, the Lake District, Wales, Liverpool, Manchester and Nottingham, sleeping in the car and eating cheap food, the quintessential British experience for skint young Australians. Big bro helped him weather the culture shock – "without him I would have packed up and come home," he writes in *True Colours* – and things soon settled down on the piss as they had on the pitch. "Gilly was able to participate socially," says Brown, "but without going over the top. He learned when to duck out. He also managed to study for his A-levels in a party house. For a 17-year-old, he was massively impressive."

On the field, Richmond went five mid-season MCL games without a win: four draws and an abandonment. Gilchrist started this run with 67 in a see-saw game at Ealing, Richmond finishing on 234/9 in pursuit of 243, followed by 15 against Hampstead, bowled by the left-arm spin of Middlesex staffer Alex Barnett.

That same day, a mile south down the Finchley Road, three stops on the Jubilee Line, Steve Waugh, having made his first Test hundred in Leeds a fortnight earlier, was busy flaying 152* with only the tail for company, Australian prime minister Bob Hawke watching on from the visitors' dressing-room balcony at Lord's as his compatriots eased toward a commanding 2-0 lead after the opening two matches. At that stage, 'Tugga' was averaging infinity for the series, by the end of which it had only come down *slightly* to 126.5. Meanwhile, England skipper David Gower marched out of a hostile press conference that evening, informing his interrogators that he had tickets for the theatre (to watch *Anything Goes*). The well-mannered young Gilchrist didn't brag too hard – after all, England had won three of the last four Ashes and were surely likely to turn things round; if not this time, then definitely at some point over, say, the next six or seven series – but he was watching the real-time emergence of an Australian juggernaut he would himself later turbocharge.

A third draw came in Richmond's cagey top-of-the-table clash with Teddington, whose opening bowler was Dawid Malan's father, Dawid Malan. Teddington made 205/8 from 70 overs, 'Penguin' taking 6/50, while Gilchrist was stumped for a duck in a chase that finished on 184/7 off 56. This was followed by an abandonment against Wembley and a losing draw at home to Shepherd's Bush, Richmond hanging on at 99/9 (of which Gilchrist made 28) to preserve their unbeaten record. The five-game winless streak was finally ended by a thumping 107-run win over Uxbridge, Gilly chipping in with 32 against future Australian Test leg-spinner Peter McIntyre, while Brown scored 92, one of seven half-centuries in a campaign yielding 630 runs at 63.

On the final Saturday in July – the day another stylish left-handed keeper was fidgeting his way to an Ashes 128 up in 'Madchester', appropriately so with this being the second Summer of Love and RC Russell Esq. being fond of a Stone Roses-style bucket hat – Gilchrist made just 11 in a draw at Finchley. It was now six league games without a half-century for Boy Wonder.

Not that these middle months were a drought, exactly. There was 129* against North London in the Middlesex Cup, while those hard-boiled friendlies brought 144* against Horsham and 110* against East Molesey. Two more Gilchrist tons adorned Richmond's Cricket Week: 141 against The Stage and 102 against Pamplonian Flyers. Jazz-hat, maybe, but runs is runs. Even so, and although Gilly was never *not* in nick, Richmond were hoping that, with the coming of August and the sharp end of their pursuit of an elusive maiden MCL title, the prodigy would go gangbusters.

By this time, the burgeoning Gilchrist legend had even reached the BBC, who sent a local reporter down to Old Deer Park to interview the young batter and his captain at midweek practice (unfortunately, there was no Internet or WhatsApp for him to send the link home to Lismore's Goonellabah suburb). Saturday's game against Winchmore Hill duly brought a four-wicket win, Boy Wonder's 52 and 76 from Cox the backbone of Richmond's chase, but the following week saw him dismissed for a single in a losing draw with national club champions and erstwhile title rivals Enfield: 186/8 plays 115/5. "I was determined that we would not lose, so declared as late as possible," says Goldie. "They took the winning draw, but I'm pretty sure it knocked them out of the title race."

Four league matches remained. The first, against Brentham, Mike Brearley's club, saw Gilchrist run out for 12, but 64 from Goldie secured a tense three-wicket win. Next, as the final Ashes Test was being played out at The Oval, Gilchrist scored 55 in an abandoned game against a Hornsey team also still just about in the title race. The penultimate game was against lowly North Middlesex, who were skittled for 106 thanks to Peter Ray's 13-6-18-4. Gilchrist made 60 in the chase, falling to future New Zealand off-spinner Paul Wiseman with the game as good as won.

Going into the final game, then, away at third-placed Southgate, Richmond were joint-top with Teddington on 88 points, with their hosts just a couple of points back. All sorts of permutations were possible. Since they were ahead on the number of wins, seven to six, Richmond simply had to match any positive result Teddington achieved at bottom-placed Brondesbury (who had only one victory all year) to secure the title. Should Teddington manage only a losing draw, however, then matching it would not be enough, as this would necessarily mean a winning draw for Southgate, who would thus come up on the rails to snatch it. The winning draw was simply determined by scoring rate, so a team batting first could only pick up the four points if they bowled more overs in the second innings than they had received, something else that might enter the equation as the day unfolded.

The club was abuzz all week. Rumour has it Master Gilchrist would go on to play bigger games later in his career, but this was arguably the heftiest so far. Richmond went into it without their Penguin, however, whose second wife – "a Russian he met on the Metropolitan Line from Pinner into the City who could never quite cope with the cricket schedule," says Goldie – had already booked holidays, unaware that September's second Saturday was, unusually, a league fixture. "As Peter left the Richmond bar late the week before," Goldie adds, "he declared that if we won the league in his absence, he would streak around Brondesbury's ground when we travelled there the following Saturday for an end-of-season friendly. Given that leaving the visitors' changing room at Bron in those days meant going through the bar, it was going to be something of a spectacle."

Three days prior to the final-day showdown, Teddington had won their maiden National Club Championship, beating Old Hill in a replay at Edgbaston to earn £1,250 and a trip to Barbados courtesy of sponsors, Cockspur Rum. However, as word filtered through to Southgate that their game against Brondesbury was not following the formbook, it appeared the euphoria and rum-fuelled festivities had left them nursing something of a metaphorical, if not literal hangover.

At Southgate, meanwhile, the home team had been knocked over for 136 in 62 overs, recovering from 56/7, and Richmond had set about the chase. Gilchrist contributed what turned out to be a top-scoring 22 before being caught and bowled, all the while his captain was desperately trying to get current information on the Teddington game. These days, it would simply be a matter of following live updates fed directly from computerised score-boxes to a phone app. Back in 1989, it wasn't so straightforward, recalls Goldie: "Mobile phones in those days were very much the preserve of the wealthy and the only person to have one in our side was Nick Morrill, who was, or is, a successful banker. He had one in his car and it was rumoured that the call rate was £1 per minute. That's about £2.50 in today's money."

By a coincidence of the fixtures, Richmond's third team, 'the Cronksquad', had played and won that day on Southgate's second pitch, keeping them on course for their own title, and were now offering vocal support from the sidelines. Their colleagues had slipped to 115/6, though, top six all gone, a dismissed Goldie giving Brown what Boy Wonder might call 'a spray' as he walked off for failing to keep him posted on events at Bron. Amid the tension, Morrill was now off phone duties and at the crease in deteriorating light. The station was being manned, however, and news arrived confirming that Brondesbury had pulled off a shock and turned Teddington over, meaning Southgate now had to take the final four wickets inside a couple of overs to deny Richmond the title. Six runs were needed from the final over, still four wickets in hand, but Goldie issued pragmatic instructions via the time-honoured hand-gesture and three dead-bats later the deal was sealed. At which point, bedlam.

Richmond had their maiden MCL championship, and at the end of a summer in which he'd scored 3,821 runs, more than Bradman ever managed on these shores in a single visit, Gilchrist threw himself manfully into the night's revelries. A week later, around the time Boy Wonder's plane touched down in Brisbane, Peter Ray upheld his pledge to streak at Brondesbury.

Back in Lismore, on the banks of Wilson's River, a tributary of the Richmond, Gilchrist prepared for his exams, yet still found time to pen a loved-up letter to the club: "I have felt privileged to be associated with such a fine group of people and feel we were all rewarded for our hard work this year by finishing 1-2-1. I wish you all happiness in the future and hope that, within the next few years, I can return and be as accepted as I was this year. Maybe I'll be as experienced *off* the field as the Penguin is on by then (crucial!)."

He did return for one further season of British club cricket, failing to register a competitive hundred as the paid man at Perthshire CC, whose North Inch ground had been flooded in April by the River Tay, making life difficult for an emerging destroyer who, by then, was well into his long apprenticeship in state cricket. The destination, of course, was to become the ultimate game-changer – both micro and macro: individual matches and the sport as a whole, redefining the keeper's role – a revolutionary counter-punching Test No.7 who famously won his first 16 games in the baggy green.

Richmond landed the title again in 1998 and 2004, the year the first recipient of the Adam Gilchrist Scholarship arrived at the club, established to allow its eponymous sponsor to help young Australians from country backgrounds benefit from the type of experience he had enjoyed. "I still see those five months of 1989 as the most influential time in my development," he wrote in 2008, "really the end of my childhood, my coming of age, both as a cricketer and a person: learning how to be independent, fending for myself, cooking for myself. Mum had given me a book of recipes and I did a mean potato fritter!"

In 2009, Goldie's champion team held a 20-year reunion. Boy Wonder was there, albeit now on the cusp of middle age, a decorated and universally admired superstar who played scrupulously fair and always batted selflessly, doing so now off the international treadmill while seeing out his playing days on the Twenty20 circuit. Thus it was that, the following summer, during a short stint in the Blast, he completed the circle, skippering Middlesex against Glamorgan at Old Deer Park. Opening the batting with David Warner, he biffed 51 off 31 balls, with three sixes launched somewhere in the direction of the ha-ha he had cleared all those years ago.

"It's the only section of it that remains," says Goldie. "We're thinking of having it restored. If we do, we should probably have a blue plaque put up: This ha-ha was cleared by Australian Test cricketer – ... No: The clearing of this ha-ha was supervised by Adam Gilchrist in 1989."

2

Gordon Greenidge and Malcolm Marshall
at Leyland CC

The cricketing stories of Cuthbert Gordon Greenidge and Malcolm Denzil Marshall were interwoven across 444 professional appearances together for Barbados, Hampshire and West Indies, yet there is a fourth and little-known link that further binds these giants of Caribbean cricket's halcyon era.

In back-to-back seasons, Greenidge in 1993 and Marshall in 1994, the West Indians with the most first-class runs (37,354) and second-most wickets (1,651) – icons identifiable à la Michael Jordan by the high-kneed silhouettes of that swivel-pull, that gather – were engaged as uber-glamorous professionals of Leyland CC, a small and not so glamorous town just south of Preston in Lancashire, chiefly famous for its post-war car manufacturing industry. Forty-one and 36 years old they may have been when they first stepped out at Fox Lane, the lofty peaks of their international careers behind them, but for the awe-struck policemen, schoolteachers, sales managers and engineers who shared the Leyland dressing room, a few of whom were on the other side of adolescence when the Calypso juggernaut settled into its pounding Eighties rhythms, this was a fairytale experience. Fantasy cricket made flesh.

Leyland were one of the 12 founding members of the Northern League, formed as a breakaway competition from the Ribblesdale League in 1952 by aspirational clubs looking at the nearby Lancashire League – crowds of four and five thousand to watch Everton Weekes in his pomp – and wanting a piece of the action. From Rohan Kanhai, Mushtaq and Hanif Mohammad in its first decade, to David Boon, Ravi Shastri and Javed Miandad in the 1980s, the league has had its fair share of star quality, yet the early 1990s were its undoubted heyday, when it was among the strongest in the country. Blackpool had won the National Club Championship in 1990, Kendal were beaten finalists in 1992, and between 1994 and '96 Chorley would become the first and only club to make three straight Lord's finals, winning the first two. Despite this national success and several local cup wins, the decade brought no league titles.

The year before Greenidge's arrival, Richie Richardson had pro'd at Blackpool, scoring 1,056 runs at 88, while Fleetwood availed themselves of a young Trinidadian left-hander by the name of Brian Charles Lara as sub-pro for Atul Wassan, the Indian Test seamer. Lara was in the country to follow his childhood friend Dwight Yorke's breakthrough season at Aston Villa, and made just one half-century in three knocks, yet urged the club to sign him up for the 1993 season. Fleetwood declined, having already agreed terms with the future USA batter Richard Staple, who was subsequently injured and unable to take up his contract. One that got away, then.

The man responsible for bringing Greenidge and Marshall to Lancastrian club cricket was John Farrar, Leyland's hard-headed fortysomething-year-old skipper and hard-handed wicket-keeper. "He was a legend, Faz," reflects teammate Tim Barry, "but as a keeper he could just about stop it. There were times, keeping to Malcolm, he'd come off black and blue."

A larger-than-life character who had briefly been a goalkeeper on Preston North End's books, the garrulous, bespectacled Farrar's career as a local sports impresario started with trading memorabilia. The big break came with his contribution to Lancashire stalwart Jack Simmons' highly successful benefit year in 1980 (£490,000 in today's money), after which he became much sought after to organise black-tie sports functions and after-dinner speakers. All of which gave him a bulging contacts book. Indeed, in 1988 Farrar had enticed Javed Miandad to his previous club, Preston (he made no centuries and even fewer friends), although 'Faz' would finish the season with a 12-month ban from the Northern League for "mooning", later rescinded when it was established that a teammate had pulled his trousers down as they left the field. Life was rarely dull around him.

Freed from the mooning ban, Farrar took his little black book to Leyland. In 1991, with former Lancashire and Gloucestershire stalwarts Ken Snellgrove and Phil Bainbridge as skipper and pro respectively, they won the league. More intriguingly, they had two ex-England players, Graham Roope and Geoff Miller – coincidentally, both excellent after-dinner speakers and both travelling far across county lines for their Saturday hit – ostensibly among the amateur ranks. They weren't the only ones receiving a little off-book remuneration for their cricketing services, as Farrar lured a clutch of Minor Counties players and battle-hardened league cricketers to Fox Lane to supplement the official pros: Mark Greatbatch in 1992, fresh off a blistering pinch-hitting World Cup, then Greenidge the following year. "I think I was the only one in the team not being paid that season," says Douglas Green, a solicitor who had moved from Preston with Farrar. "As a joke, I painted 'Leyland Amateur, 1993' on my coffin."

Among the new intake for 1993 was Paul Berry, coming off 1,697 runs for Roe Green in the lesser Lancashire County League – only once failing to reach fifty all season – and good enough to be offered a contract by Northamptonshire two years earlier. "I didn't know Gordon was coming when I signed," he recalls. "All John Farrar told me was he was going to get 'a decent pro'. Anyway, we got called up to training early one day because John said the new pro was going to be there. I nearly fell on the floor when I saw Gordon Greenidge standing there. I thought: surely it's not going to be him?!"

It was going to be him, although Greenidge was unavailable for the season opener, something about which the league's blazers were notoriously strict, as the *Leyland Guardian* explained: "Northern League cricket chiefs have taken the unusual step of allowing Leyland's new club professional Gordon Greenidge to start the season a week late." Which was good of them, considering the 108-Test veteran was in Barbados collecting a lifetime achievement medal from the West Indies Cricket Board. Nevertheless, Farrar was forced to thumb through that little book of his, and so it was that Leyland's second-change bowler at Lancaster was the world's then leading Test wicket-taker.

Sir Richard Hadlee was in the middle of a six-week speaking tour, during which he would drop in at Leyland's nets to roll over his arm and keep himself limber for occasional exhibition games. He was also two years on from double heart by-pass surgery, and not particularly match-fit, which may have explained why the Sky Sports cameras that descended on Lune Road were kept waiting for a glimpse of that familiarly regal approach, all wrist-cock and finger voodoo, Hadlee catching his breath at the end of Miller's two-minute overs to send down 12-4-11-2 in two spells as Lancaster declined to pursue the target of 158, finishing on 75/7. In the return game, they would grind to 57/7 off 47 overs, taking just two runs from the final 20 overs as Miller returned the remarkable figures of 18-15-4-4.

It was very much be the story of the season, recalls Doug Green: "The opposition, as you can imagine, all had the hump for Leyland and did anything not to lose. I don't think John was really bothered about winning the league, which you'd do by batting second and knocking off. He wanted to bat first and watch all the lovely batting he'd signed. Me and Geoff Miller would be six and seven and rarely got in. We'd usually sit doing the *Telegraph* crossword."

The one departure from this template came on Greenidge's debut the following week – his 42nd birthday and the two-year anniversary of his final Test innings – when Farrar elected to bowl and Fleetwood were hustled out for 43, Leyland knocking off without loss by 2:30pm, whereupon Miller cordially invited the visitors to join them for centre-pitch practice. They preferred to hit the bar, they said, conveying their inclinations in a robust Anglo-Saxon.

With teams regularly and sometimes resentfully shutting up shop against the 'Leyland all-stars', the first half of the league campaign brought seven winning draws – they had the opposition nine down at stumps three games running – and only two outright wins. Greenidge had taken a while to get going, with scores of 28*, 1, 58, 10 and 37 in the first five league outings, telling Barry that "he found it much more difficult playing club cricket once a week, often on dodgy pitches, than county cricket, where you're batting every day, fantastic pitches, and the ball feels huge."

Still, he soon found some rhythm, posting scores of 64, 55, 94, 64 and 99 into the halfway mark, the latter a self-inflicted run out against Chorley courtesy of a direct hit from mid-off. "The only person on the ground who thought it was out was the umpire," recalls Leyland opening bowler, Bob Cuthbertson. "Gordon wasn't a happy chappy at all. Paul Simmonite, his opening partner, then started ribbing him: 'What's the matter Gordon, have you never had a hundred before?' It then comes out that Gordon had been dismissed for 90-odd in both innings of a Test match on *two* occasions – the only player to do this."

"It was a very good innings on a difficult pitch," adds Chorley's Nigel Heaton. "Afterwards, he hung around for a quick drink then left. Once he'd gone, the barman said he had left his collection money behind to buy everyone a drink, but had told the barman only to announce it once he'd left."

Despite all the draws, Leyland were just four points off leaders Netherfield at halfway, two behind Kendal (it was eight points for a win, three or one for a draw, with a couple of bonus points available). Meanwhile, Sundays brought progress in the cups, with the team occasionally including a promising 15-year-old seamer by the name of Liam Botham – his father an acquaintance of Farrar's – a boarder at the nearby Rossall School. They had navigated the opening rounds of the Lancashire Cup – the top four teams from a dozen leagues duking it out to play a final at Old Trafford – and had advanced to the final of the Matthew Brown Cup, the first of the Northern League's two annual domestic knockouts. Greenidge made 74, 32 and 99* as Preston, Chorley and cross-town rivals Leyland Motors were dispatched, but was dismissed for single figures by Morecambe in the final, which Leyland nevertheless won by two runs after Tim Barry successfully defended six from the final eight-ball over, prompting a late evening chez Farrar, who hosted regular boozy soirées.

Socially, Greenidge's teammates found him a serious, reserved figure, but never aloof. "He wasn't a party animal, or one of those who'd be last at the bar, like Malcolm was," says Berry, "but he'd always stay and have a drink. He got that about league cricket." He lived in Nottingham during the week, but would occasionally stay over in the north west. Simmonite invited him along to the Skipton Building Society hospitality box for the Old Trafford Ashes Test, where they witnessed Shane Warne's 'Ball of the Century'. And having played a season for Greenock in Scotland two years earlier, he asked teammates to arrange for some fresh salmon to be sent down. "He paid for it, marinated it and cooked it himself, barbecuing it up for us outside the clubhouse after a game," says Green.

Greenidge was "fully integrated into the life of the team", adds Barry. "There was no ego with him, nothing about him being one of the all-time great opening bats in one of the greatest teams that ever played the game. He was a team player, and always willing to help." Such an attitude would be important if they were to keep pace with the two Cumbrian sides over the second half of the season.

Things got off to an ordinary start with defeat at St Annes, whose 15-year-old opener Andrew Flintoff biffed 48. The following week, Greenidge arrived late and had to bat at No.5, albeit with the mitigation of a delayed flight from Barbados, having returned to attend the opening of a school named in his honour. A week later, at Darwen, one of the loosening Leyland wheelnuts came free when Farrar sent off new-ball spearhead Brian Tennant for refusing to bowl.

Fiery and wiry, with a temperamental and physical resemblance to Robert Carlyle's Begbie in *Trainspotting* – "He was about eight stone wet through," says Berry, "but could cause trouble in an empty house" – Tennant had erupted when Greenidge spilt a difficult chance off his bowling. Words were exchanged and Tennant had not cooled off by the time he was asked to bowl again, so Farrar banished him to the dressing room, despite the damage to their chances of winning and thus their title challenge. Tennant subsequently apologised, but was made to serve a three-game ban: two cup matches and the derby with Leyland Motors, who hung on, eight down, when a dollop of lively in-swing might have finished the job. "John wasn't everyone's cup of tea," says Cuthbertson, "but he was a man of principle."

With seven games left, Leyland's hopes hung by a thread. They won three of their next four, however, Greenidge contributing 86, 28, 93* (his ninth half-century) and 38, and headed to Kendal for the third-last game still in with a mathematical chance of the title, at which point the team had another shock, recalls Barry. "Dennis Lillee walked into the dressing room – John was doing some work for him – and he says, 'I've got a charity match coming up and haven't bowled for a while, do you mind coming out onto the edge of the square?' So Paul Berry and I went out to warm up with Dennis Lillee, which was bizarre."

With DK watching on, Leyland crashed to a nine-wicket defeat. Greenidge was nicked off for a duck by his sometime West Indies colleague Eldine Baptiste (10 Tests, 10 victories), the Antiguan all-rounder eventually finishing second in the batting averages and top of the bowling – taking 52 wickets at 9.73, with a 'what am I supposed to do with this?' economy of 1.86 runs per over – as Kendal won the title, becoming just the third team ever to go unbeaten through a Northern League campaign.

As for Greenidge, he finally notched a century in the last game, his unbeaten 120 in the win over Fleetwood taking him past the club record aggregate and leaving Leyland in fourth, which meant qualification for the Lancashire Cup. A commendable 976 runs at 57.41 placed him third in the averages, and with Berry, Gary Wells, Green and Simmonite also featuring in the top 15, it was clear where Leyland needed a little extra bite, so Farrar had the ingenious idea of signing the man with the lowest bowling average of anyone to have taken 200 or more Test wickets as pro. That ought to help.

Having had Greenidge in the ranks, and Hadlee and Lillee in the fanbase, one might assume the Leyland players were becoming accustomed to the presence of cricketing megastars. Not so, says Berry. "The buzz around the place coming into Malcolm's season was incredible. I was starstruck. He had an aura about him, a swagger."

Marshall had finished his 14-year association with Hampshire at the end of the previous summer, yet unlike Greenidge he was still playing first-class cricket when he came to Fox Lane, skippering Natal in the Castle Cup through the South African summer. There was gas in the Ferrari's tank. Unfortunately for Leyland, however, Miller and Tennant – 44 and 47 wickets respectively the previous year – had left the club, thinning out the bowling stocks. Farrar pulled in a couple of veterans of Lancashire club cricket – one of whom, medium-pacer Dick Powell, had 19 wickets to Maco's 17 after five games – but Marshall would end up getting through a staggering 448.3 overs, the most in the league. Farrar was evidently keen to squeeze out his money's worth.

Initially, it worked. By the end of May, unbeaten Leyland had won six out of seven and sat atop the table, seven points clear of champions Kendal. Marshall had begun with 4/44 in victory over soon-to-be national club champions Chorley, followed by 6/39 against St Annes, cleaning up the now 16-year-old Flintoff in the first over for a duck in front of the watching Lancashire coach, David Lloyd, who observed that the young triallist's front leg had been "a little stiff" ('Freddie' was handed his first professional contract later in the summer and was rumoured to have enjoyed a decent career thereafter).

'Maco' started just as well with the bat, plundering 85 in the win at Darwen and a crucial 53-ball 60 in the victory over Blackpool, although it took a pair of last-over sixes from Barry to get them over the line. "Malcolm ran on the pitch and carried me off," Barry recalls. "He said, 'I've never done that for anyone before in my life'." A week later, Marshall's 6/50 blew Netherfield away. Leyland had momentum. Then they went a month without winning.

A more hands-on presence than Greenidge, Marshall lived in the town, attended practice nights and often stuck around to socialise, as competitive on a pool table as he was in the middle. "Training with him on Tuesdays and Thursdays was testing," recalls Berry. "He'd tell you what he was going to bowl, 'two outswingers, then one inswinger', and even though you knew what was coming there wasn't usually much you could do about it. You'd be mesmerised by that run-up, which we'd all seen so many times on TV."

If not quite possessed of the extreme pace of his youth, Marshall still had that high-grade skill-set and those years of sharp-end experience to fall back on. And yet, by the end of May, he had already taken two of his three five-fors. "Malcolm bowled too short," asserts Green. "He seemed to have a dread of being hit through the covers, which only happened two or three times all season. I fielded slip all year and counted the amount of times he beat the bat before getting the edge: it was 12 on average."

"The workload may have been an issue," adds Barry, whose doctoral thesis was on spine curvature in fast bowlers. "You can't bowl flat-out for 25 overs on the trot. Impossible. But there was *a lot* of playing and missing. Maybe he could have bowled a bit fuller, but who's going to tell one of the all-time greats how to bowl? The fact is that pitches were slow and the standard was high. Players would do their all to survive against Malcolm."

That was amply illustrated in the next game against Morecambe, for whom opener Graham Fisher carried his bat for 111* – the only century Leyland conceded all season – as Marshall sent down 25 wicketless overs for 67. More Lancastrian guts and grit were on show a week later, a humdinger against local rivals Chorley in which Leyland's total of 182 owed much to three Paul Berry sixes in the final over from 43-year-old quick-turned-leggie Keith Eccleshare, who had the distinction of dismissing Richie Richardson, Greenidge, Marshall and Jacques Kallis in consecutive seasons, the three specialist batters all clean bowled.

'Boy Wonder' in the bar: a teenage Adam Gilchrist puts on a brave
face at Richmond ahead of a few post-match ales

Jim White / Richmond CC

Gordon Greenidge (back row, third left) celebrates Leyland's narrow
victory over Morecambe in the 1993 Matthew Brown Cup

Lancashire Evening Telegraph

Brian Lara looks on as Malcolm Marshall thanks Leyland CC lynchpin
Jenny Crook during his star-studded benefit day at the club
Leyland CC

Netherfield treasurer Mike Rigg reunites with 'Jock' Kallis at his This is Your Life in 2019
Mike Rigg

The King cover drives: Viv Richards gives the Rishton fans a
glimpse of greatness on debut against Haslingden
PA Photos

The North Staffordshire & South Cheshire League XI for the inaugural President's Trophy inter-league final in 1965. Garry Sobers sits on the front row with fellow professionals Wes Hall, Denis Cox and Nasim-ul-Ghani

The Sentinel

Marvel superhero in the Malverns: 'Dre Russ' with his Barnards Green team in 2010

Ken Williams

Wasim Akram walks out to bat in his first game for Smethwick, wearing
a hat bearing the logo of his sponsor (and, briefly, skipper)
Birmingham Post

Having a ball of the century: Shane Warne (front row, second right) enjoyed
himself during a tough summer at Accrington in the Lancashire League
Accrington CC

The name's Bond: Kiwi quick Shane scared the living daylights out of visitors to
Furness CC's bouncy Oxford Road ground during a glorious summer in Cumbria
Shane Bond

Cuddy and the Gang: Courtney Walsh and Tynedale CC celebrate
victory in the 1983 Alcan Trophy final at Jesmond
Tynedale CC

Two ton route to cup final

GREENMOUNT emerged triumphant from a semi-final tie which produced more than 500 runs on Sunday afternoon.

They amassed 278 for 2 against Astley Bridge, thanks largely to two individual hundreds, and were then forced to sweat it out as their visitors made a tremendous effort to snatch a place in the Bolton League's Hamer Cup final.

The home side were 42 for 2 when 17 years old Gary Neville, an apprentice footballer with Manchester United, strolled to the middle to join 21 years old Australian professional Matthew Hayden.

Some 40 overs later the big Queenslander, who has high hopes of a place in the Aussie Test squad, was 140 not out and his less experienced partner (right) was unbeaten on 110, Neville's maiden first team 'ton' after a previous best of 49. It was Hayden's fourth century for the club this summer.

Bridge professional Brendan McArdle (102) and Mark Warren (74) bravely led the reply but when they both fell to Mark Stewart (6 for 74) in the same over, the chase became a lost cause and they were eventually all out for 256.

Matthew Hayden is organising cricket coaching for all juniors of any age. The sessions, at Greenmount CC, are from 10am to 4pm on August 4, 5 and 6 and then 11, 12 and 13, each week costing £20 per person. For details telephone 0204 883807 or 0204 883667.

Class of 92: Matthew Hayden and Manchester United's Gary Neville celebrate their match-winning cup semi-final partnership for Greenmount

Bury Times

Greenmount's other Australian: Mark Taylor (front row, third right) poses with teammates at the end of a successful Bolton League campaign

Greenmount CC

Junior jumps on Jimmy: Mark Waugh launches Kearsley's
Mohinder Amarnath at Egerton CC in 1985
Mike Latham

A very, very special experience for Pudsey Congs' Colin Chapman as he
opens the batting with VVS Laxman in the Bradford League in 1996
Pudsey Congs

Nec plus Ulster: Carrickfergus captain Barry Cooper (second left) with his lodger and the club's overseas pro AB de Villiers (in cap), flanked by Snehal Parikh and Robin Stewart

Carrickfergus CC

Tugga the Slugger: Steve Waugh with his Nelson teammates during the 1987 Lancashire League campaign

Lancashire Telegraph

Boom Boom in the Room: Shahid Afridi in Leek CC helmet
reaches another milestone in quick time

The Sentinel

From Delhi to Derry: Kapil Dev (back row, second left) with the Limavady
team during a one-off guest pro appearance in the 1980 North West Cup
final, prior to a full year over the water at Nelson in Lancashire

Limavady CC

White Lightnin' Fever: Allan Donald sends down another rocket at Rishton

Bill Yates

Recipient of the 1986 Vivian Richards Scholarship, Curtly Elconn Linwall
Ambrose (back row, tallest) with his Chester Boughton Hall teammates

Chester Boughton Hall CC

No gimme, despite Immy: Moddershall 1st XI celebrate success with their
reliably brilliant leg-spinner Imran Tahir (back row, third from left)

Chantal Lemaitre / Staffordshire Newsletter

"Marshall tried his nuts off when we batted, revved up by Farrar at every opportunity," recalls Chorley skipper Roland Horridge. "He hit Nigel Heaton on the grille a couple of times while I was out there. It was tough going. Then Neil Senior, our keeper, who could be really devastating, comes in with no helmet. He never wore one. At the end of one Marshall over, Neil signalled for a lid. Farrar shouts up: 'You've won the battle, Maco. The soft twat is crapping himself.' The helmet came out, but Neil pulled out a baseball cap. It was probably a set-up. Steam was coming out of Marshall's ears. First ball of his next over, Neil hits him out of the ground over backward square leg off one knee. Fifth ball: exactly the same, only further."

Senior eventually fell for 40, and with the top six back in the hutch and only 120 on the board Chorley might well have shut up shop. Instead, they chipped away and eventually needed four with two balls left. "Mark Richardson hit the ball to square leg, toward the pavilion where we were all sat, and Doug Green fielded it three feet over the boundary. There were stud marks. We were apoplectic. When he was asked later, Doug said he couldn't tell. I told him he'd cheated." Contentious it may have been, but it was also evidence for Marshall that his colleagues were up for it.

The following weekend's top-of-the-table showdown with Kendal was lost to rain, however, and the end of Leyland's winless June saw the two sides level at halfway. At which point, Farrar's men reeled off three straight wins, the third, at Fleetwood, something of a heist. With seven wickets down, eight overs left and 72 needed, No.9 Powell supported Doug Green as they inched toward the target, then, with 13 still needed, he clubbed Australian Test all-rounder Shaun Young for six from the first ball of the final over and Leyland scrambled home from the last ball. It was the sort of win that screams 'name on the trophy' to a team's glass-half-full faction, 'underlying problems' to their glass-half-empty colleagues, and two cup exits to Kendal inside a week seemed to confirm the more pessimistic view. Next game up, against rock-bottom Preston – for whom David White, a postman from Horwich, batted through for 97* – they needed Marshall to uproot a tailender's stumps from the final ball of the game to secure a scores-level draw.

If things were wobbling on the field, then cracks were appearing off it – specifically, over some of the off-book money that Marshall had been promised by Farrar, whose mouth regularly wrote cheques that his chequebook couldn't cash. Perhaps it was this growing irritation that fuelled Marshall's next two performances, when his colleagues were given an up-close glimpse of what happens when that plumage was ruffled, a flash of the old, A-list Maco. The first was only a vignette, prompted by his former Barbados colleague Terry Hunte – Kendal's more than useful support act for Baptiste – having the temerity to pull him for four, first ball, off the front foot. "We said, 'I can't believe you're letting him do this'," recalls Berry. "The next three balls were absolute lightning. He gloved the third one and thankfully, John Farrar, one of the worst wicket-keepers I've ever seen, managed to hold on."

Hunte was in the process of adding a league-record 1,351 runs to the 1,136 he'd amassed the year before, yet Marshall had handed him a swift and brutal reminder of those upper gears, those levels. "The change in Malcolm that day was frightening," Berry adds. "I thought, 'Christ, I wouldn't have fancied facing this in his pomp'. It must have been horrible."

This was very much a panther who shouldn't be unnecessarily poked. Or so you would think. Yet there is a certain breed of northern English club cricketer – thick-skinned, foghorn-voiced wind-up merchants – who are either (delete as appropriate) 'no respecters of reputation' or 'psychotically indifferent to the welfare of their opening batters'. Usually, they are wicket-keepers. One such was John Isles of St Annes, who the previous year, playing for Fleetwood, had chirped Greenidge with "NFI, this lad" (short for 'no f**king idea'), only for Greenidge to turn to him later – walking off with that unbeaten 120 – and say: "Not bad for someone with no idea, eh?" It was obviously tongue-in-cheek from Isles, but then Greenidge couldn't bowl quick. His successor? Well, he could, so perhaps a different approach was called for.

"I was stood up to the wicket and heard an edge, so I appealed," recalls Isles of his tussle with Marshall. "Not out. So I says to him, 'What did that hit?' and he just glared at me. Next ball he Chinese-cut down to fine leg. So I start saying, 'Playing by numbers, this bloke'. Anyway, end of the next over Paul Berry says to me, 'Bloody hell, Shag, what have you done?' 'Why, what's up?' He says Marshall had just told him, 'I hope the keeper's as noisy with the bat as he is with the gloves on.' *Okay* then…"

Not long after, Isles dropped Marshall off the pro, Stuart MacGill; he went on to make 80, Berry 85, and Leyland declared at 226/6. Chirp still ringing in his ears, Marshall roared in after tea and, despite some top-order resistance from Australian amateur Ross Wintle, knocked over five quick middle-order wickets. "The skipper had asked me if I'd bat 11," Isles continues. "I'm like, 'Yeah, no problem'. Wickets start falling and I'm searching for any bit of padding I can find. Anyway, we get nine down with about 12 overs left and I walk out there like Tutankhamun. I can still hear Maco saying, 'This is him! This is the 'keeper!' I'm thinking: Oh for f**k's sake."

Isles dug in, protected his castle, and even frustrated Marshall into a few balls of leg-spin. With three overs left, Maco switched ends and trapped the stonewalling Wintle lbw for 61. "Missing leg," says Isles, "but it was Malcolm Marshall appealing so what are you going to do?" Marshall had finished with 8/39, a season's best, although his haul didn't include the tempestuous 23-year-old MacGill, on the cusp of receiving an unprecedented lifetime ban from the Northern League. "He was constantly swearing at umpires," recalls Isles, "calling them 'f**king cheating c**ts' because they'd given something not out. It got worse and worse. He was even abusing his teammates for misfields. It was non-stop."

MacGill had dropped out of the Australian Cricket Academy to take up St Annes' offer, but by this stage the club had told him his form didn't warrant another deal. The news wasn't well received, and his already questionable on-field behaviour started to unravel. Blackpool batter John Wright had so taken umbrage at MacGill's verbals that he head-butted him during the tea interval, the police later showing up at the ground to investigate a possible assault, with MacGill turning out alongside Flintoff in a cup match the following day sporting two black eyes and a plaster on his bloodied nose. Wright was given a 10-match suspension, MacGill six, although he appealed and was able to play the following week at Kendal, where the umpires took the players off after 40 minutes due to abuse received from MacGill and compatriot Chris Sainsbury, the overseas amateur, after Eldine Baptiste was contentiously adjudged not out. St Annes skipper John Cotton agreed to withdraw Sainsbury from the game (he was banned by the club a day later), which then resumed. The court case against Wright for assault leading to ABH was thrown out when MacGill failed to show up at Lytham Magistrates Court five days before the end of the season. He also failed to attend a league disciplinary hearing at which he and Sainsbury were given *sine die* bans, scaled back on appeal to "expulsion from the league", which kept open the possibility of him playing elsewhere. By then, MacGill was AWOL with his club car, recalls Cotton. "He sold it in south Wales – where his mother was from – never to be seen again. We wrote to the Australian governing body explaining what had happened and never heard a thing back!"

Things at Leyland may not quite have gone full MacGill, but they were starting to fray. Marshall had enjoyed an early-August benefit game at Fox Lane, with Brian Lara skippering an International XI and Marshall a West Indian XI featuring Courtney Walsh, but money issues lingered and with five games left and a league title to play for, his form collapsed. Fears his teammates had about him potentially clocking off, if only subconsciously, were seemingly confirmed when he failed to turn up for the third-last game, the derby at Leyland Motors.

"The chairman, Terry Wilson, went to look for him," recalls Cuthbertson, "and he was just sat there in the house the club rented for him. He eventually came an hour or so late. I don't know the details, but Leyland would have been paying him so much, declared, but that wouldn't have been all he was getting. I suspect John [Farrar] had a lot to do with how the rest of the money was raised. John was the sort of fellow who, when he had money, liked to throw it around. But he didn't always have it."

Averaging over 53 with the bat heading into August, Marshall signed off with scores of 5, 1, 14, 14 and 1, and took just 10 wickets in 99 overs across those final five games: a strike rate of 59.4, compared to his Test figure of 46.76. Still, Leyland won the penultimate game at Lancaster – before which Marshall had picked up his 1,600th first-class wicket in a spell of 3/60 in Scarborough against the South Africans, his sole first-class outing of the summer – and thus headed into the finale, at home to Darwen, level on points with Kendal but with the advantage of having won more games. One more and they would be champions.

As it was, they stumbled to 96/8 from 40 overs, which were knocked off without any major worries. Farrar expressed his disappointment to the *Leyland Guardian* and announced that Marshall would be heading to Denton CC in Manchester the following year, having been offered £25,000: "He wants to stay, but we can't compete with that." Marshall finished with a haul of 64 league wickets at 17.39, Baptiste 81 at 9.71. Strange old game.

Any sense Marshall might be washed up would be quickly dispelled by his performances in South Africa, en route to which he bumped into Fleetwood batter John Whalley at Manchester Airport, himself heading off to the southern hemisphere for the winter. "I was waiting for the shuttle flight down to London," he says, "and out of the blue Malcolm came up to me and asked where I was heading. He then went to the desk and sorted it so that we sat next to each other on the 40-minute flight, during which we knocked back three dark rum and cokes. Doubles. I was blown away by the fact he had arranged for us to sit together, and when we landed, we shook hands and he said, 'Enjoy your time in Tasmania'. It's a memory I will cherish forever."

Marshall would finish top of the Castle Cup wicket charts with 35 at 16.17 (Baptiste: 27 at 24.55) as Natal were crowned champions. In April, Denton thus welcomed one of the five South African Cricketers of the Year for their Lancashire County League campaign. "Malcolm was a lovely guy, a true gent," reflects club treasurer, John Foxall, "although he did tell me he was going to burn John Farrar's house down – joking, obviously, but I think he'd been let down over money. He said he was paid £12,000 up at Leyland. We actually paid him £30,000 [£55,000 in today's money], and this for someone a year older and playing in a lower league! Crazy, really. He couldn't believe it. I only became treasurer in April that year and I couldn't believe it either! In the end, he agreed to £25,000. He took 82 wickets at 9.62 and we won the league, for which we received a cheque for £200."

There was one more South African winter before he called time, but the peerless, immortal-seeming Marshall would be dead within four years, cruelly taken by colon cancer in November 1999, aged just 41. The following year, Farrar also died a premature death, suffering a heart attack at Manchester Airport while waiting to collect an autograph. He had brought a sprinkling of stardust to Leyland – and to the Northern League as a whole – but, when the money dried up, the hired guns drifted away to reveal a structure built on sand. It would be 14 years before Leyland managed even a top-half finish, with 10 bottom-three placings in the 12 years after Marshall's departure. There are few things quite so desolate as a morning-after visit to the site of a party, but while the revelry was in full swing it bequeathed magical experiences for teammates and opponents alike, memories that will never be forgotten.

"I remember walking out to bat in one of Gordon's first games, taking my guard and thinking: blimey, that's Gordon Greenidge at the other end," says Berry. "I was so nervous, because I didn't want to let him down. But if you played a good shot, he'd tell you so and make you feel 10-foot tall. He was quite reserved, Gordon. Malcolm was a bit more outgoing, a lovely man and great company. We had many good nights at Squires in Preston on a Thursday after training, and he certainly didn't spoil his rum with much else. It was such a privilege to play with them both. When we were kids, me and my mate used to play cricket all day, every day in the holidays, making up our own teams. Greenidge was always in there. Marshall was always in there. So to play with them both was totally surreal."

Not the sort of thing you can easily put a price on.

3

Viv Richards

at Rishton CC

Many's the time in club cricket you'll turn up to a game without the proverbial Scooby Doo about the opposition's pro: his name, what he looks like, his credentials. This probably wasn't much of a problem for Lancashire League cricketers visiting Rishton CC in the summer of 1987, for the new pro at Blackburn Road had by that stage of his career amassed 6,472 Test runs at 52.61 with 20 hundreds, one of which was, at the time, the fastest in the history of the game.

No, no one needed telling that the hip-swaying, shoulder-rolling strut or the coiled power of that familiar, gum-cudding figure standing on the square belonged to Isaac Vivian Alexander Richards. They probably recognised him from off of the telly – maybe from that game three years earlier and 40 miles down the road when he bludgeoned the highest ever ODI score, an undefeated 189 out of 272/9; or from 11 years earlier, when, rather than *grovelling*, he opted instead to rub Greigy's nose in just the 829 runs in four Tests. Yep, they may have had an inkling, these savvy men of the Lancashire valleys, that Rishton's new pro was strong through mid-wicket.

His Vivship missed the season opener at Bacup, and only touched down in London around noon on the day of his debut, meaning he got to the ground just half an hour before the start. This isn't entirely unheard of among club cricketers, so you could argue that it was an immediate adaptation. Conversely, his mode of transport was the less-conventionally-clubby chartered helicopter, paid for by *The Sun* newspaper, who were part of the sort of media scrum that doesn't greet your bog-standard overseas pro from, say, Khan Research Laboratories or Chilaw Marians. Film crews from the BBC and ITV Granada were also present, along with national and local press. But then, this was the Master Blaster, captain of the all-conquering West Indies team and fourth in the world batting rankings, although still the undisputed *numero uno* in most eyes. It was like Lionel Messi signing for Accrington Stanley or Stocksbridge Park Steels.

Viv's availability was possible due to the acrimonious fall-out that had engulfed Somerset the previous year, when the decision was made mid-season to release the club's two long-serving West Indian greats, Richards and Joel Garner, which they knew would almost certainly prompt the departure of Ian Botham in solidarity. Club captain Peter Roebuck's choice to replace the two legends would be the bright and preppy Martin Crowe. However, given Richards' 56-ball evisceration of England in Antigua just prior to that toxic '86 campaign – followed up with the English professional season's fastest hundred, a 48-ball effort for Somerset against Glamorgan – it was fair to say he was still in possession of his mojo. He hadn't sought another first-class home, however, later writing in one of his autobiographies, *Hitting Across the Line*: "I did not want to be involved with another county. I needed something else, something pure."

Rishton's chairman, Wilf Woodhouse, was ahead of the curve, and his dogged persistence eventually persuaded Richards to dispatch his manager to Lancashire, to run the rule over this village of 7,000 people. He reported back that this "nice community" with the cricket club at its heart was just what the maestro needed. And as luck would have it, Rishton's secretary was out in Australia watching England in the Benson & Hedges Tri-Series alongside the hosts, and with the West Indies also competing, Richards put pen to paper.

It was, patently, a major coup, not that Richards was the first big name the club had engaged – Michael Holding had played there in 1981 – and nor would he be the last, with Mohammad Azharuddin coming the following season, and after him the likes of Allan Donald, Jason Gillespie and Vernon Philander. In fact, it is a Lancashire League rule – C 1.i. since you ask – that clubs must field a professional – no ifs, no buts – presumably to help cultivate interest, with failure to do so incurring either a fine or points forfeiture. But still, this was Viv: the biggest draw in world cricket! The Rishton first XI skipper, David Wells, even went on national TV, discussing the club's new signing with Frank Bough on BBC's *Breakfast Time*. "I was wearing a horrendous jumper. But then, so was he."

Having fought his way through the paps, Viv was soon donning the pads. The first ball he faced in Lancashire League cricket was bowled by Eddo Brandes, pro at that season's eventual champions Haslingden. "I had him absolutely plumb lbw," recalls the Zimbabwean, yet the presence of a couple of thousand spectators dissuaded the umpire from pooping the party, and Richards went on to score 87, one fewer than Rishton's margin of victory. "I saw him in a hotel foyer at the World Cup later that year and he admitted he was stone dead," laughs Brandes.

Next victims of the Richards Roadshow were Accrington, alma mater of David 'Bumble' Lloyd, who was 40 years old and making a return to league action 23 years on from his last outing. Lloyd chiselled out an unbeaten 51 in his team's 181/6, which proved nowhere near enough thanks to Viv's 98* in reply.

It was Lancashire League tradition that any player scoring a fifty earned a collection – money tossed into a box taken round the crowd – and Bumble pocketed £105 for his efforts, with Accrington pro Bharat Arun picking up £135 for his 72. Better than a kick in the proverbials. However, Richards, to use a Bumbleism, was *absolute box-office*, and with the 2,500 on the ground primarily there to see him in the up-close, King Viv's half-century added a nice little £400 to his take-home. Alas, he missed out on a double-collection when, sitting on 94 with the scores level, stalwart seamer Alan Worsick served up a deliberate full toss, which he narrowly failed to launch over the ropes. Still, gate receipts came to £1,700 – around £4,500 in today's money – at the time the highest in the history of Lancashire League cricket and enough to finance Accrington's urgently needed new clubhouse roof. With all this came important logistical considerations. "I played in some big finals, but those were the biggest crowds I played in front of on a consistent basis," says Wells. "Because Viv was turning up at, say, Haslingden or Burnley or Lowerhouse, instead of ordering 100 pies for the day, they'd order 300, you know…"

An average of 185 was going to prove difficult to sustain, even for the great man, and in the next match, the return fixture at Haslingden (in one of many obstinate local quirks, fixtures were played in blocks rather than standard symmetrical half-seasons), Viv was trapped for just 8, caught at what the successful bowler and captain, Bryan Knowles, called "deep cow", part of his sole five-for in 27 seasons. Knowles also scored 95* – the highest innings Rishton conceded all year – as the 138 runs were knocked off one down. Not bad, but then six years earlier he had become the first amateur since 1957 to top the Lancashire League batting averages, the first since 1929 to score 1,000 league runs, even hitting Rishton's pro that year – MA Holding, a few short months after *that* over to Boycott in Barbados – back over his head for a one-bounce four during an innings of 96. Not many in the country have done that.

These were no mugs, and Richards quickly realised it wouldn't be a stroll, writing in *Sir Viv*, a later and more definitive autobiography: "This was no sabbatical. Any thoughts of a hatful of runs and a handful of wickets were soon tempered by the reality of the serious cricket played on damp, difficult strips against captains who knew how to make the best of the local lie of the land. They were no respecters of reputation."

The weather sweeping in off the Irish Sea claimed four of the next seven fixtures. First, Bacup's players were denied their once-in-a-lifetime opportunity. Then, after a 10-wicket win against Accrington in which he didn't bat, a weekend double-header succumbed to the elements, with Richards' pre-deluge 91 against Ramsbottom being chalked off his final stats, as another of the local rules allowed for some league fixtures to be replayed. One such was the washout at Burnley, although unfortunately for their bar takings (and maybe for a five-year-old Jimmy Anderson, there to watch his uncle Neil) not a single ball was bowled in the rescheduled match either. In total, 10 out of 29 matches were lost to the weather, a lot of useful Viv-lucre remaining in those Lancastrian pockets. It's surprising a UN agency wasn't set up to provide economic aid.

In August, a second double-header fell victim to the rains on the weekend that the MCC's star-studded Bicentenary match against the Rest of the World was played, Viv having declined an invitation to join the likes of Greenidge, Haynes, Marshall, Border, Imran Khan, Abdul Qadir, Javed Miandad, Gavaskar, Shastri, Vengsarkar, Hadlee, Rice, Gooch, Gower and Gatting out of loyalty to Rishton. On another occasion, Richards ruled himself out of a pair of lucrative paydays for the Rest of the World XI in the Callers Pegasus Festival at Jesmond in order to play in – and then stay to the end of – a much-interrupted Worsley Cup semi-final with Ramsbottom, stretching over several nights, five overs here, 10 overs there, the heavens opening each time the game looked like reaching its conclusion, denying an already-dismissed Viv his leave of absence. But this wasn't a man to abandon comrades still on the battlefield.

Come rain or shine, Viv was a regular presence at the club, coaching kids on Monday ("Mum, just off for my two-hour batting session with Vivian Richards"), netting on Tuesdays and Thursdays, and taking on all-comers at snooker between times. Lodgings were the four-star Dunkenhalgh Hotel and Spa, a 700-year-old former manor house with turrets, porticos and crenellations that was literally one mile up the road yet still closer to Enfield CC, indicative of the league's parochial patchwork of cheek-by-jowl rivalries (Church CC was even closer). His wife and kids visited for a couple of weeks, otherwise it was Viv and his 'minder' Tony. He had a sponsored BMW to buzz about in, fulfilling his promotional obligations with Cockspur Rum, sponsors that year of the National Club Championship, and not a product whose endorsement would have caused too many pangs of conscience given his fondness for it as a tipple – not least when Ian Botham paid an impromptu midweek visit.

Amid the rum and the rains, Richards' maiden league ton against Colne – pronounced as you would the thing you use to put a bat rubber on the handle, or out of which you might slurp a consolatory ice cream having hit a full bunger to extra cover on a red hot day – was followed by a four-game mini-slump without a half-century. "The opposition, without fail, were ecstatic to see the back of him," recalls Wells. "But plenty of fans would go off the ground as soon as he got out. All they'd come to see was him get some runs."

Chief among the revenue-suppressing Viv Destroyers were a trio of bowlers who dismissed the Master Blaster home and away: Enfield's former Lancashire all-rounder Bernard Reidy, a left-arm swing bowler with one of the game's great perms; lanky East Lancs 'dibbly-dobbler' Ian Haworth, who snared him for 5 and 30; and Rawtenstall's 24-year-old left-arm spinner, Keith 'Kes' Roscoe, who 35 years later became the highest amateur wicket-taker in the history of the league.

"He came swaggering to the wicket and scored 20-odd in no time," recalls Roscoe, who today runs the family racing pigeon accessory business. "Our skipper took the fast bowler off and said, 'Here y'are, your go.' First ball he pushed back. Second ball, he danced down and put me on Bacup Road, and kept walking at me and said, in that West Indian lilt, 'I didn't even middle that one, man.' The next ball I bowled an arm-ball that popped on him a bit and he got a faint outside edge, which the keeper, Peter Barnes, juggled around him and finished up catching. Viv stood back on his bat, daring the umpire to give him out. And the umpire did the business for me!"

"By the time I had safely gathered the ball in," adds Barnes, "Kes, who was not known for his athletic prowess, even back in the Eighties, had sprinted down the pitch to celebrate taking the wicket of the great man. We looked up to see Viv just standing there, staring at the umpire and tapping the top of his pad, indicating that he had not hit the ball. We were horrified. We looked to the umpire, and after what seemed an eternity, he eventually – and bravely – lifted his finger. The rest of the Rishton innings passed in a bit of a blur, as I considered what actions Viv might take if he genuinely thought that we had cheated him out. Would I get home in one piece?"

Viv's reputation-flexing antics had not gone down well with a small section of the crowd. "As he walked back to the pavilion, one of the Rawtenstall supporters was shouting abuse at him," says Barnes, pinpointing the likely source of his own safety concerns. "He rightly took offence. Instead of heading for the changing rooms, he changed direction and headed towards the seat where the abuse had originated. Luckily, some of his teammates intercepted him before he got to his prey. I don't think the gentleman was around at the end of the match!" Nevertheless, Richards soon cooled off and, later, he and his pocket-opening charisma took round the collection box for his teammate, David Wilson, who top-scored with 66 in Rishton's 179/9.

Some intemperate weather saw that target reduced to 156 from 39 overs, and by the time Barnes walked in at No.11, 28 were still needed. Going into the last over, Viv bowling, it was down to 13, John Kershaw unbeaten on 50, Barnes on strike. "In my opinion," says Barnes, "the first two balls were both wides, but not given: the same umpire who had raised his finger to Viv. I think by now he was scared to death of him and his glares. Next ball beat me all ends up. Still 13 needed. As the fourth ball hit my bat, I thought I had launched it onto the terraces for six, but then, as we started running, I felt it may not quite get there and only be a four, leaving nine off two. It did neither. It plugged in the soft, rain-soaked ground on landing, and we only took a single. John now had to hit two sixes off the last two balls to win. I had every confidence in him. Viv bowled, John took a mighty swing, and the ball flew from the edge straight into his face, splitting his eyebrow open. Retired hurt. Instead of the fairytale ending of hitting Viv Richards for two sixes to win the game it was the nightmare of visiting A&E for several stitches!"

The final innings of the mini-slump came at Todmorden, whose ground had once been bisected by the Lancashire-Yorkshire border but which now lay entirely under the white rose. Their pro was a 22-year-old outswing bowler, South Africa's second greatest de Villiers: Petrus Stephanus 'Fanie', who had the temerity to clean-bowl Richards for 40. "The whole of bloody Todmorden was upset with me!"

For obvious reasons, de Villiers had never seen Viv bat on TV, and so was somewhat taken aback by the aggressive manner of the King's play. In the return fixture, Richards – not one to enjoy being bested by South Africans in the 1980s – made a season's best 127 out of Rishton's total of 210, de Villiers finishing with 3/92 from 18 overs. "I thought: why the hell is he slogging me? I can understand him slogging the local bowlers, but I had extra pace and swing. I never realised that's just the way he bats."

Richards had hit a patch of form more purple than Prince's wardrobe, the Tod ton sandwiched by innings of 79 and 103, both against Nelson and their 22-year-old tyro pro, Steve Waugh, who responded with scores of 54 and 93. Cameras from Australia's Channel 9 network turned up for the second game to film a small news feature on 'Tugga', who steered Nelson to 194/4 with 10 balls remaining in pursuit of Rishton's 199. "We were dead and buried," recalls Wells.

Colin Kuhn finished the penultimate over with a brace of wickets, without further addition to the total, and the Master Blaster stepped up to bowl the final over at the young pretender, six runs required. He began with two dots. Third ball, Waugh shuffled down the pitch, attempting to win it with one hit, but was defeated by the capricious Lancastrian wicket and Frank Martindale completed the stumping. Only three more runs were scrambled from the rest of the over, Nelson finishing two runs short in front of another bumper crowd privileged to witness a toe-to-toe encounter of actual and future Hall of Famers, one lent an extra sprinkling of spice by news that Waugh would make his County Championship debut for Somerset four days after the game, as a replacement for Crowe.

Viv sat on 688 runs after the Nelson nailbiter, with a possible 11 further innings. He would have had to go some to overhaul Everton Weekes' league record tally of 1,518 for Bacup in 1951, but the symbolic 1,000-run season – already achieved that decade by the likes of Mudassar Nazar, Madan Lal and Collis King – was surely a formality. In the end, Viv would only bat six more times, making just one more half-century – 66* at Ramsbottom in what turned out to be his final innings – as he succumbed to each of his nemeses once more.

Roscoe again found the maestro's edge with an arm ball that popped – "the keeper not only caught him, but stumped him as well, so you could say I got him out *three* times in two games" – and was subsequently offered a summer contract at Gloucestershire on the back of his exploits. However, with a mortgage and five-year-old son to take care of, he had to turn it down. "I couldn't afford the pay cut. Besides, I had booked a fortnight's holiday at my dad's caravan in Poulton-le-Fylde, and I promised my good lady we would go."

Despite their esteemed pro's considerable reputation and talents, not to mention his mythical aura, Rishton were unable to land a first title since 1955, ultimately finishing fourth. Viv himself ended up top of both run charts and averages (his 899 league runs at 64 from just 17 innings edging out Waugh), although he missed the final weekend with chickenpox, denying him and the club a fitting farewell to what he described as "a great experience and a lot more exciting than I expected".

Nevertheless, as Wells reflects, he left a considerable impression on those lucky enough to share a dressing room, a partnership, a pint, or even an encouraging word with the great man. "Can you imagine someone telling you you're captaining Viv Richards? Wow, unbelievable! I suppose you can play with Jordan Spieth in a golf pro-am, but in which other game can you play with someone who's the best in the world at what he does for five months? Unfortunately, those days will never return."

4

Jacques Kallis

at Old Edwardians CC and Netherfield CC

It would be unfair to describe someone with more Test sixes than everyone bar Stokes, McCullum, Gilchrist and Gayle, those four swordsmen of the apocalypse, as *vanilla* – and perhaps unfair on vanilla to use it as a synonym for bland – but for a cricketer who finished with 13,289 Test runs at over 55, including 45 hundreds, as well as 292 wickets at under 33 and 200 catches, comparatively little of Jacques Henry Kallis' career skips down the pitch at you from memory. His was a bloodless, relentless brilliance: snicks melting into massive mitts, splice reluctantly hit at 140 clicks, runs gathered in an unfussy, low-risk manner with minimal ostentation and even less emotion. Robocricketer. For the various dressing rooms he was part of, it was like a dose of cricketing Valium – all the senses that evolution had slowly tweaked into danger-readiness could be safely dialled down. Relax, Jacques has got this.

"He just batted and batted," recalls Simon Dutton, who in 1995 captained the 19-year-old Kallis at Netherfield CC in Cumbria. "He never seemed to whack it. He never got bogged down. Everyone batted around him. He blocked good balls, and if you were slightly off your length, he hit it for four, seemingly with no effort. You don't remember anything particularly outrageous. He'd be on 60 and you'd barely remember him playing a shot." By the time he left in mid-July for a South Africa under-24s tour, he was averaging 98.87 in one of the top three leagues in the country. Those mechanics and methodology were already firmly embedded.

This was a player comprehensively out-YouTubed by the select few among his peers: Lara's flamboyance, Sachin's impudence, Ponting's pugnacity, Sanga's sagacity, not to mention the various extravagances of Sehwag, Gilchrist, de Villiers and Pietersen, all of whom threw bold colours on their many memorable canvases. Kallis seemed to paint in blocks of reassuring beige, then another in khaki, and another in sand, cream, buff, tan. Twenty years of haptic apprehension later, you stepped back – clambered down from the scaffold – and realised that each block formed part of an enormous portrait, one that could only be appreciated holistically. The devil was not so much in the detail, but the monument.

It was ever thus, a teak-tough and unflappably methodical customer right from his days at Wynberg Boys' School in Cape Town, representing South Africa under-17s on a tour to England in 1993 just weeks after his final exams. The two summers he spent in English club cricket after that were simply dipping the conker in vinegar.

Kallis scored a hundred at Old Trafford on that under-17s tour, and made a first-class debut for Western Province 'B' the following January, averaging 53.33 across four games in the second-tier competition. Head coach of WP at the time was Duncan Fletcher, whose old comrade Dave Houghton was heading back for a second Birmingham League season at West Bromwich Dartmouth and had sung the league's praises. Fletcher reached out to Warwickshire coach and WP old boy Bob Woolmer, who made enquiries.

Sitting on the Warwickshire cricket committee at the time was John Winspear, an alumnus of King Edward's School in Solihull and occasional player in the Bears' second team in the 1970s. Winspear was still playing Saturday cricket for Old Edwardians first XI in the Midland Combined Counties League, which comprised clubs from Worcestershire and Warwickshire and, while a lower standard than the BDCL, was certainly competitive enough. And so it was that, through this mesh of happenstance, Woolmer came to call OE's skipper John Nicholls and a group of club cricketers from Solihull got to witness some of the first cricketing steps of the only serious rival to Garry Sobers as the greatest all-round cricketer of all time. And they paid him just £70 per week for the experience.

"Bob put me in touch with Henry Kallis, Jacques' father," recalls Nicholls. "He was very protective. Jacques' mother had died when he was 10 years old and he'd never been out of South Africa on his own before. Jacques fitted the bill of what we wanted – a medium-fast bowler and top-order batsman – and we agreed to take him on. I received the paperwork from Duncan, who had some concerns over whether Jacques was going to be able to cope on that sort of money. I was providing the accommodation at my house, and a wealthy backer had paid for his airfare. I told Duncan he wouldn't need any money, because we'll treat him as family, and everywhere we go, he'll go."

Come April, Nicholls headed down to Heathrow to pick up the 18-year-old Kallis. "The first thing that struck me was his hands were massive," he says. "We brought him back to Redditch, settled him in, but he got very homesick in the first few weeks. It was early season and raining a lot."

Still, there were enough breaks in the inclement weather for Kallis to rack up three hundreds before May had reached its second week, the first coming in the traditional pre-season friendly against King Edward's School. "It was impressive," his new skipper recalls. "My wife at the time said, 'It's all very well him hitting all the schoolboys around'. I said, 'Two of those schoolboys are Mark Wagh and Anurag Singh, who both play for England under-17s!'"

Rain claimed the MCCL opener, but it would take just four balls of batting against adults on league debut against Sheldon Marlborough for his teammates to experience the 'yep, this lad is quite decent' moment. "He came in at three," recalls opener Richard Lucas, "after we'd put on over a hundred for the first wicket. I'm at the non-striker's end, knackered, on 80-odd and leaning on my bat as he picked up his third and fourth balls over square leg for six, off a good line and length, from a top league bowler."

Six more balls were launched over the ropes en route to an unbeaten 114 – one of them sailing over a huge oak and out of the ground, with locals unable to recall anyone clearing that tree before – a score he matched the following week against Streetly, no mean feat given OEs were chasing just 156.

A week later, against Walmley, Chris Woakes' club, Kallis had moved serenely to 92* out of 156/2 when the weather intervened with 98 needed off 12 overs. Even then, the smart money was on Kallis walking off with 150-odd not out, having steered the ship home. As it was, he had to content himself with an early-season average of 330, which was probably going to be difficult to maintain, and it had indeed come tumbling to 131 by the end of the month, when he followed 13 against Droitwich with 60 against eventual champions Highway, for whom future New Zealand left-arm quick Shayne O'Connor was pro.

Meanwhile, Kallis was slowly getting over his homesickness through golf, says Nicholls. "I'd go to work about half-seven, home at half-five, and what Jacques would do all day if there wasn't any cricket on the TV was putt golf balls up and down my 30-odd-foot lounge. When he started, he had a touch like a blacksmith, but by the time he went home he was almost professional level."

Nicholls and Kallis made regular trips to Edgbaston that summer to watch Brian Lara, who had begun his season with seven first-class tons in 10 knocks, including the world-record 501*, as Warwickshire landed three of the four trophies on offer and lost the final in the other. Nicholls and his wife took Kallis away to France together, too, and as the season wore on the young lodger came more and more out of shell, occasionally pranking Nicholls by hiding gummy bears in his Chinese food. Nevertheless, his shyness meant he never took up an open-ended offer to supplement that £70 with coaching sessions in local schools.

"He was very introvert," explains Nicholls. "He only left the house three times on his own when I wasn't there. The first time, he locked himself out and spent five hours at the neighbour's house. The second time, he wanted to go into Birmingham city centre, an easy journey on the train, and ended up at Stafford station. Don't ask me how. I had to go and rescue him. The third time was when he had a call from a teammate at WP, Alan Dawson. Alan had managed to get hold of some Wimbledon tickets, and came and picked Jacques up. He was with Lance Klusener. I gave them directions, as they hadn't got much of a clue where the motorway was – this is before SatNav, and they didn't have a roadmap – and about two hours later I get a call from Alan. They were in Cardiff."

Of course, Kallis was primarily there to further his cricketing education, and June brought more opportunity in the shape of the Berry League, a 45-over Sunday competition in which OEs faced some of the Birmingham League heavy-hitters, like West Bromwich Dartmouth, Wolverhampton and Old Hill. Kallis kicked off the campaign with 107* against Moseley Ashfield and would finish with 580 runs at 64.44. "He also enjoyed the fact that he could only be called on for nine overs," adds Nicholls.

Saturdays were often a different story. A dearth of bowling options and the realisation that their South African teenager's fast-mediums were better than it had said on the tin led to a steadily increasing workload: 36 overs in the first five MCCL outings, an average of 14 per match thereafter, including one unbroken spell of 25. He would finish with a modest 32 MCCL wickets at 25.4, along with 23 at 13 apiece in the Berry League. "He could be a handful," says Lucas. "There were times I stood 20 yards back at slip to him, even at that age."

As ever, though, Kallis was principally interested in batting. And more batting. June, however, also saw the start of a mini-famine in the MCCL, with scores of 6, 43, 0, 18, 42 and 0 leading into the club's tour of the West Country, where a Monday DNB was followed by 134 at Weston-super-Mare on Tuesday and 100* at Marcus Trescothick's club, Keynsham, on the Wednesday. "He caused some damage there," says Nicholls. "There was a house 30 yards behind the mid-wicket boundary. An old fellow said he'd never seen anyone hit it before. The ball dislodged two tiles, one of which went through the top of the conservatory."

Groove rediscovered, Kallis finished the Berry League season with scores of 45, 74 (from 26 balls), 104*, 52, 38 and – in his final outing in Old Edwardians colours – a disappointing 2 at Kidderminster, missing out on a good pitch at a Worcestershire out-ground. He would do rather better at Chester Road three years later, scoring an unbeaten 171 there for Middlesex, with Nicholls turning up to catch the end of the match.

"Afterwards, Jacques told me he had to head down to Somerset that night," Nicholls recalls. "The game was starting the next-but-one day, but as the Worcester game had finished at about two o'clock, he asked if we could play golf. So we went to Bromsgrove Golf Club. I won, and he wasn't happy. He was playing off about 20 at the time. I was off 16. He was very competitive. So he phoned the Middlesex coach and asked if he could turn up a bit later to Taunton. The coach spoke to me and I said it was fine. What I didn't tell him was Jacques wanted to stay so he could beat me at golf in the morning. Or try!"

Kallis' post-tour form in the Combined Counties was even more impressive than in the Berry, with scores of 93*, 63, 129*, 27, 21, 56* and 81. The final game was rained off, however, denying him the chance to break the 1000-run mark.

The first innings of that sequence helped knock off Walmley's 254 in just 40 overs, with Lucas making 116 at the start of his own high-summer purple patch, which also brought him 73 the following week against Aston Manor (his opening partner Mike Hughes slammed 135* as Kallis wandered in at 132/1, OEs eventually racking up 357 from 50 overs). A week later, it was Lucas' turn to register 135* as OEs knocked off 285 in just 38 overs, Kallis' 129* containing 10 fours and 10 sixes. "We put on 269 in 215 balls," says Lucas. "It's a club record for all wickets. I have a transcript of the scorecard on my wall. I had the pleasure of batting with him for three partnerships over a hundred, all in winning efforts, and I am unashamedly proud of those achievements in my career. Who wouldn't be?"

In the end, Kallis had to settle for 972 MCCL runs at 74.44 as OEs finished second (a feat they would repeat a year later, before winning the title in 1996 with Marais Erasmus as pro). Throw in his Berry League efforts, and the haul was 1,552 runs at 70.54. Add in the friendlies, and Kallis racked up over 2,000 runs for the club, including eight hundreds. None of which seemed beige to his awestruck teammates. Nevertheless, since Kallis' career is so often reduced to the bottom line, perhaps the most impressive number was the initially homesick homebody's average on home turf: a chunky 112.86 in all competitive cricket. Get the deck chairs, pack some fine cheeses, Jacques will be batting at the Old Memorial this afternoon! Little wonder his skipper was fielding inquisitive calls from the Birmingham League big boys.

"It was obvious he was going on to bigger and better things," says Nicholls. "We weren't daft. But we did try and contract him for 1995. We were constantly in touch with his dad. We spoke to Duncan Fletcher. Two months before the season we got a call saying, 'No disrespect, but we want Jacques to play a higher standard'. At the time, the Northern League was probably the best in the country alongside the Birmingham League. I had a call from the chairman of Netherfield, basically asking if this guy was any good. I had to think twice about putting him off!"

By the time the 19-year-old Kallis was being collected from Heathrow by Nicholls the following April, he had spent an unspectacular year in the West Province 'A' team, although had registered twin fifties against the touring Pakistanis. After an overnight stop in Redditch, he was picked up by Netherfield first-team colleague David Otway, who drove Kallis up to the flat that the club owned in Kendal town centre. Ideal, you would think.

"On Thursday," recalls Nicholls, "I got a call from him. 'Skip, do you mind if I come and stay with you?' I asked him what was up. 'The people are fine, nice ground, but they've put me in a flat with a loaf of bread and pint of milk.' I says, 'Right. And?' He says, 'Well, what do I do with that?' I told him he must have known what he was getting into and that he couldn't stay here because he was 140-odd miles away. He suggested driving down to Redditch on Sundays, staying for the week and going back on Friday. 'What about practice?' 'I'll say I'm practising with you.' So the first week he drove down straight after their match. They finished early and he was here before I got back from my game, 10 miles away! He did this a few times through the season. I'm not sure the Netherfield lads even realised. We even took him on tour with us again!"

Prior to that jaunt south, a beaming Kallis had been featured in *The Westmorland Gazette*, Kendal's local paper, crouching beside his complementary car and describing his first ever experience of snow. A day later, he was stumped for 11 on debut at Fleetwood in what the *Gazette* described as "trawler-deck weather", a slow start compared to his early season fireworks at OEs. With Netherfield never before having won the Northern League, and cross-town rivals Kendal coming off an unbeaten league campaign that delivered their second consecutive title, it was imperative Kallis fell quickly into the swing of things.

"We had built a reputation of finding professionals who later went on to play international cricket," says Netherfield secretary, Ian Heath. "David Boon had been the first, back in 1981. Iqbal Sikander, later part of Pakistan's World Cup-winning squad, followed from 1983 to 1985. We had Kenny Benjamin in 1991 and '92, Steven Jack in 1993, and Colin Miller in 1994. Jacques arrived fresh-faced and with a very pleasant manner, but also with a 'little boy lost' look about him."

Heath was playing in the second team at the time, and after a comfortable away win at Leyland on the second weekend sped back north to catch the new pro in action. "We watched from the car just inside the ground and saw this massive expansive off-drive with full follow-through. Our eyes lifted, expecting a lofted drive, but in fact the ball went like a rocket along the floor to the boundary. I thought, 'Jesus, that was class', and a few other expletives were let out."

Kallis finished unbeaten on 89 as Leyland's 187 was comfortably overhauled. A week later, he made a chanceless 115* from 109 balls in a 67-run win over eventual wooden-spoonists Preston, giving him a three-game average of 215 – something of a drop-off from the previous season's 330, but tidy all the same. On the Sunday, he added a round 50 in victory over Workington in the first round of the county cup, smiting an enormous six over Netherfield's bowling green and into the road. Kallis' feet were firmly under the cricketing table, and the club did everything they could to make him feel at home (which, considering he couldn't use a microwave, was a more sizeable task than it seems).

"He was a bit lost in the flat at first," recalls treasurer Mike Rigg. "We got him a load of cricket videos through the club, but he came back after a week and said, 'I can't watch them, Mike. The flat doesn't have a VCR.' So I gave him the keys to my house and he would come round and watch them while we were at work, studying them obsessively."

Rigg's wife worked at Marks & Spencer, which helped in attending to Kallis' copious appetite – Nicholls quips that he's "only just paid off Jacques' food bill from 1994" – while they regularly had him over for Sunday roast. "He was very polite, with perfect manners," adds Rigg, "but it was hard work to get a conversation out of him at times."

As ever, Kallis was letting his bat do most of his talking, and with the young pro having already proven his chops, optimism grew at Netherfield that they could improve upon their three runners-up finishes in 36 years of NCL membership and land a maiden title. It would not be easy. One gauge of the stiffness of the challenge was the quality of professional engaged by the three clubs Kallis had hitherto encountered. Fleetwood had four different Test players in four years at the start of the 1990s; Leyland's pros in the previous two seasons had been Gordon Greenidge and Malcolm Marshall; while recent years had brought Javed Miandad and Mark Greatbatch to Preston. Elsewhere, Richie Richardson, Stuart MacGill, Ravi Shastri and Maninder Singh had sprinkled their stardust.

In addition, Northern League clubs were dominating the Lancashire Cup – contested by the top four teams from 12 of the county's leagues – winning 13 of the previous 16 finals. They were making an impact in the National Club Championship, too, Blackpool winning it in 1990, Kendal making the final two years later, while Netherfield's next opponents, Chorley, were the reigning champions, having beaten Ealing at Lord's the previous September.

Chorley tended to avoid signing high-profile pros, which doubtless helped them on the national stage, where overseas players were ineligible. Indeed, their paid man from 1978 to 1984 had been local legend Keith Eccleshare, one of the league's great characters and named in a *Test Match Special* interview by Jim Gledhill, the man who ran Lancashire Schoolboys from the 1970s to the mid-1990s, as the most talented player to come through the system on his watch, Atherton, Crawley, Fowler, Fairbrother *et al* included. Lancashire offered Eccleshare terms 20-odd years earlier, but his father had answered the phone and told them, unilaterally and unequivocally, that his son was going to be a footballer. He went on to play for England Schoolboys and in the Football League for Bury before dropping into the semi-pro game in his early twenties. Sliding doors.

Eccleshare had been a sharp, splice-bothering fast-medium bowler during that first seven-year spell at Chorley – bagging a phenomenal 547 league wickets at under 13 apiece, an average of 78 wickets per 22-game season – and returned for two more years as pro in 1989, by which time he was starting to morph into a high-quality leg-spinner. During his four years away, playing in the Bolton League, 'Eck' had combined the two, even going two-and-a-half seasons without being removed from the attack. Three years before training his crosshairs on this strapping teenage South African, Eccleshare's googly had bamboozled Richie Richardson, who later told him he was the best spinner in the country, so he was unlikely to be phased as Kallis cruised serenely into the twenties.

"I was at first slip, Eck at second," recalls Chorley skipper Roland Horridge. "We had a bowler from Liverpool in Sydney grade cricket, Ronnie Davis, whose claim to fame was knocking over Steve, Mark and Dean Waugh. Good bowler, low-80s, no rubbish. Kallis came in and second ball leant on one that went whistling through extra-cover. He did it three or four more times. Eck and I looked at each other and said, 'Oh yes, this guy can play'. It was absolutely effortless. Pure class."

With Kallis on 29 and looking set, Horridge tossed the ball to his 44-year-old leggie. "He bowled Kallis fourth ball," chuckles Horridge. "It pitched leg and took the off bail. Unplayable. Kallis said in the bar that he'd never faced a ball or bowler like it. After he was out, he went and stood by the sightscreen behind the keeper to watch."

Eccleshare finished with 4/14, Davis 5/22, and Netherfield were 76 all out. However, Chorley soon slipped to 13/3, two of them falling to Kallis, given the new ball after his early season spells had impressed keeper-captain Dutton.

"He told me he was medium-pace at first," says Dutton, who combined those roles in the Cumberland team as well. "I used to enjoy standing up to the seamers, so I said to him, 'Do you want me to stand back or up?' He said, 'I think you should stand back and have a look'. The first ball nearly took my head off. I looked at slip, who looked at me, and said, 'F**king hell, where did that come from?!' They were rock-hard wickets at our place and he already had a big barrel chest, even at 19."

Nevertheless, Western Province, perhaps learning from Kallis' experiences with OEs, had insisted on a clause in his contract limiting the number of overs he could bowl in a game. Not that it would have prevented Chorley inflicting a seven-wicket defeat on Netherfield, the first of three on the bounce that took the early-season wind from their sails. The second came 24 hours later in the Vaux Samson Cup to a St Annes team that had a 17-year-old Andrew Flintoff in the ranks, the first iteration of what would become a classic *mano a mano*. "Kallis won hands down," says Rigg. "Freddie was out for a duck and Jacques made 1!"

Kallis was again undone by spin, stumped by a chirpy John Isles off the slow left-arm of John Cotton, a regional manager of Blackburn-based Thwaite's brewery and future league chairman. "I'm saying, 'Come on, JC, give him the wrong'un'!" recalls Isles. "Two balls later: 'There it is! He's not picked it!' Obviously, there isn't anything going on with these balls, I'm just blagging it." Welcome to the north, young man.

Whether or not any of this had punctured the usually impervious Kallis bubble, Isles nevertheless decided to pick up the thread at tea, now in full 'cultural attaché for the Fylde Coast' mode. "I said, 'Done by the oldest bloke on the field. You weren't stumped, you were fossilised.' Then I told him, 'I hope you can bowl, son, because you can't f**king bat'."

Spoiler: it turned out Kallis could bat. In fact, in a further dozen innings for Netherfield, he was only twice dismissed for under 50, with his lowest score coming in the league fixture with St Annes: c&b Cotton for 29. "I met him in 1998 at Langan's brasserie in London," recalls Cotton, "and he said he'd never in his life faced anybody so slow!"

The problem for Netherfield was that, despite Kallis' rock-solid contributions, few of these games were won outright, which was largely down to Dutton losing 10 consecutive tosses in the league, decidedly sub-optimal for a team stacked with batting. Grahame Clarke, the carrot-topped counter-punching opener, would top the league run charts with 937 at 52, including three hundreds; Dutton himself would contribute 408 runs at 31.4; four others chipped in with fifties; and Kallis finished a full 40 runs clear at the top of the league averages. A team built for chasing.

Kallis' sequence began with 73 out of 156/9 in defeat to table-topping Morecambe, 15* against lowly Leyland Motors before the game was abandoned, then a grafting 42 on a sticky dog in the Kendal derby, where he renewed his acquaintance with Eldine Baptiste, against whose Eastern Province team Kallis had taken a one-day hundred in March. The Antiguan was pound for pound the best pro in the league, finishing top of the bowling averages in all three years he spent at Shap Road, snaring 206 wickets at 9.6 apiece while scoring 1,955 runs at 48.88.

Even so, Kallis saw Baptiste off before falling to left-arm spinner Andy Wilson, and with Clarke scoring a chancy 60, Netherfield battled to 172/6. In response, Kendal mustered just 87/8, the ninth-wicket pair stonewalling for the final seven overs. The lack of knockout firepower would encapsulate Netherfield's frustrations – Kallis chipped in a few wickets here and there but would not manage a single three-for in league or cups – and they would again finish below their neighbours in the table.

The derby was the first of five winning draws in six games, the only exception coming when St Annes decided it was too hot to bowl first and handed Netherfield a straightforward chase. Either side of being Cottoned for the second time, Kallis made 69* from 70 balls against Darwen, 76* against Blackpool, 64 against Lancaster, and 54 against Fleetwood – a game in which he left a few out there, having smashed a low full-toss to mid-off with almost 30 overs still to bat ("shite takes wickets" is John Whalley's succinct verdict of his most illustrious scalp). But there were no wins. They just didn't have the dynamite needed to blow out the last rocks. Darwen finished 40 short, seven down; Blackpool 31 short, eight down; Fleetwood 64 short, six down.

In an effort to force a result against Lancaster, Dutton had gallantly declared two overs early with himself unbeaten on 96. It almost backfired. Despite Kallis turning the game by running out Lancaster's top-scorer with a direct hit from the cover boundary, the home team went into the final over needing just four to win, but the scores finished level after the last-ball run out of wicket-keeper Brendan Hetherington, who remembers being impressed by the opposition pro. "He played the best shot I have ever seen in a Northern League game. Phil Dennison was bowling medium pace. Kallis steps inside it and lifts it over extra cover for six, full face, elbow high, centre of the square. It landed the other side of the bowling green at Lune Road, in the days before sixes were hit over extra. A *huge* hit. It was that good I didn't even slate him. I just said 'shot'."

Netherfield had known since the start of the campaign that Kallis would be jetting off for South Africa under-24s' tour of Sri Lanka in mid-July, and at the start of the month confirmed his WP colleague Herschelle Gibbs as his replacement. 'Scooter' usually played rugby union in the southern winter, representing Western Province under-21s as fly half, but he had picked up a cruciate injury so decided to fly north to take over Kallis' £6,500 contract.

Announcing the news, *The Westmorland Gazette* described Gibbs as "a black South African" (which they corrected a few days later) and "a batsman who bowls" (which they didn't). Gibbs went on to bowl six deliveries in 361 international matches. Still, he did manage to trump Kallis' best Northern League figures in a short and hedonistic stay in the Lake District. "He was like a cat in heat," recalled Otway. The club flat would not have been primarily used for poring over old cricket videos, even if it came with a VCR.

Before Gibbs got started, however, Kallis had four games to leave his mark on the Kendalians, starting with an unbeaten 47 against Millom to nudge Netherfield into the semis of the county cup. The following weekend he fell for 54 in a losing draw at Leyland, while on the Sunday, with Dutton, Clarke and Mike Scothern away with Cumberland, his 88 anchored the innings in a famous 10-run win over full-strength Morecambe in the Vaux Bitter Cup.

Gibbs arrived that week, via a layover with Nicholls in Redditch, and was introduced to his new colleagues at an impromptu exhibition game on the Friday night. "Hersche was tonking it all over the place," recalls Rigg, "while Jacques was hitting a lot of fours but wasn't being silly. I came on to bowl and said to Jacques, 'You hit me for six and we'll have to think about how much money we give you'. He said he wouldn't do that to me and just blocked me. He had good manners, as I say."

A day later, Kallis signed off with 71* in victory against Preston. 'Jock has a final fling,' trumpeted the *Gazette*, to whose reporter Kallis gave the usual "great bunch of lads" and "I'd like to come back, if it's possible" bromides, but deep down the Netherfield players knew they had seen the last of him. Five months later, he was making a Test debut against England in Durban.

"Within a month you could see how good he was," says Dutton. "By the time he left there was no doubt he was going to be an utter world-beater. It helped that he played on a quick, bouncy wicket that every South African batsman would have loved."

Indeed it did. His average at Parkside was 147 (combining this with his figures at OEs, Kallis' final home batting average in competitive club cricket in England would be 125.27: 1,358 runs for 11 dismissals). Overall, Kallis finished 19 runs short of four figures in all competitions for Netherfield, despite missing a possible 12 games. In the league, it was 791 at 98.87. Nine of his 14 innings were fifty-plus scores. Pro rata, a full NCL season would have brought 1,243 runs, the fourth highest in the league's history. When a 20-year-old David Boon pro'd at Parkside, he made 485 at 27.

All that remained for the near-teetotal Kallis to do was play a few last games of pool with an old supporter by the name of Vince Crawford and swerve the farewell beers his teammates attempted to foist upon him. His replacement needed no such chaperoning.

"The difference between Jacques and Herschelle was as big as you could imagine," says Dutton. "Kallis was utterly driven. I don't think he drank a drop of alcohol while he was here. Hersche was great for the club, great in the clubhouse, a lovely bloke, the best fielder I've ever seen, but he did enjoy a beer. Not long after he arrived, he went to the nightclub down the road from the club after the Saturday game. We had a cup game on Sunday, and they found him asleep under the covers in the morning."

That afternoon, a Vaux Bitter Cup defeat, Gibbs fell to Eccleshare for 24. Eight days earlier, on debut, Eck had nicked him off for 36, also a defeat. Between times, Gibbs' medium-paced filth took 4/52 – backed up with a freewheeling unbeaten 50 – in that hard-celebrated victory over champions-to-be Morecambe. The following weekend, he crunched 66* in a win over Leyland Motors and 118 in the county cup semi-final win over Cleator, at which point this most gifted of shot-makers was averaging over 100 for the club.

Thereafter, he tailed off, scratching out scores of 8, 36, 28 and 3 in the league, although he did pull off one typically astonishing run out from cover before the batters had even crossed. And he chipped in with a vital 40 in the county cup final win over Vickers Sports, before then ensuring the beers flowed until the small hours. "He was spending his money faster than he was getting it," recalls Rigg, "and left himself with bugger-all for the last two or three weeks."

It was Netherfield's ninth Meageen Cup success in 12 years, a satisfying end to a campaign that saw them finish fourth in the Northern League. Morecambe were worthy champions, having won 15 of 20 completed matches. Cross-town rivals Kendal came third, and overcame Walsden of the Bolton League at Old Trafford to triumph in the Lancashire Cup. Blackpool lifted the Vaux Samson Cup, while the Vaux Bitter Cup was won by league runners-up Chorley, who also retained the National Club Championship crown, beating Bristol's Clifton Flax Bourton at Lord's by 12 runs. This was tough cricket, an important undergrad module on Kallis' journey toward his eventual professorship of batting.

The following summer, both of Netherfield's pros toured England with South Africa 'A', Kallis averaging 32 to Gibbs' 66. In 1997, inspired by the memory of Kallis' professionalism, Netherfield landed that maiden Northern League title, the first of four in five seasons. Meanwhile, Kallis began methodically painting his way toward immortality.

The full dimensions of that career were honoured in 2019 with an edition of *This Is Your Life*. In attendance were Mike Rigg and Ian Heath, who travelled out to South Africa, cloak and dagger, after Desmond Haynes – Kallis' former WP colleague and the initial choice for the two sponsored airline tickets provided by the producers – had insisted on first-class travel from New Zealand. "So they opted for a grassroots option," says Heath, "and we had been very prompt in responding to their request for information at the outset of planning for the event." The pair of them got to hobnob with the great and good of South African cricket, Rigg even helping correct some details in Duncan Fletcher's speech. "He had to revise it at the last minute, because he thought he'd sent him to a club in Manchester."

By then, of course, Kallis had retired. And when the bright light of the battle had receded, grown softer, those beige panels – all 13,289 of them – were finally revealed as iron and bronze.

5

Mohammad Azharuddin (and friends)

at Rishton CC

It would be reasonable to assume that a village cricket club in Lancashire whose outgoing professional was Isaac Vivian Alexander Richards would find it impossible to trump that the following year, yet in many ways what Rishton did in 1988 was even more remarkable. And that was despite only landing their fourth choice as pro. Imran Khan had been first pick (other commitments), Javed Miandad second (he wanted to be a match-day pro only, so ended up playing for Preston in the Northern League), while third was Abdul Qadir. "And he wanted more money than Viv," says Rishton's skipper that year, David Wells. In the end, they had to slum it with the only batter in history to score centuries in each of his first three Tests: Mohammad Azharuddin.

Azhar's ultimately brief stint in the Lancashire League began with a tie against Bacup in which he made 58. Scores of 1 and 15 followed – the former in defeat to reigning champions Haslingden, whose pro Geoff Lawson had him nicked off – before those silken subcontinental wrists rattled off a quickfire 97 in a season-launching win over Colne, his last act before pulling up lame with a groin strain. As Rishton gave Azharuddin time to regain his fitness, there began a parade of sub-pros that would have made a more than serviceable 1980s World XI.

Over that summer of '88, the Rishton stalwarts – Wells, a distribution manager for Whitbread Brewery; his opening partner, Craig Smith, an accountant who finished the season as the league's leading amateur run-scorer; David Wilson, logistics; Robbie Walsh, surveyor; Phil Sykes, bank manager; Frank Martindale, sales rep; John Ainscough, teacher – shared their dressing room with men who would collect a total of 1,719 international caps, more than Tendulkar, Dravid and Dhoni between them.

Only two of Rishton's sub-pros failed to win international recognition. Both were Bajans: Franklyn Stephenson, one of only three men ever to take 10 wickets and score twin hundreds in the same first-class game, so hardly a second-rate option, and Neal Phillips, who made a brutal match-winning 101* against Enfield in the first post-Azhar game.

It was one of only two tons that year from the Rishton *galácticos*. The other was made the following weekend by Mark Greatbatch, who had been seconded from Yeadon in the Bradford League. The New Zealander, fresh off a Test debut earlier that year, warmed up with 85 out of 181 in Rishton's first round Worsley Cup exit to Haslingden. On the Sunday, four miles down the Blackburn Road at East Lancs, Greatbatch made 138 out of 228, although Rishton's derby rivals knocked off from the final ball. Two games, two defeats, the Kiwi scoring 54.52 per cent of their runs.

The following Saturday's visit of Church saw the pro's hat donned by the world's third-ranked ODI batter, Dean Jones. The Victorian only managed 15, however, playing Test colleague Peter Taylor with ease but yorking himself charging at the other offie, Roger Watson. "It was bizarre," recalls Sykes. "Quite often we would pick the team plus AN Other, the pro, and no one would have a clue who was playing until Wilf Woodhouse, the chairman, rocked up on Saturday."

Woodhouse was no super-agent or jet-setter, mind. He ran a small shop on Rishton High Street, but in 1981 found himself in the Caribbean alongside club president Eric Whalley, a cardboard box tycoon, when the latter had signed Michael Holding. Woodhouse had plenty of front, and his can-do attitude toward luring superstars to the Lancashire valleys saw Viv sign six years later.

And as the search for a long-term replacement for Azharuddin floundered, with a reluctant knock-back from Clive Rice, the next batch of games featured a trio of Indian internationals.

Off-spinner Arshad Ayub would win 13 Test caps, the following January locking down one end as Narendra Hirwani took 16 wickets on debut. The first of his two games after being parachuted in from the Bolton League saw him score 64 out of 130/9 before returning figures of 22.1-12-24-4 in a 14-run win over Bacup. Promising, although the following week brought a second defeat to pacesetters Haslingden.

Next in was Maninder Singh, then pro at Blackpool in the Northern League, a gifted bowler once anointed Bishan Bedi's left-arm spinning heir before his form nosedived. Accrington were seen off – Bumble retiring hurt with a ruptured Achilles – but the sub-pro only took 3/74. Wicket-keeper Frank Martindale rated Ayub the better bowler. "He had more control. Maninder spun it more, although he gave you more chances to score, and Lancashire League players back then played the ball, not the name."

The following week, Woodhouse brought along RS Ghai, an Indian seamer who had already played the last of his six ODIs. "He was one of the few to raise eyebrows," recalls Sykes. "Especially when his first ball went straight over the keeper's head for four byes. I thought: bloody hell, what have we got here?" In the end, Rajinder bowled tidily and Rishton were set 228, which had come down to a daunting 110 off 10 when Sykes suddenly went doolally, finishing unbeaten on 116. "It was shit or bust," he says. "Wilf had actually taken the pro to the station with about 15 overs left and couldn't believe it when he heard we'd won the game with two overs spare."

Rishton had five wins, five defeats and a tie heading into July, and finally the stability of a regular pro arrived with Salim Malik, signed on a long-term deal for the rest of the season. Or so they thought. As it turned out, he was only in the UK on a visitor's visa and the Home Office stopped him playing. But he made quite an impression across the six games he played in Rishton colours – four wins and one defeat – contributing steady if unspectacular scores of 40, 9, 57, 30, 40* and 68, as well as tidily effective slow medium-pacers. "Salim was great," says Smith. "A real gentleman. He didn't fit the mould. He liked a drink back then and was very personable, which is why, I suspect, he got involved with the stuff he did."

That sole loss came in Malik's second game, against Burnley, with his Pakistan teammate Mudassar Nazar following his 67* with a spell of 5/49. "Salim was actually 45 minutes late for the game," recalls Wells, "and then we noticed him stood outside the car park gates, which had been locked. Fancy that: your pro locked out of the ground!"

Next through the mystery door was a diminutive Guyanese scrapper who had become an 11-year-old David Wilson's hero in 1975 after taking down Lillee and Thomson in the World Cup. "The lads were winding me up when Wilf rocked up with Alvin Kallicharran: 'Oh Dave, you can't believe who's coming up the path'. He ended up giving me quite a bit of kit: shirt, sweater, batting gloves…"

Opponents for the day were Church, whose own sub, Carl Hooper, was seen off by a classic three-card trick: two outswingers followed by an inswinging yorker from Colin Kuhn, a bus driver from Zimbabwe who finished the year as the league's top amateur wicket-taker. 'Kalli' then made a classy unbeaten 59 in a straightforward nine-wicket win. "He was dropping the ball at his feet and not even calling," chuckles Smith. "You had to be looking at him."

By late August, with three double-header weekends remaining, Rishton were in the thick of the title race. However, four comprehensive wins were sandwiched by fatal home and away defeats to Rawtenstall. The solitary point taken from a possible 10 proved decisive (it was four for a win, with a bonus for bowling the opposition out), as they finished nine points behind Haslingden in the final reckoning. And who were the two sub-pro fiascos who couldn't deliver those vital home-stretch wins? Michael Holding and Dennis Lillee is who.

"Michael remembered all the members' names from 1981: 'How's it going, Betty, love?'" recalls Wilson, and his 4/46 helped reduce Rawtenstall to a perilous 77/8, at which point they were rescued by a 53-run partnership featuring some "pogo" from number nine Brett Storey.

"Brett just unloaded," says his partner, Keith Roscoe, "and was on for the fastest fifty of the season, off 26 balls. But being numb as a piss stone, as he was – nothing there at all – he ran me out when he was on 49, then ran himself out two balls later. But he did smite Michael for a massive six, which hit the chippy on Bacup Road without bouncing: 30 or 40 yards out of the ground! Mikey just shrugged his shoulders, turned round and ran back in off about eight paces."

Rishton's reply went from the promise of 75 without loss to hanging on at 113/9, but they got the show back on the road 24 hours later when FD Stephenson – one-time title-winning pro at Rawtenstall, 100 first-class wickets already bagged that year – took 7/41, mainly with slower balls, including the big wicket of Tom Moody. Zimbabwe all-rounder Kevin Curran, father of Sam and Tom, was hired for both the following weekend's games, and two solid performances – 3/37 and 4/52, plus two red-inkers – brought two more wins.

The penultimate game's guest pro was the Barbadian who, two years later, on Test debut in Trinidad, would break Graham Gooch's hand, the England skipper's grimace captured in a famous cricketing photograph. Ezra Moseley bowled skiddily fast from wide of the crease, and wasn't shy of putting it up club cricketers. Ideal, then. He took 6/31, rearranging Ramsbottom pro Wasim Raja's stumps second ball for a duck in "one of the quickest spells" Martindale ever kept wicket to. Job done.

All of which meant that going into the final game, five points for Rishton and none for Haslingden would force a title-deciding playoff match. The need for wickets saw them sign DK Lillee, 39 years old and struggling through a half-season as Northants' overseas pro. He returned 19-2-86-0. "I think he gave us some of his money back," recalls Smith. "Dennis said 'That's me done' and gave all his kit away," says Martindale. "It was a real shame," adds Roscoe, "but his pace had gone. Our lads climbed into him. He shrugged his shoulders in the bar: 'Sometimes you have bad days, and this is one of my bad days!'"

Having finished fourth with Viv and third with the World XI, Rishton aimed to go a couple of steps further in 1989 and signed county cricket's most fearsome bowler of the 1980s, Sylvester Clarke, although he had to drop out with injury before the season. His replacement was another of county cricket's nightmare-inducers, Wayne Daniel, who played most of the games in a back corset.

'Black Diamond' was unavailable for three matches, prompting Wilf Woodhouse to revisit his Rolodex. Ezra Moseley came back. Martin Crowe appeared, too, picked up by Sykes at the Tickled Trout in Preston and then "run out for 30-odd by Wellsy," recalls Smith, "who dropped it into the legside, which was only being patrolled by one man. Unfortunately that man was Roger Harper." Third up was Patrick Patterson, a veritable treat for club batters! "We were playing against the elite of the world with little or no protection on cabbage patch pitches with no helmets," recalls Wilson, "you wonder how no one was killed."

It was truly a golden era for Rishton, all inspired by the chutzpah of the man who rented out TVs and top-loading video sets on Rishton High Street. "Why was Wilf doing it?" wonders Sykes. "There was no financial gain, no improved gate. Rishton were well supported, so there was no sudden influx of people. Often, no one knew who we were having. There was no social media, no mobile phones, no awareness, and unless you signed them by Thursday lunchtime, there was no press. He was just trying to get the best possible side to win the league, which they did eventually, after I'd left, with Phil Simmons in 1995, and in 1996 with Allan Donald."

Chuck in Jason Gillespie (2000) and Vernon Philander (2006), and it was a surreal time at Blackburn Road. But nothing quite matched the absurdity of that 1988 summer, when a possible Rishton 'Team of the Year' would read: MJ Greatbatch (wk), AI Kallicharran, DM Jones, Mohammad Azharuddin (c), Salim Malik, FD Stephenson, KM Curran, DK Lillee, MA Holding, EA Moseley (Arshad Ayub on a turner), and Maninder Singh. "We'd rock up on a Saturday," laughs Wilson, "and someone would say: 'Who've we got pro-ing today?' 'Well, I don't know yet'. Then 15 minutes before the game Wilf would walk in with Michael Holding."

6

Garry Sobers

at Norton CC

In common with most breakaway competitions, the North Staffordshire & South Cheshire League was cooked up by a cabal of self-interested grandee clubs who didn't much care for the threat of relegation and so decided instead to form a protectionist, closed-shop structure.

Its inaugural season was 1963, the year the wider cricketing landscape was transformed by the birth of limited-overs cricket in the shape of the Gillette Cup, and among the NSSCL's dozen founding clubs – eight clustered in Stoke-on-Trent and four from the nearby towns of Crewe, Nantwich, Leek and Stone – was Norton, whose enterprising chairman, Tommy Talbot, a local plumbing and decorating magnate, had given his money, and thus name, to the new confederation's limited-overs cup. That same year, he reached an agreement with one Garfield St Aubrun Sobers to become Norton's professional.

It was certainly a coup, although not entirely a shock, for Talbot had also enticed Frank Worrell and Jim Laker to the Potteries in the final years of Norton's membership of the North Staffordshire & District League. Worrell was introduced to his new teammates on the eve of his first match at a lavish dinner featuring an Al Jolson impersonator singing 'Mammy', while Laker, having arrived early for his debut and headed out to loosen up, returned to the dressing room to find a policeman's uniform on what he thought was his peg. "He may have taken 19 wickets in a Test match," said Norton's incumbent off-spinner, PC Frank Reynolds, "but nobody nicks my spot".

Talbot had signed Sobers on a five-year deal worth £50 per week. Ordinarily, a contract of that length might be considered something of a risk; the professional can become a little too comfortable and play in third gear. Was this a wise move from Talbot? Let's consider the evidence.

At the time, the 26-year-old Sobers had played 42 of his 93 Tests and was averaging a cool 60.9 with the bat, which included a highest score of 365* against Pakistan in Jamaica in 1958, a world record that stood for 46 years, all of which was probably a solid tick in the pro's 'pro' column. His Test bowling average was a less spectacular 36.66, which would come down to a tick over 34 by the time he retired – not all-time great stature in itself but, for many a judge, good enough for him to have been selected as a bowler alone, not least because he offered decidedly lively swing, left-arm orthodox, and wrist-spin, which Talbot would have been correct in thinking comprised a useful package at club level.

Another factor to weigh in Talbot's calculations was Sobers' record from five years of pro-ing for Radcliffe in the Central Lancashire League, where he had also followed in the footsteps of his great Bajan friend and mentor, Worrell. The supremely elegant Sobers' box-office appeal alone, Talbot may have reasoned, would have made the deal attractive from an economic standpoint – the jingling of coins at the gate, the clinking of glasses at the bar – but what about those on-field 'KPIs' he had put together further north? The hard stats. I mean, sure, he had a Test triple-hundred, but could he do it on a showery Saturday in Stoke?

Sobers had only just turned 20 when Radcliffe's chain-smoking committeeman John Lowe snapped him up in late-summer 1956 on a contract worth £500 for the season (around £9,120 in today's money), out of which would come accommodation costs and income tax. When he eventually arrived at the Racecourse ground in April 1958 – a year later than expected, having been picked to tour England in 1957, and six short weeks after that 365* – the fee would no doubt have seemed something of a bargain. He duly caressed 127 on debut against Milnrow.

"In those days there was a lodge at the back of the pavilion," recalled a future teammate of Sobers of that innings, "a stinking rectangle of stagnant water which provided a natural barrier, discouraging any intruders from the adjoining council estate. It was filled with old prams, tyres, the odd unwanted cat or dog, and not much else. By teatime that day, it had also laid claim to several new, and very expensive, cricket balls. If memory serves me right, within weeks it had been filled in."

Sobers amassed 1,232 runs at 72.47 in that first CLL campaign, a figure he bested the following year when his final tally of 1,454 at 90.88 – still some way short of Worrell's 1,694 eight years earlier – included what remains a club-record score of 186* against Ashton, one of eight centuries he made that season. There were also 83 wickets at 14.96 in 1958 and 86 at 13.08 in 1959. Solid.

However, despite Sobers completing the rare feat of a pro's 'double' in 1960 – 101 wickets at 10.27 and 1,113 runs at a scandalously paltry 48.39 – Radcliffe still had not won anything. Nor had they under Worrell, mind, although he too was a tremendous draw on the gate, the BBC even televising Radcliffe's match with Crompton in May 1953, three weeks before the coronation of Queen Elizabeth II. Truly, a bygone age.

Worrell fell for 98 in that game, which was ironic given that one of the first lessons Sobers learnt from him was the value of the collection box. "Frank was shrewd," writes Sobers in his autobiography. "He used to tell me when I reached 50 not to give my wicket away until I heard that last penny drop in the box. He told me that he used to look around the boundary and he knew where the fellows were with the £5 or £10 donations and he would make sure the box passed by them first before he lost his wicket. Frank used to work out all these things. He knew that when a player was out, the collection would stop."

There were bigger fees on offer for Sobers in the neighbouring Lancashire League – likewise in Yorkshire, where he might receive £25 per game and £50 for the collection, astronomical in comparison to the £5 per week he received for West Indies duties – although officials there imposed strict rules on how many games pros could play elsewhere, which would have severely restricted his earnings from the various exhibition games he played in midweek.

It was en route to one such game at the back end of the 1959 season that Sobers' Ford Perfect slammed into a 10-tonne cattle truck at a quarter to five in the morning. In the car with him were a couple of teammates from West Indies' 1957 tour of England, his best friend Collie Smith and seamer Tom Dewdney, although not Roy Gilchrist, whose no-show at the rendezvous had delayed their departure for London. Clambering from the wreckage with a dislocated bone in his wrist, a cut eye, and a severed nerve in a finger on his left hand,

Sobers heard Dewdney screaming and hysterical then went to ask the prone Smith how he was. "I'm alright, man. Go look after the big boy." But Smith was not all right. He had suffered spinal injuries, from which he would die three days later in hospital, casting a long shadow over the rest of Sobers' career, ultimately pushing him toward his famously copious dual-ended candle-burning.

"I was devastated. I could not believe it had happened. It just took everything out of me," writes Sobers, with the £10 fine he was handed for driving without due care and attention only adding "to the burden of responsibility that I already felt". O'Neill had been a soul mate, "a restraining influence", and over the coming winter, as he prepared for a series against England, "the events of that late summer morning were still fresh in my mind and I thought about them every minute of the day and night". His drinking increased, and although "always something of a night owl", Sobers "started to live more by night than I had before, not wanting to go to bed to think or dream … I used to stay up all night and drink. It didn't touch me. So much that was going on in my head was stronger than alcohol, it had no effect. Sometimes I would drink from one day to the next without even sleeping. Scotch or brandy, whatever was there."

Nevertheless, Sobers went quite well in that Test series, scoring 709 runs at over 100. But Collie Smith never left his thoughts: "It suddenly struck me forcibly that I no longer had to play for Garfield Sobers. I had to do two men's jobs – Collie's and mine."

Drinking had become part of the Sobers lifestyle, the Sobers mythos. Back in Radcliffe, it had served the less destructive function of social lubricant. "You cannot find friendlier people than the Lancastrians," he writes, describing how, despite the many warnings, he found no trouble with the flick-knife-wielding teddy boys on the regular stroll back to his lodgings above the Boar's Head in the centre of town. "Everywhere I went [the locals] would pat me on the back, ask how I was settling in and how I was coping with the weather. I could walk into a pub by myself and instantly find someone to talk to … I enjoyed the social scene of the pubs and clubs in England even though they often wanted to know what a professional sportsman was doing out so late."

Sobers was already a global superstar by the late-1950s, but he became a true local hero in his fourth year at the Racecourse when his still-club-record 144 wickets (including a phenomenal 20 five-wicket hauls) at 9.8 and 1,008 runs at 63 – a second straight pro's double – propelled Radcliffe to a CLL and Wood Cup double. He followed up in 1962 with another 15 five-fors as he bagged the *second* most wickets taken by a Radcliffe player, 118 at 9.84, along with a relatively modest 901 runs at 50.06. It was a good way to sign off, and although Sobers is perhaps the ultimate in irreplaceable players, the blow would have been softened somewhat when the following season's pro, Sonny Ramadhin, took 10/26 in his second outing, finishing the season with 117 wickets at an absurd 5.73 apiece.

Talbot would thus have contemplated this five-year stint – 5,708 runs at 63.42, 532 wickets at 11.23 – and no doubt reckoned he was on terra firma offering Sobers a five-year deal at Norton. The bona fides stacked up. Very probably, he would do them a job. Even so, the newly signed Sobers was unable to play that maiden NSSCL season as he was busy touring England with the victorious West Indies, 3-1 winners of the inaugural Wisden Trophy. Instead Talbot engaged the famously sweary Australian leg-spinning all-rounder Cec Pepper, who took 87 wickets at 11.2 and chipped in with 366 runs as the team finished joint-third.

Playing alongside Pepper in the Norton team that year was Sobers' brother Gerry, a wicket-keeper and hard-hitting batter who would accompany his famous sibling throughout the duration of his time in north Staffordshire, although not without some minor stretching of the rules, observes Vince Lindo, the new Jamaican professional of neighbours Sneyd, where David Steele had learnt the game in the 1950s.

"At the time, if you were an amateur, like Gerry was supposed to be, you had to live within a 10-mile radius of the club you played for," says Lindo. "If you were a professional, you could live anywhere. So, Garry lived in Manchester. And Gerry lived with him. But Tommy Talbot got him a flat on High Lane in Burslem so he could be within 10 miles. Gerry never slept there once. It wasn't even a flat: it was Tommy Talbot's office!"

Garry eventually made his entrance in late April 1964, straight from a tour of the Far East with EW 'Jim' Swanton's XI, playing alongside the likes of Richie Benaud, Seymour Nurse and MAK Pataudi in Hong Kong and Malaysia, against whom he took five wickets in five balls at the august Selangor Club in steamy downtown Kuala Lumpur, none of which could be classed as acclimatisation. A few days later, he was greeted under soupy Potteries skies by a Pathé News crew, to whom he explained he was looking forward to "getting away from the sunshine" in "a class of cricket that had done a lot for me".

The Norton ground was owned by the National Coal Board. Although well appointed, it was not much of a looker. The vista south toward the ground from High Lane took in the first bricks of a new, low-cost brown-field housing development at Smallthorne, while looming over the ground's northern boundary like a sagging Goth pyramid was a jet-black spoil heap from the Ford Green pit, topped up throughout the day by heavy, rumbling belts.

The Norton faithful's first sighting of Sobers' insouciantly upturned collar came during a sprightly 44 on his home debut against Stone, although the game succumbed to the weather not long after tea. The next two Saturdays brought a pair of comfortable wins – Newcastle & Hartshill's declaration on 87/9 an hour from the end of another damp day was generously gobbled up by Sobers, who slammed an unbeaten 47 – setting Norton up nicely for their Talbot Cup first round match, in those days 25 overs each on Sundays or 20 on a weekday, with no restrictions on bowlers' overs. The game brought Sobers head-to-head with his West Indian teammate, Wes Hall, who was picking up a cool £60 per week at Great Chell, a fee reflecting three consecutive 100-wicket campaigns for Accrington in the Lancashire League. Around 1,800 people flocked through the gates at Norton to witness a low-scoring thriller as the visitors fiercely defended a paltry total of 63, a task helped immeasurably by Roger Blank knocking out Sobers' leg stump for 25.

The previous week's *Evening Sentinel* had reported that the future Reverend Hall "bowled with scrupulous fairness, scorning the use of bouncers when a lesser man might have been tempted", and here again he kept it pitched up to Frank Reynolds as Norton stumbled to 61/8 in the final over. "My cousin, John Bailey, was wicket-keeper at Chell," recalls the Norton tailender. "Wes Hall's run-up was so long that I remember turning round and having a conversation about family matters, what we were doing with the wives the next day. But Wes was bowling fast, and I wasn't sure where the runs were going to come from. Then he clean-bowled me, and the ball ricocheted to the boundary. But the umpire had called no-ball, so it counted as four byes, and we won the game."

The teams would lock horns again in the league a fortnight later, Norton having picked up a couple of wins in the interim, the first of which, against reigning champions Crewe LMR, featured an astonishing over-the-shoulder catch from Sobers just in front of the sightscreen – off his own bowling! For all Sobers' manifest brilliance with bat and ball, says Reynolds, it was his fielding prowess, anticipatory and agile, that most frequently left his teammates awestruck. "It was as though he had a sixth sense of where the ball was going to go."

A week later, as pitched battles between Mods and Rockers raged on Brighton seafront, Norton beat Sneyd in the local derby, although not without a large and expectant home crowd grumbling at skipper Jim Flannery for inserting the visitors upon winning the toss, fearing they might not see Sobers bat. Indeed, Norton's home crowd was never short of a word or two. On one occasion, when the pro was flattening out divots with the back of his bat, one wag yelled out, "Steady on, Sobers. There's men working under there."

The turnout and excitement for the Talbot Cup encounter had prompted the *Sentinel*'s cricket correspondent 'EGS' to pen an editorial asking, 'Why not run league matches on knock-out lines?' However, an even bigger crowd of 2,500 turned up to Chell for the league fixture, with takings of £160 on the gate and a further £90 in refreshments (just shy of £4,000 in today's money), a welcome boost for a club that had recently built a swanky new pavilion. Top of the bill, of course, was the Bajan showdown, and the locals didn't have to wait too long for Sobers' entrance, which began with him picking up his bat in the upstairs dressing rooms before pitter-pattering in his spikes past a full-sized snooker table, then out through a door and down the shallow steps of a viewing gallery with three long rows of leather-backed seats, sweeping left to the top of a grand staircase that folded back on itself before disgorging him onto a ballroom floor whose parquet floor he crossed on a rubber mat, before another door then threw him down a dozen or so concrete steps flanked by rows of wooden-slatted benches on which the members nestled, then finally out into the arena, with its covered stand down the Western flank. It was the closest thing the Potteries had to Lord's.

Sobers was soon treating them to those trademark whiplash pull shots and back-foot slaps, bat finishing its mighty arc down by his backside. Watching from the other end as the maestro made 59 was the 21-year-old Dave Brock, who finished unbeaten on 66, an innings from which he was still floating as Sobers' 5/47 secured a fifth win from five completed games. "It was a great day," recalls Brock. "Batting with Garry was marvellous, although he never really gave us advice, other than to play your own game. Wes was very sharp, and even broke my bat. It took me a few months to save up for another. But he bought me a drink at the end of the game and, after someone had popped out to fetch food, we stood and ate tripe and chips at the bar."

Norton made it six from six against Leek, Sobers this time bagging 8/45 in front of another home crowd in excess of 2,000. 'Sobers-Hall grumblers should remember the advantages' honked a *Sentinel* editorial, its author having been briefed about Norton fielding enquiries from Manchester, Birmingham and Derby over their upcoming fixtures, such was the Bajan all-rounder's pulling power. The investment was paying dividends, on the field and off, the club abuzz with *Saturday Afternoon Fever*, as Norton's Peter Gibbs, an Oxford Blue and future Derbyshire opener, later the author of 53 episodes of the 1950s-set police drama *Heartbeat*, would describe in *Wisden*. "During his seasons with Norton, Worrell was never short of a fan to help carry his kit from the car park, but when Sobers rolled up, a whole troupe of helpers would greet him. One would carry his bag, another his bat, another his pads – all keen to grab a piece of their idol. Thereby unencumbered, the leading man did his 'Stayin' Alive' walk to the pavilion."

While Sobers was strutting his stuff in Stoke-on-Trent, wider political events – provoked by that caustic brew of imperialism and racist oppression – were starting to convulse through this most tumultuous of decades, as armed liberation struggles caught fire across Africa, Martin Luther King and Muhammad Ali became figureheads of the American civil rights movement and, in the Caribbean, where only Jamaica and Trinidad of the cricket-playing nations were independent by 1964, a more peaceable though no less fervent decolonisation process came to a head. Two days before Sobers added an unbeaten 62 to his 5/50 in a seven-wicket win over Porthill Park, a South African lawyer by the name of Nelson Mandela was convicted of plotting to overthrow the government and imprisoned for life.

Unlike Worrell, who became a Jamaican senator, Sobers wasn't a particularly politicised soul – indeed, a few years later, he created something of a furore by visiting Ian Smith's white-supremacist Rhodesia to take part in a double-wicket competition for which he was paid £600 – and he insists that, aside from being refused entry to a couple of "dancing clubs" in Manchester, he never really experienced any racial discrimination in England. Perhaps he simply wasn't attuned to it. After all, Roy Gilchrist had been called a "black bastard" by a spectator while playing for Great Chell in 1961; he responded with his fists, and was banned for life by the North Staffs & District League. Sobers' immunity from all this may or may not have been a function of his celebrity, and whether or not he was breaking down barriers, or even saw himself as doing so, he was adored in the Potteries. Venerated, even.

As is the way, local concerns muffled out these wider historical tremors, and Norton progressed serenely on through that 1964 season, reaching the Talbot Cup semi-finals courtesy of a two-run win over Bignall End in which they defended 67 as Sobers "worked up a terrific pace" and sent down six maidens out of 10 overs. Still, the *Sentinel* went on, "only an acrobatic, full-length save by Sobers, off the fifth ball of the last over, prevented a certain two runs and a resulting tie". This was showmanship, but also commitment. "He was always very down to earth," says Reynolds. "He didn't put himself above others."

In the league, Norton had reached the mid-point of the season with a six-point lead. The format was a decidedly uncomplicated three points for a win and one for a draw, so this was a useful buffer, particularly given that no batter had yet made a century (Gerry Sobers' 81 was the highest score across the entire league at half-way).

July began with a trip to Stone, a journey that took Sobers past the site of that fateful car crash on the A34 five years earlier, and Norton won a tight affair by 22 runs. They would pick up four further victories from the opening seven games of the homeward stretch, with the other two abandoned. One of those wins came against Crewe, Sobers avenging their Talbot Cup semi-final exit with an unbeaten 58 and 6/67, although Brian Griffiths made 64 in defeat – astonishingly, the only half-century scored against Norton all season. Heading into the final four games, then, unbeaten Norton still held a six-point advantage over Longton, who were the next team to visit.

Longton's professional and main threat was left-arm spinner Nasim-ul-Ghani, who knew all about Sobers having been a 16-year-old novice in Jamaica when the great man made his unbeaten 365. At the time, Nasim was the youngest ever Test cricketer, and he still holds the record for the youngest man to take a Test five-for, which came in the next game in Guyana and included Sobers, Everton Weekes and Rohan Kanhai. Sobers made a hundred in each innings of that game, however, and would have fancied his chances of getting the upper hand in front of another heaving home crowd.

Sobers landed the first blow, catching Nasim for 31 off the bowling of 18-year-old Richard Downend, who took 6/39 and would make his Minor Counties debut against Bedfordshire at Walsall the following day, appearing alongside club colleagues Bernard Newton, David Wilson and the 20-year-old Gibbs, who in 2012 penned an essay for *Wisden* about chaperoning – at the behest of former England batter and Staffordshire skipper Jack Ikin – a 91-year-old SF Barnes through the first day of the game, in which Gibbs conspired to record a first-day pair as Staffordshire followed on. "Ikin introduced me to SF as an 'opening batsman and recently dubbed Oxford Blue'. The old boy reacted as if he had been asked to accommodate a scorpion in his pants."

Still, Gibbs attempted to placate the old goat, mentioning that he played in the humble surrounds of Norton, which prompted Barnes to rattle off a list of their professionals. "I could hear the clink of cups and saucers inside the pavilion. 'Would you like a coffee, Mr Barnes?' But he was lost in deliberation. 'Sobers I like. Batting or bowling, he attacks. That's the thing – attack, attack. A gamble, of course, for a left-hander against someone like me.' Holding an imaginary ball, SF sketched three deliveries with a flick of his long fingers – the first two pitching and beating the outside edge, the last breaking the other way through the gate." Sobers versus Barnes: now that would have been worth a bob or two.

Nasim's was the chief contribution to Longton's middling score of 118, which left Norton three hours to chase the runs and, with it, almost certainly wrap up the league title. Gibbs opened with Newton – the former scoring 26 in 111 minutes, the latter 13 in 57 – and the restive home crowd were soon barracking them, reported the *Evening Sentinel*, as they "let a score of possible singles go begging and their strokes became so rare that each was greeted with ironical cheers. The crowd slow-handclapped and made frequent appeals to the umpires to give them out."

Gibbs would later describe this "impatient heckling" as a "character-building feature of [his] Saturday afternoons" in his *Wisden* essay, 'Stars that shone beside the slag heaps': "After dismissing the opposition for a modest total, and with the pro's collection box already doing the rounds, Garry had the disconcerting habit of putting his feet up and inviting our first three batsmen to knock off the runs. So together we would nudge and push our way towards victory in the hope of not bothering our star attraction. The crowd, however, were less than delighted. They may have seen Sobers bowl, but they had paid to see him bat as well. In a matter of a few overs we three stooges had outstayed our welcome."

Sobers eventually emerged at No.5 and was "subdued in the poor light" before being caught in the deep off Nasim, who proceeded to whittle through the lower order, finishing with 7/39 as Longton took the final wicket with just three minutes remaining and Norton 11 runs short. "[Norton] ought to have had the game in the bag an hour before," contended the reporter. The title race was back on, although Norton would have to slip up at least once more in the final three games.

First up, they took care of Porthill Park (for whom Barnes had taken 893 wickets at 5.38 in the nine seasons prior to the First World War), Sobers coming to the party with 6/38 and a cameo 19*, finishing the game with an enormous six on to the car park before heading back to Manchester as visiting Everton fans tore up Stoke town centre. He was back at the party a week later against Nantwich, chipping in with 9/41 in a 100-run win. Meanwhile, Longton had won twice – one more, coupled with defeat for Norton, would take the season to a playoff. It wasn't to be, rain having the last word with Norton precariously placed at 35/5 – Sobers in and out – chasing Knypersley's modest 86. Tommy Talbot's investment had indeed paid off (and, according to Brock, the pro "was far from the only one picking up a brown envelope").

Sobers finished with 549 runs at 49.9 (second behind his brother, who averaged 50.1), and 97 wickets at 8.4 – a league record haul that would stand until 2002, and a full 30 more than the next best. Handy. "Sobers stood out as the ideal league cricketer," asserted the following year's *Wisden*, "in that he regards the game not just as a medium for obtaining personal records in batting and bowling but as a match to be won in the shortest possible time and at the sacrifice of personal performance if necessary." Remind you of anyone?

Garry and Gerry stayed for a couple of celebratory drinks with their Norton teammates before heading back to Moss Side. In early October, Garry joined the Bermuda leg of Yorkshire's North American tour and by the time the Norton team saw him again he was West Indies' captain, having been hand-picked by Worrell as his successor. He didn't accept immediately, however, concerned that his leisure habits, tolerated by Worrell, might make a leadership position untenable. Over the summer, he had talked through the ramifications with his Norton skipper, Jim Flannery, and eventually resolved the dilemma by applying the same (uncurfewed) rules to everyone else: a free pass on nocturnal activities, provided they delivered on the field. It was much the same at Norton, recalls Reynolds: "He enjoyed the nightclubs, like any young man. But he was remarkably fit and was always up to the task of playing cricket, even after a heavy night out on the town, boozing."

Sobers' first engagement as Test skipper – a five-match home series against Australia, wrapped up with one to spare – meant that he arrived four weeks late for his sophomore NSSCL season. Norton engaged his fellow Bajan Clairmonte Depeiaza as sub-pro, picking up three wins and a draw to set things up nicely for Sobers' introduction at home to winless Leek, who soon found themselves in the mire at 9/4. Enter a teenage Stan Trafford, recently signed for Port Vale FC, who eked out two runs in his first 45 minutes at the crease, 51 in the next 45, although not without a mishap or two, recalls teammate Steve Cartledge. "His box was turned inside-out by a pretty sharp delivery from Garry that left a seam mark on impact with his flannels. The repairs that ensued included the box being somewhat restored by repeated hammering with a bat handle. I don't know about any repairs to Stan's bits."

Trafford considered that innings of 53 to be the pinnacle of his cricket career, and it allowed Leek to post 103, which started to look useful when Brian Tatton nicked off the great man for just 5. Roger Lancaster held things together for Norton with 42, but with 10 minutes remaining, they found themselves 100/9. The *Sentinel* reports that Stuart Sharratt, who already had 6/42, "summoned one last effort" and the ball "flew from the edge of David Wilson's bat, high over the slips and on its way to the boundary and a win for Norton, but Ken Brew, at short third-man, found enough height to pluck it out of the air and make the catch of his young life". It would be Leek's only victory of the season.

Norton registered a pair of wins over the Bank Holiday weekend, Sobers making a breezy 52 against Porthill then being castled for 17 on the Monday by Bignall End off-spinner Arthur Burgess' first ball, "a friendly offering which the West Indies' captain tried to clout into the next parish", according to the *Sentinel*. With just 126 to defend, Sobers then knocked over Jack Ikin in his first over, finishing with 6/44 as Norton won by 18 runs. "He would always ask who the opposition's best player was," recalls Brock, "then step it up a level, and he was very quick that day." Nevertheless, added the newspaper report, No.11 Burgess "despatched a ball from Sobers out of the ground with uncharacteristic violence, as if to say 'That's how you should have hit the one which I bowled you'."

"As a batsman, Garry went out to enjoy his game," reflects Reynolds, "certainly compared to Frank Worrell, who played a steady, grafting game and got his head down. Garry was a flair player and went in to play shots and entertain. He took chances. He was so good with the ball and with his fielding that the batting was almost incidental, really." So incidental, in fact, that he would finish the season averaging a preposterous 25.4 with the bat. There for a good time, not necessarily a long time.

"Garry would often say, 'I've done my job, now you do yours'," adds Brock. "He did what he wanted. The captain couldn't control him and neither could Tommy Talbot. He would often disappear at tea and go for a tot of brandy in the secretary's office. An attendant would bring him his sandwiches. Tommy made sure he was always looked after. Everyone wanted a piece of him, so he would sit and chat to spectators or reporters. Occasionally he would say, 'Right, I'll go in next skipper' if it was a game against a rival at the top."

This he did on his next outing, albeit making just 13 at No.4 against the thrumming backdrop of motorcycle engines in defeat inside the speedway track at Crewe LMR, who duly displaced Norton at the top of the table. He followed up with 70 in the 161-run demolition of Nantwich, which would be his second and final half-century of the season, still two games shy of the halfway mark. The game after that, at home to Great Chell, amply illustrated Reynolds' thesis, Wes Hall flattening his opposite number's stumps for just 6 in Norton's total of 98, before Sobers fired back with 5/24 as the visitors were routed for 44.

Sobers' multi-faceted bowling could invariably be relied upon to secure the rattle of coins in the bespoke biscuit tin that he brought along with him for the purpose. Indeed, the final game of the outward stretch, a draw against Knypersley, was the last time all season he failed to pick up a five-for – although Norton managed just one league win in eight after the turn, Sobers snaring 7/22 at Leek.

There was also 8/61 in the derby draw against Sneyd, although Sobers had earlier been bowled for 28 by his friend Lindo, a regular companion to star-studded exhibition games at Colwyn Bay featuring the likes of Kanhai, Nurse, Lance Gibbs, Conrad Hunte, Charlie Griffiths, Gilchrist and Hall. The standard appearance fee was £50 – very attractive to Lindo, who received £8 per week from Sneyd – although on one occasion the crowd swelled to over 7,000 and the organisers paid them £105 each (equivalent to around £1,700). Be it these fees or Saturday afternoon collections, the overseas pros were always looking for ways to supplement their earnings, although Sobers was more speculative in this than most.

"Garry always needed money," says Lindo. "He'd say 'tonight I'm staying with the Dexters' and he'd tell me he needed to buy a new suit, because they were high society and Garry wasn't. He once gave me £100 to put on a horse, which was two weeks' cricket wages for him. I'd never been in a bookies before. I told Garry, 'You can't put £100 on a horse' and he said 'don't you tell me what to do with my money'. I went into the bookies in Etruria, laid this bet, and the bookie told me you should always back a grey horse. I told Garry this, although I don't know if he took any notice. I don't even know whether he won the bet!"

Norton's frustrating eight-game stretch encompassed three consecutive abandoned home games, causing a dent in both club coffers and league position. By the time Crewe visited, the teams were joint-top of the table. Fires duly roused, they found Sobers "in his most militant mood," reported Monday's *Sentinel*, taking "five for 45 in 21 consecutive overs of hostile bowling", after which, batting at five, he contributed an unbeaten 42, which "contained seven turf-singeing boundaries and a six onto the bowling green". It was the business end of the season, and Sobers meant business.

Twenty-four hours later, it was the Talbot Cup final against holders Longton on a sticky dog at Newcastle, where, the *Sentinel* reports, "the large crowd … stretched the capacity of the ample car park to its limits." Sobers slipped in at first drop this time, but was undone by "a beautiful delivery" from Nasim-ul-Ghani, which apparently "swung in, then cut back sharply to take the top of off stump". Norton could only muster 90, although this proved ample as Sobers bagged 5/31 to complete the first part of the double, before a fourth washout in eight at Nantwich left Norton on the brink of back-to-back titles: three points clear with two to play.

A further treat for the Potteries' cricketing public that year was the inaugural inter-league competition, the President's Cup, sponsored by Rothmans (everything was fags back then). The NSSCL had breezed past the Birmingham, Bolton and Northumberland leagues in the opening rounds, the latter blown away by Wes Hall's 7/13, including 6/6 in his opening spell. By late August, they were in the final against Yorkshire Cricket Council, played on a sunny day at Great Chell, with the four professional berths in the team filled by Hall, Sobers, Nasim and Crewe's Denis Cox, a member of the Magic Circle and future Surrey CCC president. The fifth member of the bowling attack was Stone's Peter Harvey. "One of the most bizarre things about the final was the Tannoy system," he recalls. "The announcement came on, 'Replacing Garry Sobers at the scorebox end is Peter Harvey'. I had to pinch myself when I heard that."

The home team had batted first, Sobers falling for 13, a huge disappointment for the estimated 4,500 crowd. Stone's Paul Shardlow, a goalkeeper at Stoke City, top-scored with 32 in a total of 102 that contained a quintet of ducks. YCC had 40 eight-ball overs to chase them, not a straightforward task with Hall and Sobers sharing the new cherry, although the former's opening over took 15 minutes to complete thanks to two wickets and a couple of no-balls. "There was some rain overnight," recalls Harvey. "It was still wet because I remember when Wes was bowling, Paul Shardlow was at short leg and scrambled to take a catch, but slipped. It was the days before sawdust."

The visitors themselves slipped to 49/7, mounted a partial recovery to 81/8, before Sobers returned to seal a 20-run win, finishing with 5/10. Champagne corks were popped and the sponsors brought some complimentary product into the victors' dressing room. "The smokers in the team are probably still wondering where all their free Rothmans fags went," says Harvey. "A lot of them were upset when Garry quickly put them in his kit bag!" It's unlikely his friends in Manchester went short over the coming weeks.

Back with the NSSCL bread and butter, the penultimate round of fixtures produced four washouts, although both Norton and Crewe were able to record wins, leaving the gap at three points. Once more, a possible a playoff loomed; again, Tommy Talbot hoped his hired gun could turn things on. The chairman may have been fretting when Norton were bundled out for 134 by Knypersley, although by then they knew Crewe would have to knock off Longton's 179, which was odds-against.

It was all immaterial. After six balls to find his radar, Sobers' second over went like this:

Sherratt lbw Sobers 0
Lowe lbw Sobers 0
Henshall b Sobers 0
Dot ball
Worrall c Sobers (Gerry) b Sobers 0
Dennett b Sobers 0

That was the day's collection tin sorted inside an over, and there was no way back from 7/5 for Knypersley, although when Sobers later switched to spin in fading light they were able to dent his figures slightly. Still, for a title decider, 9/41 was a solid day's work. Norton had secured a double, and Sobers once again sat atop the

NSSCL bowling averages with 76 wickets at 8.04, effectively from 14 games.

The following season, with Sobers skippering the West Indies' victorious Test tour of England (a blow softened somewhat by the football team's World Cup triumph at Wembley), Norton signed his compatriot Vincent Brewster, an unheralded left-arm spinner who had turned out for Warwickshire the previous summer against Oxford University (taking 7/58, including Gibbs, who may have oversold him). Without their special sauce, Norton finished fourth-bottom, picking up just four wins as Longton won the league.

The winter then took Sobers to India, where he averaged 114 with the bat and 25 with the ball across the three-match series, as well as striking up a romance with Bollywood actor Anju Mahendru. They had become smitten on the dancefloor and were briefly engaged, although the relationship was never viable given Sobers' globetrotting cricketing commitments, starting with an abandoned St George's Day season-opener for Norton at home to Bignall End.

NSSCL had tweaked the rules slightly for 1967, offering a bonus point for the faster scoring rate in drawn games, which continued to earn a point, while upping the reward for a win to four points, which is what Norton collected at Leek in front of a Pathé News crew who had come to film the now 30-year-old legend. Sobers sent down 19-9-24-4 as the home team subsided to 61 all out, before the cameras captured the West Indies captain clipping future Notts teammate Billy Taylor to mid-wicket for 11 in an otherwise routine run chase. Slow start. Could do better.

A week later, focussed by the visit of the reigning champions, Sobers brought something pretty close to his A-game (Club Cricket Remix), spanking his sole century in Norton colours – 113 out of 171 – before taking 8/40 as Longton went home with their tails between their legs. It almost wasn't fair.

To the chagrin of the NSSCL representative team's selectors, the summer of 1967 saw Sobers turning out most Sundays for the International Cavaliers XI against the first-class counties – exhibition games, in essence, although invariably broadcast on BBC2 and generating enough interest to prompt both the demise of the rules excluding overseas players from county cricket and, a year later, the birth of the John Player Sunday League. The Cavaliers games often meant Sobers scooting off immediately after play. On May Bank Holiday weekend, an abandonment at Great Chell allowed him to set off early to Hove, where he stroked 47 princely runs and sent down 9-0-18-2 before driving back for a game against Stone on the Monday, an eight-wicket win to which he contributed 18-7-28-5 and a sprightly 18*, including a huge six over the pavilion. Then back to Manchester.

Sobers was approaching his fiftieth NSSCL appearance and still no opposition batter had made more than 67 against him. At which point, Staffordshire opener Dave Hancock played arguably the innings of his life. "It was a glorious afternoon and a hard wicket," he told the *Sentinel* over half a century later. "Norton were undefeated and top of the league. Behind me, keeping wicket, was Gerry Sobers, Garry's extrovert brother. He had a mouth full of gold teeth and when he smiled, it dazzled you. Garry started with some very quick bowling and I was dropped off him a couple of times by Gerry, which caused a bit of family friction. I was riding my luck. It was the only way to play against someone of Sobers' class."

Wickets tumbled at the other end, but Hancock rattled along regardless. "I can clearly remember putting up my hundred with a leg glance, down towards the pavilion. While I was in my 90s, it had all gone quiet. Then when I reached a century, everybody came out and cheered. It was a privilege and pleasure to score a century in such illustrious company. The day was made complete for me when I caught Garry off Peter Timmis' bowling. We got him out cheaply as well, for 17. But we were denied victory as the match ended in a draw. Afterwards, Garry came up to me and said they'd tear us to ribbons when they got us back to Norton. But he was out of luck. That match was rained off!"

Indeed it was. However, between times, Norton did not lose a match, the biggest scare coming at Bignall End, for whom Jack Ikin's 108 helped elevate the home team's total to 221. In reply, Norton reached the final ball of the game nine down and needing two runs for victory, only for David Wilson to block it, later claiming he thought there was one more left in the over. Earlier, Gerry Sobers had top-scored with 62, and he was roped into following day's International Cavaliers game against Leicestershire. He was also offered a late-season trial with Northamptonshire second XI, but was unable to get there due to heavy traffic. "Garry always did say Gerry was talented but a clown," says Brock.

Norton followed the Bignall End humdinger with six straight wins. Sobers was only required to bat in three of them, making an unbeaten 49 against Longton, a crucial 79 in the 10-run victory over Great Chell, and a brisk 32* against Stone to follow up his 9/43. By that stage, he had returned a combined 73-11-176-20 in the International Cavaliers' fixtures, which offers some indication of the difficulties faced by humble NSSCL batters. Norton's six-game winning streak brought Sobers 36 wickets at 6.3, all but sealing a third league title. With four games left, they needed a single point to wrap things up. Then came the Porthill washout and it was job done.

Three titles in three seasons with the world's greatest cricketer created a good deal of chatter about the competition being distorted, and Talbot duly went on the PR offensive in the following week's *Sentinel*, which ran the headline: '"We don't buy success," says Norton chief'. Talbot took the opportunity to point out that it was Sobers that had requested to join Norton, and that his presence was a net benefit to the league, providing opposition clubs with their best earner of the season, which was inarguable. He also confirmed that, although Sobers was on a five-year deal, Norton wouldn't stand in his way should he wish to play county cricket. "Obviously the considerations of this club would have to be discussed and we have a special committee to consider this very question should it arise."

The one remaining target was to complete the league season unbeaten. Newcastle almost put paid to that, finishing on 151/9 in response to Norton's 152, Sobers taking a relatively expensive 8/72. That night, he drove to London, playing for the Cavaliers at Lord's under Denis Compton's captaincy and in an attack featuring Fred Trueman, Lance Gibbs and former Norton pro Laker, before returning north for a 41-run home win over Knypersley on Bank Holiday Monday. Norton rounded things off at Crewe with a ninth draw of the campaign to go with 13 wins, giving them 65 points, 15 clear of the runners-up. They were Invincibles.

Sobers had taken 95 wickets, third in the bowling averages. He finished fourth in the batting. Remarkably, his overall run aggregate of 1,381 (at 38.36) across his three years at Norton was fewer than he had managed in the 1959 season at Radcliffe. Still, he did take

268 league wickets at 8.63, a sizeable contribution to the team's record across those three title-winning campaigns: 39 wins, 24 draws (11 of which were abandonments) and just three defeats. It was domination, and as Tommy Talbot sipped a celebratory brandy under those autumnal skies, taking in a facility with triple-banked seating for 2,750 spectators, with tennis courts, bowling green, football pitch and a full-size snooker table to keep the club's almost 2,000 members entertained, he would have contemplated at least two more years of local supremacy, if not more. But they would never win the league again. These days, there is no cricket played on the ground.

That winter, the MCC opened up the county game to overseas players and Norton's special committee was duly convened. "Tommy Talbot sold me to Notts," writes Sobers. "I was probably the first transferred cricketer. I have no idea what sort of money was paid, but knowing Mr Talbot, I'm sure it was to his benefit!"

Some 363 days after Norton's third NSSCL title was celebrated, Sobers sealed his cricketing immortality by launching six sixes off one Malcolm Nash over in Swansea. Tommy Talbot did not live to see it. Still, he had been the architect of an unrivalled period of glamour for both club and league, and for that a small corner of Stoke-on-Trent would be forever grateful, as the veteran BBC Radio Stoke presenter Nigel Johnson summed up. "Worrell, Laker, Sobers – all these players were visible. They were approachable. And that was a very important thing. To go home on a Saturday night and say 'I saw Garry Sobers', 'I spoke to Garry Sobers', 'I had a drink with Garry Sobers and I shook his hand when he left...' What memories. What memories."

7

Andre Russell

at Barnards Green CC

Late March 2010, and with spring settling over the picturesque Worcestershire spa town of Malvern and the summer approaching fast, the cricket committee at Barnards Green CC were fretting. Their initial choice as overseas pro, the Geoff Lawson-recommended Sydney Grade seamer Charles Matthews, had suffered a stress fracture of the back and the club were now scrambling to line up a replacement, a player who could help a team that had just finished second in the Worcestershire County League go one better, bootstrapping them into the Birmingham & District League, not only the world's oldest cricket competition but also one of the strongest in the country, a league whose clubs had dominated the National Club Championship through the 1980s and 1990s. It was the Promised Land, and Barnards Green had never been there before.

Most clubs are acutely aware that the fate of their season can be decided before it even gets going, hinging on their choice of pro. It's a stressful business, a dance through the usually well-meaning though not always objective patter of agents, an anxious attempt to peer through stats at potential, a feverish whirl of doomsday and best-case scenarios. You look for a match-winner, an impact player, ideally someone whose 60 average would take the 140, 20, 20 route rather than a glut of Steady Eddie 70-odds, someone who'd achieve his three-wickets-per-game with an unlucky one-for, an off-colour one-for, and a blitzkrieg seven-for, everyone in the bar by four o'clock. So, with the clock ticking, Barnards Green skipper Tim Williams went back to the agent Steven Hirst, who told him about a 21-year-old Jamaican all-rounder with seven first-class appearances and one List-A game to his name. "He's a bit of a risk," said Hirst, "but he could also be a gun…"

Were a top-secret human-cloning lab somewhere in the New Mexico desert to attempt to bioengineer cricket's ultimate impact player, the result might look something like the quick-bowling, livewire-fielding, monster-hitting Andre Russell. This, presumably, is the reason Kolkata Knight Riders have been paying him $930,000 per IPL season. Barnards Green managed to land him for just a tick under that, with Williams, interest duly piqued, initially discussing matters with the former West Indies captain Jimmy Adams, then technical director of Jamaica Cricket. "Jimmy was looking after Andre's interests at the time," says Williams, "and he was very keen to find the right club and not just a big pay packet."

Which was just as well, since the club had never before paid an overseas player, offering instead a mix of cricket experience, help finding casual work and free accommodation, even to the likes of future New Zealand Test batter Daniel Flynn, who had worked on a building site between matches. Russell's visa category meant he couldn't be paid, adds Williams, "so Jimmy and Steven asked that we provide him with some pocket money and accommodation. But I still think what sealed the deal was the lure of the free kit-package Duncan Fearnley Cricket always offered our overseas. Andre loves his 'gears'!"

In the end, the total cost to Barnards Green was around £4,000, which has to be considered something of a bargain. Three weeks out from their final pre-season friendly, however, they still could not be sure if it would turn out to be money badly spent. So when news filtered through to Malvern that Russell had slammed a maiden first-class ton for Jamaica against Ireland – from just 62 balls, with seven fours and nine sixes, following a spell of 4/42 – the sense of excited anticipation started to build. Even more so when he followed up with 5/42 in a one-off one-dayer.

With his arrival delayed by the ash cloud from a grumbling Icelandic volcano, Russell eventually flew into the chill of Birmingham International Airport, rolled out 4-4-0-0 in that pre-season friendly along with a sedate 30-odd, and settled into the first of his digs.

"Initially," says batter Jez Clarke, "he stayed with Chris Grubb, a young postie in Malvern who was a social member of the club but not a cricketer. I don't think they got on, or got each other on any level. Andre would cook at all hours and just leave things how he left them. So that didn't last long. He also stayed with Smeds' mum [previous captain, Chris Smedley] for a bit. Then he lived with Kev

Golder, our top-order batter, who'd just bought a new-build house in Malvern with some pretty decent patio furniture included. Kev's very particular about his possessions and careful with the things he owns, but one night Andre had gone outside and carved his name into the patio table. Kev should have sold it on eBay after the T20 World Cup!"

Having celebrated his 22nd birthday two days before the WCL campaign got underway, Russell was ready to roll for the season opener at Astwood Bank. It didn't go well. Barnards Green were restricted to 173/9 from their 50 overs, the home team knocking off the target for three wickets down with 15 overs spare, Russell's contribution an underwhelming 29 and 1/45.

"It was very clear that he liked to play his shots and that he was quick," says Williams of his first impressions. "It wasn't clear if this was going to translate to runs and wickets at a prolific rate. We'd had some rapid bowlers before, but they hadn't worked out. Andre was in my car on the way home and he was absolutely gutted we'd lost and gutted that he had underperformed. He said it wasn't good enough and he wanted to do much better, although I do remember being woken at around 6:30am on that first Sunday and the voice on the phone saying, 'I just need some drugs'. Turns out he had a stiff back and wanted some painkillers!"

Although Russell wasn't yet the bulked-up, gym-honed beefcake he later became, he was still unlikely to be unduly taxed in finding (or clearing) the boundaries at Barnards Green's compact, leafy ground, with houses on three sides and a 50-metre hit, pitch included, toward the road that ran along its southern flank. By the time he got into his stride on his home debut, he may even have fancied launching one to the Malvern Hills Area of Outstanding Natural Beauty, a mile or so to the west.

The game was reduced to 34 overs each, and title rivals Worcester Nomads scratched out 152/9, Russell taking 4/45. He then came in at 56/1, with 97 required, and walked off around an hour later having slammed six sixes and six fours in his unbeaten 77, giving his teammates the first taste of his outstanding natural ability to hit a stratospheric cricket ball. "Not that we needed it," says Adam Binks, the wicketkeeper. "I knew he was a tasty cricketer from the first game's warm-up. He picked up this ball one-handed, off balance, about 30 metres away, undulating outfield, and rocketed it into me. It frickin' *stung* my hands. There was just a different level of athleticism in everything he did."

Russell's familiar method of muscular, mid-pitch chin music soon adapted to the slow-and-low conditions at North End Lane, the Jamaican going full and straight the following week against Bewdley to bag 7/38, with five bowled and one lbw. Chasing 139, Russell entered at 64/2 and promptly fell without scoring to Jack Mills' left-arm spin. "He'd got me out for a fourth-ball duck, so I was returning the favour," recalls Mills. "He had hit the first three balls to point, cover and extra cover, the hardest I'd ever seen a ball hit. Then I bowled him an arm ball, and got him through the gate." Barnards Green folded to 107 all out to make it two defeats in three. "While there was concern in the wider club," says Williams, "there was none in the first team. We were calm."

This calmness may have begun to ebb slightly a week later when they found themselves 10/3 chasing Bromyard's 47 all out – Russell having taken 6/22 – with two very handy first-class bowlers, Lundi Mbane of Border and Zahid Saeed of Sialkot, nipping it about at a decent lick. It's the type of game in which you crawl agonisingly toward the finishing line, inching home in thick inside edges and scruffy leg-byes. Or, if you have Andre Russell batting at four, it's a game he wins in around 20 minutes, launching five sixes and one four in a 13-ball 35* that left Zahid with the somewhat unusual figures of 3.2-2-21-2.

These, then, were the foothills of Russell's transformation into the T20 circuit-bestriding megastar 'Dre Russ': a Marvel superhero origin story being moulded in Malvern. Binks remembers someone with bulletproof confidence who was "1,000 per cent committed to winning," even while turning out in semi-competitive Sunday games, midweek knockabouts, anything for a game of cricket. "When he was here, he was all in," adds Clarke.

That competitive edge was on full display in the following weekend's league double-header, which began with an 89-run stroll against Colwall in which Russell smote 105 in quick time. Then, on a hot Bank Holiday Monday at Droitwich Spa, came the paciest pitch of the summer. Russell contributed 70 to a workmanlike total of 202/8, but had apparently been upset (and mightily revved up) by some ill-advised verbals while batting. He duly tore in after tea, with Binks and what became a six-man cordon pushed back toward the 30-yard circle, finishing with 8/21 in 12 overs of shock-and-awe that included a burst of five wickets in six balls, with his chief irritant's stumps demolished first ball.

Besides the heavy tremors he was sending through WCL circles, drawing curious new cricket folk through the Barnards Green gates, Russell was fast becoming a recognisable figure around a town not exactly renowned as an ethnic melting pot, often spotted pursuing teammates' dubious barber recommendations or doing his grocery shopping in the Caribbean style. "He would drive around in this silver automatic Mondeo," recalls Clarke, "which our sponsors used to give the overseas players. It wasn't stickered up, but everyone knew it was the cricket club's car. One day a bloke I work with told me he'd been down to Morrisons the day before and seen it outside the main door, not in a parking space, with the window down, radio on, and engine still running. He hadn't even bothered taking the keys out!"

Next in the Russell firing line were derby rivals Malvern, who had certainly become well aware of the Jamaican's presence around town, off-pitch and on (and if any of them hadn't, friends in the Barnards Green team had helped paint the picture for them). The chatter in the build-up seemed to have inadvertently pushed Russell's competitive instincts up to 11, and after being furious with himself for falling on 98, he steamed in and peppered the opposition, hitting three of them on the helmet (two of whom switched to Barnards Green the following season) in a fiery spell of 4/44. The 122-run victory consolidated the team's momentum, with Russell's contribution at that stage a reasonably handy 414 runs at 82.8 and 32 wickets at 7.56. At which point Barnards Green lost him for two months, initially to the West Indies 'A' tour of England: two first-class games against India 'A' (a five-for in each), two 50-over warm-ups against Ireland, and a triangular series against India 'A' and England Lions (119 runs at 39.66 from 64 balls).

Losing their star man for so long might easily have derailed things, but a team of gnarly, streetwise veterans had banked a lot of confidence from their two recent promotions, while some younger players were starting to make their mark. Among them was a 16-year-old George Rhodes, the son of former England wicketkeeper and Worcestershire coach Steve Rhodes, a frequent spectator at Barnards Green that year. 'Bumpy' invited Russell up for regular training at New Road and later signed him for the Rapids' 2013 T20 campaign.

Immediately after the triangular series, Russell flew back across the Atlantic for the inaugural Caribbean T20 competition, another unforeseen interruption to his Barnards Green duties. "A lot of people thought we'd seen the last of him when he went back to the West Indies," says Williams, "but I always had faith he'd come back." Still, the club couldn't afford another air fare, so were thankful that Russell sorted things at his end, determined to return to Worcestershire to complete his unfinished business. He had missed eight games, only one of which had been lost, with three wins and three winning draws pushing Barnards Green up from third when he left to pole position. "We rubbed that into him a lot," quips Clarke, "that we'd actually *improved* since he'd been away."

Even so, Russell just about squeaked into the XI for the first game of the home stretch, away at Colwall, surviving a drop on 30-odd – after which the fielder *literally* burst into tears – to slam 18 fours and seven sixes in a 103-ball 161, setting up a crushing 183-run win.

The next two games, against Droitwich Spa and Malvern, were lost to inclement August weather, which may not entirely have disappointed their opponents, given their bruising earlier encounters with the Jamaican. All of which left Barnards Green in the box seat heading into the final four games, just needing to hold their nerve over the bank holiday double-header to get one hand on the trophy, one foot in the Promised Land. They took care of the first part, strolling to victory over Redditch, Russell bagging 4/43 on the day the Pakistani spot-fixing scandal was engulfing Lord's.

By this point, Russell was on his fourth Malvern abode, lodging with another social member, club sponsor Julian Hall. "We found him the right home eventually," says Binks. "Julian was a kindred spirit, if only because of his love of rum, although Andre wasn't a massive drinker." Be that as it may, the pro had to withdraw from the Monday game at Romsley & Hunnington after mysteriously injuring himself falling down the stairs at home in the aftermath of a long, hot and pretty relaxed Sunday six-a-side tournament.

No matter, though. His colleagues bagged 16 points from a winning draw and the following week completed the job with a seven-wicket win in their final home game, against Stourbridge, Russell bludgeoning 98*, including a six that cleared the houses on the other side of North End Lane, the only time anyone can remember it being done. "To be fair," says Binks, "I don't remember him plinking many over the boundary. They'd have been sixes anywhere." When a call came through that Worcester Nomads had failed to win, the celebrations could begin. "We had 'Champions' t-shirts ordered by 11pm that night," jokes Binks.

However, before the end-of-season send-off – a Caribbean-themed party with jerk chicken, rice and peas, rum punch and, um, a bucking bronco – there was their final-day victory parade at Worcester to take care of, complete with trophy presentation. Dre being Dre, he wasn't in the mood for a hit-and-giggle, declining the offer to open the batting and insisting on his usual chair at No.4, from which he raised himself to biff a 60-ball 110 with 11 fours and nine sixes of typically vast magnitude. "The boundary's big enough there as it is," says Clarke, "then there's a bit of a road, and then the barracks, which are four stories high. Andre hit James Wagstaff two thirds of the way up the barracks. Waggy says, 'Bet you can't do that again'. The next ball sailed clean over the building."

The September rains swept in to end Worcester's forlorn chase of 309, and Barnards Green repaired to HQ for the party. Yards of ale were quaffed, songs were sung, farewells were said, with Andre again to be found in his usual spot. "Notoriously, if we have a do," says Clarke, "they'll put a disco on in the back room and no one will go in there. Not Andre. He'd *always* be in there dancing, absolutely loving the music. He wasn't a big drinker, but he never sloped off early. He was always about somewhere."

Re-signing him for 2011 was never an option. Russell was on a fast-track to superstardom via a Test debut in November, an ODI debut in March 2011 at the World Cup, and after that the IPL, CPL, BBL, BPL, PSL and many others besides. He took some Malvern mementos with him on the journey, though, including a pair of framed photos presented by Williams' father that were later spotted on his bedroom wall in a Facebook post, but mainly in the form of his beloved 'gears'. "The done thing with pros is to give away all your spare kit at the end of the year," says Binks. "Absolutely not with Andre. Everything he was given was definitely going back to Jamaica, excess baggage or not!" He even persuaded a third-teamer to give him his bat after taking a fancy to it.

For all the mementos he took, there were many indelible memories he left behind, memories of brutal hitting, thermonuclear bowling, and the all-in, switched-on professionalism that shaped an unforgettable season in which his 799 WCL runs at 99.9 (strike rate over 160) and 37 wickets at 9.2 helped squeeze Barnards Green through the narrow Birmingham League doorway, a vital helping hand on a wider journey that saw the club win back-to-back promotions over the next two years, establishing themselves near the top of the local pyramid. Russell popped in for a visit during that 2013 T20 stint at New Road, although had to ask several people how to get to "the Greens" from Worcester, and whenever he appears on the TV in the bar, whether playing for West Indies, KKR or Jamaica Tallawahs, he always brings a smile to members' faces, especially those lucky to have shared a dressing room with him.

"For all the amazing on-field stuff he did, though, one of my best memories was walking to the top of the Beacon with him," says Clarke. "Just before he went back, I'd asked him if he'd been up the Malvern Hills. He said, 'No, I don't know how to get up there'. So I told him we'd have a walk up, and the chairman was waiting up there with a slab of Guinness, a tray of 24 cans. It was a blustery old day and we stood around chatting and getting stuck into these cans, Andre as well. Then he stood on top of the plinth up there and shouted, 'I'm on top of the world! I'm on top of the world!'"

Well, not quite. Not yet. But it wouldn't be long, as Steven Hirst's glass-half-full hunch proved bang on. He did indeed turn out to be a bit of a gun.

8

Wasim Akram

at Smethwick CC

A sweltering Sunday morning in June 1999 at Smethwick CC, a couple of miles west of Birmingham city centre, and the members who had roused themselves for a hair of the dog and/or to watch the juniors in action start funnelling into the pavilion for a unique occurrence in the history of English club cricket. It was the toss for the World Cup final, Australia versus Pakistan, and both captains had a connection to the club: Steve Waugh had played three games there in 1988 (scoring 2, 124 and 135*), while Wasim Akram had been signed in December and was due to get going once the World Cup was over. Or rather, he had agreed to play, with no written contract signed and the fees to be covered by a local garden furniture magnate of Kenyan extraction, Abid Mir, who had apparently promised a £30,000 investment. Smethwick also engaged the former Warwickshire cult player Asif Din as captain, who in January gave an interview with the local *Sunday Mercury* that bore the headline: 'Akram can do a job for Smethwick – old pal Asif'. You reckon?

The early announcement had certainly afforded local players plenty of time to consider their options, which were: (a) sign for another club in a different division, (b) bring forward plans to pivot to Saturday afternoon golf, (c) consult the fixtures and book a judiciously timed holiday, (d) purchase a chest-guard, (e) write a will, or (f) as West Bromwich Dartmouth skipper Richard Cox did, pick Graham Gooch's brain on a coaching course, go through visualisation exercises, have a bowling machine replicate the Wasim wizardry, and join the Warwickshire squad for routine pre-season vision tests. Still, in the Birmingham League batters' favour, YouTube didn't yet exist, so there were no 'Wasim Pace God: Top 10 Toe and Head Crusher' videos to get the popcorn (and whisky chasers) on for.

It was an astonishing coup, and the club, as one might expect, was humming with anticipation. Smethwick had secured the services of an A+ cricketer, elite of the elite, at the time the only man with 300 wickets in both Tests and ODIs, one of eight players to make both *Wisden* and ESPNcricinfo All-Time XIs (along with Jack Hobbs, the Don, Sachin, Viv, Garry, Shane and Malcolm), and they wouldn't have to pay a penny for it. What could possibly go wrong?

Akram wasn't the first bona fide superstar bowler to have been engaged by Smethwick either. Having started out at the club as a teenager, local-born SF Barnes returned home as pro in 1936, aged 64, and took 70 wickets, the terms of his contract stating solely that he received half the gate money. Certainly nearer the peak of his considerable powers in 1999 than SF had been 63 years earlier, Akram recalls being paid £2,000 per game, "which was a lot of money. More than I got for playing a Test match, and I was one of the top players in the world then." Indeed he was, a high-grade weapon about to be inserted into the ancient rivalries of the country's oldest league, inspiring both teammates and trepidation, perhaps even a first Smethwick title since 1968. That was the dream, although Wazball wouldn't quite pan out that way.

The deal had been set up by a former Smethwick junior, Raja Khan, a PE teacher, agent and much else besides who, thanks to a chance meeting with PCB chief executive Majid Khan in 1996, became an "informal media officer" for that year's World Cup and an "ad hoc liaison" for the Pakistan World Cup squad in 1999. Late one night the previous summer, Raja was browsing the teletext news service Ceefax at home in Small Heath, where he lived with his parents, when he read that Lancashire captain Akram's benefit year would be his 10th and last at the county, the 33-year-old stepping down to stay fresh for the last few years of his international career, World Cup included.

Wheels were set in motion, with Raja taking a Smethwick official to Trent Bridge in September to meet Wasim, two valedictory one-day trophies by then safely pouched. Once the financing had been agreed, with A Mir & Co receiving prominent sponsorship at the club, the deal was announced. The plan was that Wasim would play whenever permitted by his commentary commitments for Channel 4, debuting that summer as the UK's live international cricket broadcaster after they had outbid the BBC. Channel 4 also commissioned a documentary, *When Wasim Came to Smethwick*, a unique occurrence for an English club pro's season. And in another slightly surreal turn, Raja arranged for the full Pakistani squad to play a charity game cum World Cup warm-up against Smethwick first XI in early May for victims of the ongoing war in Kosovo, one of the more unusual friendlies in the club's history, albeit a match that would later prove central to Wasim's already truncated stint being further trimmed amid an acrimonious fall-out. "It was Shoaib Akhtar, Wasim, Waqar: the full cast," recalls Smethwick opener Steve McDonald, "and an absolute minefield of a wicket. It shouldn't have been played, really. It was a farce."

Smethwick would not be Wasim's first spell of English league cricket. In 1986, he had arrived as a teenager – one with 28 wickets at 24.57 from eight Tests – to play for Burnopfield, just outside Newcastle-upon-Tyne, in the Tyneside Senior League on £50 a week. "Imran Khan organised for me to go there," he recalls, "because in 1987 Pakistan was touring England, so he said, 'Why don't you go and play league cricket?' I left Pakistan with my sunglasses on and landed in London for the first time at four o'clock in the afternoon in April and it was pitch black. That was the first shock."

Wasim's brother, who was studying in London, picked him up from Heathrow and put him on a train at Euston. He was greeted at the other end by club officials and taken to a one-bedroom riverside flat in Newcastle. "I enjoyed it," he says. "The club were very helpful. It was boring for the first two or three weeks because practice was only once a week and it always rained. But I performed well. I got my first hundred, first eight-for and first hat-trick. They were uncovered wickets, sometimes muddy, and I learned to bowl cutters. The boundary was 25 or 30 metres on one side. Wasim Raja was playing in the league and I roomed up with Mohsin Kamal. It was a very pleasant experience."

He was a very different animal back then from the 33-year-old legend who arrived 15 minutes late for his Birmingham League debut in a cobalt blue Porsche loaned him by Abid Mir, having sped 130 miles up from Taunton after filming for Channel 4 that morning. The anticipated four-figure crowd had not materialised – perhaps because the large local Pakistani community had been turned off by the humiliation at Lord's, perhaps because of the £3 admission fee – although there was a media scrum outside the ground, which Wasim pushed regally through, his kit lugged in by a flunky. Not many of them were there for his thoughts on opponents West Bromwich Dartmouth's batting line-up. The Porsche, the press pack: it was a league pro's grand entrance bested only by Vivian Richards landing on a Lancashire outfield in a helicopter 12 years earlier.

With his star man somewhere on the M5 when he won the toss, Asif Din had little option but to bat first, and while openers McDonald (48) and Sohail Mohammad (54), son of Pakistan legend Mushtaq, were quietly going about their business, Wasim met his new teammates, a number of whom had played or would go on to play professional cricket: there was Abdul Hafeez and Maneer Mirza, who each had a smattering of games for Worcestershire; Kasir Shah, who did the same at Derbyshire; and Kadeer and Kabir Ali, 16 and 18 years old, brother and cousin of Moeen, who briefly appears in the C4 documentary, milling about as his father, Munir, and uncle Shabbir build the fabled backyard net that set him on his way.

Akram's entrance at 129/3 was a curious mixture of big-time and village: on the one hand, he was doubtless the first Birmingham League batter ever accompanied to the middle by a documentary crew and press photographers; on the other, he was sporting a gaudy A Mir & Co branded cap and shirt, which wicketkeeper Adam Binks recalls being "handed to us out of a bin bag before the game. Terrible quality, no club crest, just the yellow and purple Mir logo, which weren't even club colours. I never wore mine, and they were binned off pretty quickly." Never one to dally too long in the lower gears, Akram slog-swept a six over the pakora stall off Worcestershire's Matt Rawnsley, crunched another four, and was then castled by the part-time offies of Warwickshire's Mark Wagh for an eight-ball 11 as Smethwick closed on 247/9 from their 60 overs.

During the interval, he held a press conference on the outfield, most of the questions concerning Pakistan's nine-wicket trouncing at Lord's six days earlier, defeated with 35 overs unbowled. The Smethwick pro was asked about rumours of the players partying the night before, and even whether the game had been fixed, a reminder that the Black Country would provide no escape from wider cricketing currents. By then, the Qayyum Commission had been running for nine months, a government-backed attempt to get to the bottom of the corruption and match-fixing rumours bedevilling the Pakistan team since Imran Khan's retirement. Salim Malik was at the centre of allegations, but Wasim, Ijaz Ahmed and a strong support cast were all heavily implicated. Indeed, these were especially chaotic times in Pakistani cricket, with 13 captaincy changes in the four-and-a-half years prior to the Commission, Akram having stepped down in early 1998, then played under Aamir Sohail in South Africa and Rashid Latif in Zimbabwe before his final Lancashire summer.

Four days after the Commission opened on September 9, shortly after the County Championship game at Trent Bridge during which he first spoke to Smethwick, Wasim announced his retirement from international cricket. He soon unretired, however, playing in back-to-back 1-0 home Test series defeats: the first to Australia under Sohail, during which Latif presented secret tape recordings to the Commission; the second to Zimbabwe under Moin Khan, during which Sohail gave explosive testimony to Qayyum, much of it fingering Akram. Nevertheless, Akram was then restored to the captaincy for the two-Test trip to India, winning the Chennai epic by 12 runs before losing in Delhi as Anil Kumble took all 10, Wasim later accusing his 10th-wicket partner Waqar of suggesting a deliberate run out to deny Kumble his glory.

Wasim stayed on as captain for the victorious Asian Test Championship campaign, where there was another away win against India, followed by hat-tricks in consecutive games against Sri Lanka. Pakistan then won an ODI quadrangular in Sharjah – coach Javed Miandad stepping down afterwards, citing five players who had fixed a defeat to India – before a World Cup that brought four wins, a shock defeat to Bangladesh, losses to South Africa and India in the Super Sixes, the semi-final roasting of New Zealand and that capitulation in the final, which had the effigy-makers of Lahore and Karachi digging out the glue and paraffin. "Anger over the World Cup final had been intense," writes Osman Samiuddin in *The Unquiet Ones,* his history of Pakistan cricket, "the loss a vent for an entire population's building fury over six years of corruption paranoia."

And so, six days later, Akram was being asked about it all on the Smethwick outfield while his teammates enjoyed a sandwich and cup of tea, maybe a smoke, and tried to figure out how they'd knock over WBD. Plan A, presumably, involved the new lad from Lahore. However, the league was a high standard – between 1980 and 1999, its clubs would win nine National Club Championships, with four final losses as well – and Wasim wasn't necessarily going to have everything his own way. "Those were tough cricketers," he recalls. "I was surprised, but in a good way. None of them backed down."

And then, finally, it was show time: that short-stepping sharp sprint through the crease, the arm coming over as quick and savage as a fan's blade, the wizard's wrists, the improbable trajectories, the laser-guided intimidation. "Good luck, fellas. Get stuck in!"

West Brom would certainly be no pushovers. Taking strike was Wagh, who would retire with 12,455 first-class runs. His opening partner Mike Rindel had played 22 ODIs for South Africa, scoring a hundred against Pakistan, Wasim and Waqar included, in one of them – a Mandela Trophy final in Johannesburg pinpointed by Qayyum as one of eight key suspicious games, before which an irate Latif had the Pakistan team swear on the Qur'an that they weren't involved in fixing after Salim Malik had unilaterally u-turned on strategy at the toss. At No.4 was Bedfordshire batter Richard Dalton, good enough two years earlier to crash a 59-ball 76 against Derbyshire for Minor Counties, then 69 from 47 against Worcestershire four days later. Nine overs into West Brom's reply, however, they were all back in the shed, courtesy of Akram: one bounced out, the other two comprehensively bowled. "Rindel creamed one through the covers for four off Wasim," recalls McDonald, "cracking shot, and you just saw something change in him. You often felt he was bowling within himself but he really let the reins off. That little spell was absolutely electric to watch."

By now, the Waz pills were starting to kick in (side effects: delusions of slaughtering 12 teams in a row and romping from eighth to first in the table), and the high would last around an hour and a half, extending into Akram's second spell when he decided to terminate Rob Fenton's middle-order resistance. This he did by breaking his toe and then his jaw in a three-ball burst, the latter delivery dislodging two teeth as it came in under the grille and back out above it.

At 59/6, with another in hospital and almost 40 overs still to bat, West Brom might have been forgiven for chucking in the towel.

However, led by skipper Richard Cox, who dug in for over two-and-a-half hours and 138 balls for 42*, taking a pummelling in the process, they survived Akram's third, fourth and fifth spells, escaping with a draw as last man Paul Swainson held firm for the final nine overs. These efforts earned Cox not one but two features in the local press. "Once I got out there it was every bit as difficult as I imagined," he said. "But I refused to be intimidated and I enjoyed the contest."

For Wasim, it was time to put the feet up and block out the background noise and drama as best he could, which was easier said than done. Raja, Abid and Asif had all spoken of Smethwick using their icon's status to tap into Birmingham's large South Asian-heritage population, coaching and talent-spotting, but that didn't really take off. He had his house in Altrincham, near Manchester, and still does, but was given use of a smart two-bedroom flat in leafy Edgbaston, his late wife Huma and young son flitting between the two. "In Altrincham, you meet Indians and Pakistanis, but not so much," he explains. "Over there [in Birmingham], whenever I went out for a walk with my three-year-old boy, it was just people from my part of the world and I was always being recognised and stopped. That was tough, especially after losing the World Cup the way we did." The Edgbaston flat would be the scene of the next drama.

Akram had been diagnosed with diabetes a couple of years earlier – he ascribed its onset to stress – for which he needed three insulin injections a day. On the eve of the next game, at home to Stratford-upon-Avon, he suffered an attack at 7:30am while alone at the flat. He was discovered curled up on the floor at 10am by Raja who sensed something amiss when Wasim failed to answer the intercom or respond to stones being thrown at the window. It was a potentially life-saving intervention. Akram skipped the day's commentary duties down the road at Edgbaston, but just over 24 hours later was back at Broomfield for his second Birmingham League outing, where there would be more off-field drama.

Smethwick batted first, McDonald continuing his good form with 86 as the innings closed at 217/9. Akram fell for just 5 to a one-handed, *wrong*-handed caught-and-bowled from Mike Palmer, who observed, magnanimously, "I had nothing to lose and he was on a hiding to nothing". Kabir Ali then struck early for Smethwick, before Chris Howell (68) and 18-year-old Huw Jones (67), in only his second Birmingham League game, added 130 in a 38-over partnership during which Akram left the field after receiving news from his brother that their father, back in Lahore, had suffered a heart attack not long after hearing that two bookmaker brothers jailed for his kidnap in October 1998 had been released (and were due to testify before Justice Qayyum).

Declining the offer to withdraw from the game, Wasim returned to remove Howell in his second spell, with left-arm spinner Firoz Otha snaring Jones, who told the *Birmingham Post*: "[Wasim's] second spell was very, very pacy and it was as hard as I thought it would be. I did ride my luck a bit, but I enjoyed every minute." Otha then whittled through the middle-order, including future Warwickshire skipper (and grandson of Doctor Who) Jim Troughton for a single, but was clattered for a couple of late sixes by David Graham, whose 40 threatened to win it until a trademark Akram yorker detonated his stumps. Stratford finished seven short, eight down, Akram contributing 15-3-40-2 to a second winning draw that put Smethwick into the top half for the first time.

Yet still, like Radiohead playing the Red Lion, he wasn't really *feeling* it. "Going from international into league cricket – I found it tough," he says. "Maybe 'boring' is not the right word, but I was used to playing with big crowds. League cricket wasn't exciting for me as a player."

If not quite Eden Gardens, the following week's trip to Old Hill, a natural amphitheatre with grass banking at both ends, nevertheless drew a crowd of over two thousand. Dressing-room areas were cordoned off, and Wasim had his minder hand out pre-autographed photos as he shuffled to their sanctuary. Old Hill were four-time national club champions and had destroyed Smethwick in the first half of the season, winning by 180 runs. It was probably best not to read too much into that, though, given they didn't have one of the greatest pace bowlers who ever drew breath taking the new ball that day, one who had now been revved up by teammates looking for atonement.

For most of the Old Hill side, it was comfortably the biggest crowd they would ever play in front of, and out into the cauldron strode Harshad Patel and Jonathan Wright, experienced Birmingham League campaigners who had both been contracted at Worcestershire in the mid-1980s without quite breaking through. "The first thing I noticed, from ball one," says Wright, "was they were passing the new ball around the team on the bounce. We'd never seen anything like it. The second thing was that Wasim bowled a lot of bouncers early on, obviously trying to intimidate us. I'd faced quick bowling before, but with Wasim I thought, 'There's no way in a million years I'm going to try and hook this'. Kabir was sharp, but his pace paled in comparison. It was *quick* quick. He was Pakistan captain, there were a couple of thousand on the ground, and there was no way he was going to treat it like an exhibition game."

"My habit," recalls Akram, chuckling heartily at the memory of teammates expediting the removal of lacquer from the new cherry, "was to run in every ball, bowl some bouncers, and show those guys that, you know, international level was a little different. But those club players were very gutsy."

Indeed, Patel (57) and Wright (61) took the score to 133 without loss before the ball-husbandry paid off, the latter "bowled by the best ball I ever faced, which looked like it was going to pitch miles outside leg stump before reversing away and knocking my off stump out". This brought Karl 'Careless' Pearson to the wicket, juiced up on "five or six Red Bulls" according to teammate Sean Lloyd: "He was so hyper by the time he got in that he jumped on the front foot early two balls in a row, before getting the inevitable short one, which he gloved in front of his chin while still on the front foot!" Akram's fracture tally moved up to three – technically five, as Pearson now had three broken fingers. "I followed him in," adds David Banks, the captain. "He couldn't even open the gate to leave the field of play. He just stood there showing me his palm, which had already gone blue. Cheers, Careless!" Still, Banks dug in for 28* and Old Hill got up to what seemed a fairly competitive 233/6.

After a solid 60-run start from Sohail and McDonald, Akram slid in at No.4 and finally located his batting juju, slamming 17 fours and five sixes in a 93-ball 135* as the target was passed with more than 10 overs to spare. Amid the carnage, he also claimed a second hand-fracture of the day, as Lloyd, whose part-time off-spin disappeared for 50 runs in 3.2 overs, explains: "I'd gone for one run off the first eight balls, bowled mainly to Kadeer. At that point, Wasim had seen enough of my 'straight breaks' and absolutely smashed a ball to long-on that didn't get above two metres off the floor, bursting through Jamie Parks' hands and going for four. I was so disappointed to have Wasim dropped off my bowling – at least, until I saw Parksy's thumb bone sticking out the back of his hand! He was off work for months. Anyway, the 11 balls after that went for 45. Massive sixes, into the neighbouring houses. Bansky said they had to close the flightpath from Birmingham airport!"

Despite the thumping win, various off-field rumblings and grumblings were coming steadily to the boil at Smethwick. Chairman John Lumb, a no-nonsense Yorkshireman and uncle of England T20 World Cup winner Michael Lumb, was growing increasingly irate with Raja Khan, who had been appointed membership secretary at the start of the season to harness the anticipated bump in interest from the 'Wasim factor'. Raja had banked some of the subscription money in a personal account and later gave the club a cheque that bounced. There were also questions being raised at committee level – and not being satisfactorily answered by Raja, they felt – about the gate receipts from the Kosovo charity match, when cars had blocked up the surrounding streets, leading to several complaints from residents to the police, who were none too happy at not being forewarned about such a sizeable event. Akram may have been oblivious to all this, but he was trapped in a Russian-doll structure of cricketing crises.

The sense that the club was becoming a circus soon afflicted on-field matters when Asif Din, unavailable for the upcoming game against Barnt Green due to a family wedding, not only selected the portly fortysomething Abid Mir – for whom he later worked for many years as a general manager – but also made him captain, confirming the view among some Smethwick players that the whole thing was developing into a vanity project for Mir. In the Channel 4 documentary, Munir Ali, sat proudly in an England tracksuit top, asserts politely that he is "a little disappointed in the selection" as the film cuts to Mir waddling haplessly after a skied ball.

"I picked him as captain because I felt he was the one who could get the best out of Wasim," says Din, "and whether or not he was good enough to play was irrelevant. Was Mike Brearley good enough to play for England?" Adam Binks scoffs at the notion:

"An international cricketer with hundreds of wickets playing as a league professional would only listen to an ageing businessman with diminished cricketing ability? Really?! Also, although Mir was captain, Sohail Mohammad, the vice-captain, effectively skippered that game."

Nevertheless, it was Abid who marched proudly out for the toss against Barnt Green, one of the Birmingham League's new powers, who had become the first club to win the title in their maiden top-fight season four years earlier, thanks in large part to Grant Flower's 1,024 runs, before landing it again in 1997. Punchy as they were, Akram knocked over three in his first spell, including two Worcestershire staffers in Ryan Driver and Scott Ellis, before Lyndon Jones with 46 and Matt Dallaway with 53 steadied the ship. Dallaway even pulled the great man for a six to bring up his fifty, while his brother Gary, a last-minute call-up usually found in the seconds and here batting at No.11, clipped Akram for four through square leg – doubtless prompting a few fraternal clinked glasses over the years. Wasim finished with 17-2-61-5. "There was no one else in the club besides Abid who could have got Wasim to bowl 17 overs," says Asif, in apparent vindication – and the visitors were dismissed for 231. The game was following a similar pattern to the previous week, the main difference being that Akram scored 135 fewer runs.

McDonald's 112 and Sohail's 65 had all but guaranteed victory by the time Akram entered at first drop, ready for more fireworks. "By this stage Roger Hudson was on, part-time slow medium pace," says Barnt Green wicketkeeper Matt Anderson. "I'm standing up. First ball, Wasim punches it really hard to mid-off, no run. Great shot for nothing. Second ball, he starts walking down the pitch during the run-up and gets probably a yard out of his crease when Hudson pulls out. Next ball, he stays in the crease and gets pinned half-forward below the knee roll. Plumb. We all go up and Billy Smith raises the finger. Wasim walks straight down the pitch and says to Billy, 'You can't give me out, the crowd have come to see me,' to which Billy replied something like, 'I don't care, you're out. Now off you go.'"

It would be Akram's last act at Smethwick's Broomfield home. TV work made him unavailable for the next game, a straightforward home win against Moseley that took the team into fifth place, just three points off second, still with an outside chance of the title if they could beat leaders Walsall a fortnight later. The next day, Wasim learnt that he had been suspended by the PCB, along with Salim Malik and Ijaz Ahmed, at which point he flew back to Pakistan in an attempt to clear his name (although the Qayyum Report would later admonish him and others for failing to co-operate). Brown stuff now being scattered by proverbial fan, it is unlikely Wasim was keeping long-distance tabs on how the Smethwick lads were getting on in their next game, where their three-win streak was ended by a losing draw at a Wolverhampton side who a month later triumphed in the national knockout final.

The wheels were coming off at the club, with the 'Kosovo match' against the Pakistanis at the centre of things. John Lumb had been contacted by Smethwick police, who told him the correct licences and safety protocols had not been in place for a ticketed event of that magnitude, and they would not be supporting the club's pending application to renew its liquor licence, a crucial revenue stream, on the basis that management "didn't appear to have control of the club". Then there was the missing gate money from the game, all of which the committee had been told would go through club books, with ticket stubs presented. "They charged £5 admission," recalls then treasurer Gordon McKenzie, "and told us they had taken £9,000. I said, 'No, there's more than that. There must have been 3,000 people there.' Anyway, I told them, it had to go through club accounts. They opened another account in the name of Smethwick Cricket Club and put the money in there. We didn't see a brass farthing."

It had been almost three months since the game, so the committee sent solicitor's letters to five people they deemed responsible for the missing money, including Raja and Abid. The latter had already been swiftly demoted after the Barnt Green game and when he received the letter a few days later, he promptly withdrew his financial backing, citing "a personal attack on my integrity".

Having initially protested that he was too busy working with the Pakistan World Cup squad "in an official capacity" to sort out the money, Khan showed club officials a photo of a cheque for £9,000 being presented to the Kosovo Relief Fund at the George Dixon School, where he once worked as a PE teacher. "I told him, 'That proves nothing'," says McKenzie. Raja lashed out at Lumb in a stormy committee meeting, accusing him of being a racist and lying about the threat to the liquor licence: "Look, tell us: you want us Pakis to leave." Lumb was defended by Asian players in the second team. Raja was removed as membership secretary, then barred from setting foot on club grounds. None of this was in the Wazball brochures.

Rain claimed the game against eventual champions Walsall, by which time Asif Din had stopped playing, apparently over unpaid wages. The club argued that his arrangement was also a private matter with Abid, or at least dependent on moneys that had been verbally – though not contractually – promised and now would not be delivered. Din later sued the club at Birmingham small claims court and won, with bailiffs turning up at Smethwick the following Saturday afternoon, attempting to collect £2,000.

Like some sort of Kansas plains storm-chaser, Akram had departed Qayyum for this smaller-scale but no less turbid maelstrom, and on August 14, Pakistan's 52nd birthday, he played away at Moseley in what would be his final outing for the club. Asif Din was there, as were Abid and Raja. With Sohail Mohammad also downing tools in solidarity, Steve McDonald had taken over as captain and compiled an unbeaten 135 as Smethwick finished on 226/1. Akram wasn't required to bat, and sat watching in long conversation with his manager, (former) financial backer and (former) captain.

On strike for the first ball of Moseley's reply was Ian Stokes, a nuggety left-hander whose 1,236 runs in 1984 remains the highest amateur aggregate in the 134-year history of the Birmingham League (a Zimbabwean teenager by the name of Graeme Hick made two runs fewer for Kidderminster that same season). "The first ball was a little loosener," recalls Stokes, who went on to make 53, "a half-volley which I hit back past him for four. He gave me a bit of a look. A couple of balls later there was another half-volley, which I clipped down to fine leg for one. As he walked past me, he said 'that's the end of the half-volleys' and for the next three or four overs he absolutely steamed in and peppered me and Stuart Eustace, who was thanking me a lot for it, especially after he was clonked on the helmet."

Akram's second spell brought a blow on the lid for Andy Hughes, prompting the umpires to take everyone off for light. Good light, that is. A late-summer sun dropping over the sightscreen behind the bowler's arm is a nuisance at the best of times and decidedly sub-optimal when that bowler is Wasim Akram. And with that anti-climax, he was done at Smethwick: five games, 438 deliveries, 15 wickets at 13.93 and fourth in the averages, one century, one duck, one documentary, one leave of absence for a judicial inquiry, one diabetic attack, one father's heart-attack, and four (or six) fractures caused.

If Akram's premature departure wasn't an enormous problem for a Smethwick team marooned in mid-table and without title chances or relegation jeopardy, it was something of a calamity for the narrative arc of *When Wasim Came to Smethwick*. Deprived of a natural denouement, and needing to inject some dramatic thrust, the final third of a film littered with minor factual errors focuses instead on Raja Khan's frantic efforts to find what's described as a "missing" £20,000 – although quite why it is missing when Akram had played five games and his deal was a private arrangement with Abid Mir remains a mystery. In the end, the problem – of the narrative, of the cash – is resolved by an unlikely partnership with South Birmingham College, Akram apparently being made an "honorary associate lecturer".

Walking off into a bright sunset after an unsatisfactorily concluded match might have been the perfect metaphor for Akram's spell at Smethwick, but his West Midlands story wasn't quite done yet. The roiling waters in which his career sailed back then would once again bring him ashore in the Birmingham League, this time in the second tier. First there would be more Pakistani politics to negotiate, more reputational finessing, and of course some stellar performances – a reminder to both the club batters who had faced him and those still to do so that, even at 33, the autumn having come, this was still an apex predator.

Before that second act, however, Akram would be sacked as Pakistan captain in the wake of a 3-0 defeat in Australia. After a seven-month delay, the Qayyum Report was finally published in May 2000 – the eve of Pakistan's series decider against the West Indies – fining Wasim $3,750 and recommending he be permanently debarred from the captaincy. The final, feelgood scenes of *When Wasim Came to Smethwick*, depicting Wasim relieved at being "cleared of all wrongdoing in Pakistan", looked a somewhat generous interpretation. "It is only by giving Wasim Akram the benefit of the doubt after Ata-ur-Rehman changed his testimony in suspicious circumstances that he has not been found guilty of match-fixing," the report stated. "He cannot be said to be above suspicion."

Akram promptly recorded career-best match figures of 11/110 in Antigua, winning the Player of the Match award in a lost nailbiter. Two days later, the deadline for Birmingham League registration, he signed and faxed documents transferring him from Smethwick to Aston Unity, where he would join four old Smethwick teammates, including Asif Din. He then flew to Bangladesh for the Asia Cup quadrangular, during which, on his 34th birthday, Channel 4 announced they were dropping him from their commentary team for England's summer Tests. He responded with two more Player of the Match awards in Sri Lanka, making it three Tests in a row. Yep, still got it. Two weeks later, he was marking out his run at Bedworth CC on debut for Aston Unity, working through a wicketless 10-over spell as 54-year-old Dennis Oakes grafted to 59*.

Akram's seven games for Unity produced 15 wickets at 13 apiece, 217 runs at 36, six wins, a draw and promotion, which came at the expense of a Smethwick team decimated not only by the first-team exodus to Unity and elsewhere, but also by the loss of several fringe players frozen out the previous year. They finished rock bottom: four abandonments, 15 defeats, three draws, no wins, and a paltry 52 points. Champions Cannock amassed 237.

Smethwick committee members from that time are still stung by the events, several declining to speak about it, even off the record. Others have said it was "the worst thing ever to happen to the club". The most charitable explanation in a whirl of conflicting accounts is there were two incompatible visions: Raja Khan with buzz, spectacle, dreams, patter, glamour; John Lumb and other committee members with bureaucratic probity, careful financial husbandry, and transparency. Bitterness and acrimony linger. Gordon McKenzie says it took "two or three years to recover", although it was 10 before they were back in the Premier League.

Still, Wasim's two short Birmingham League stints provided lifelong memories for those who shared a dressing room with him or those who sat, with slightly elevated heart rates, on the other side of the wall – experiences begetting bar-room yarns that were intrinsically good to begin with, and which have doubtless been polished into greatness down the years. Or even immediately, in the case of Barnt Green's Richard Hall, who went back to the club after the game at Smethwick to tell second-teamers he had cover-driven the legend for four, neglecting to mention Akram was bowling spin at the time.

For humble clubbies brushing shoulders with genuine A-league greatness, even the bad stories are good stories. Like Karl Pearson's, who confirms both having imbibed several Red Bulls before batting and adopting an ill-advised front-foot strategy. "But my recollection is Wasim barely ambled in during his opening spell," he says, tongue not far from cheek. "Their skipper must have had a word with him at drinks when we're 130 for none, and only then did he start bowling the speed of light. 'H' and Wrighty will disagree, but I went in to face a completely different bowler! I was quite happy with the way I played the first two balls. Third ball I didn't even see. To be fair, though, Wasim came in the shower later and checked how my hand was. A true gentleman and legend of the game. It was an absolute honour to have my fingers smashed by the great man!"

9

Shane Warne (c)

at Accrington CC

It was June 4, 1993, not long before tea on the second day of the series opener at Old Trafford, when the cricket world's collective jaw was abruptly lowered by a young blond leg-spinner from Melbourne whose first delivery in Ashes cricket fizzed, curved and then ripped along such an improbable flightpath that England's best player of spin, Mike Gatting, had to seek confirmation from the umpire that the ball that he'd seen – or, perhaps, *not* seen – dart past the outside edge of his bat had in fact hit the wicket. It was soon anointed the 'Ball of the Century', and much like the footage of the Twin Towers collapsing or JFK's assassination, no one who saw it live will forget where they were when it happened. Cricket would never be quite the same again.

Just two short years earlier, however, and only 30 miles up the road, the same SK Warne was being booed from the field after his home debut for Accrington in the Lancashire League. "Send 'im back!" bellowed one or two members. "Go 'ome, pro!" foghorned a few more. This was a crowd accustomed to pros of the calibre of Wes Hall, Eddie Barlow and Bobby Simpson, while Graeme 'Foxy' Fowler and David 'Bumble' Lloyd were homegrown stars. They had seen enough.

Warne had just had his off stump sent cartwheeling first ball by Ramsbottom's Steve 'Dasher' Dearden, this after an earlier spell of 16-1-82-2 during which Jack Simpson (father of Middlesex's John) had swept him to distraction. "The very first ball he bowled at me pitched outside leg stump," Simpson recalls, "and I was looking to help it on its way, but I absolutely nailed it and it went for four. He came down the wicket, saying: 'What's your f**king game, sweeping leg-spin?' I said: 'If you keep bowling there, I'll keep sweeping you'."

The previous week, on debut away at Burnley, where an eight-year-old Jimmy Anderson was helping operate the scoreboard,

Warne had recorded tidy figures of 15-3-34-2 but had then been run out for 2, which wasn't all that well received by the club's hierarchy. "The committee called me," recalls Warne in his autobiography, *No Spin*, "and said, 'Listen, the pro never gets run out. You have to learn to turn your back on the bloke and burn him'. I argued back, saying the run out was just one of those things and that I wasn't going to be burning anyone. 'No way,' they said, 'the pro doesn't get run out'. End of story."

Even for someone as famously straight-shooting as Warne, it was all a bit of a culture shock and certainly far removed from his first experience of English club cricket two years earlier. With his heart still belonging to Australian Rules football, he had played for the now defunct Imperial CC in Bristol, tagging along with a friend, Ricky Gough, and sleeping in the pavilion. "I was 19 years old and began to hang out with a bunch of great guys who loved a beer and taught me how to drink a pint," writes Warne. "We're talking truckloads of them. I was 79 kilograms on the scales when I left Oz and I came back 99 kilos. I learned to drink, play cricket and, well, a few other things about life too! It was competitive enough for me to have to pull a finger out or be the Aussie pro who made a goose of himself."

He stayed home for the following southern hemisphere winter, and only learned of the Accrington offer when his bowling mentor Terry Jenner introduced him to the ex-Test player turned agent Neil Hawke, a former pro at both Nelson and East Lancashire. Hawke explained that Accrington's first choice, Shaun Young, the Tasmanian all-rounder, had sustained a serious shoulder injury and they needed a last-minute replacement – not having one would have incurred a fine from the Lancashire League – so Warne took the plunge. He was an afterthought.

"I kind of wanted to go back to Bristol," he writes, "but I was on a fiver a week there for painting the fences. At Accrington I was offered between £1,500 and £2,000 – plus car, airfare and accommodation. I thought, 'Wow, I've got to do this'. So I used to drive miles up and down the motorway to get on the piss with the boys in Bristol through the night and then, too often, arrive back at Accy the next morning worse for wear."

This home-from-homesickness and long-distance carousing may have explained Warne's early struggles, for after those two opening losses he sent down 11-0-40-0 in defeat to East Lancs, whose pro, Warne's fellow Victorian and soon to be Australia teammate, Paul Reiffel, bowled him for 2 to leave his batting average sitting at 1.33, his bowling average a portly 39. Warne had hit the ground crawling. Indeed, a couple of weeks later, having missed the game against Church after an operation to remove an in-growing hair from a somewhat delicate area, he played in a makeshift nappy, squirming his way to figures of 7-0-40-0.

Warne's indifferent start to the season had by then prompted skipper Andy Barker into morale-boosting action: "I decided to take him out to a local nightspot, Martholme Grange. Strippers and chicken in a basket. He was a bit down. You could see it in his face. He was only 21 years old, trying to be a professional in a team with a lot of guys who were older than him, which isn't easy whoever you are. We were in transition – we'd lost five or six players, and Bumble had retired – but because we'd always been there challenging for the league there was a lot of pressure on him from the members. It was the first time we'd seen him relaxed. We all had a few drinks and said: our season starts now."

Things began to improve the following weekend – personally, at least – against Rawtenstall, whose pro was another Victorian, Colin Miller, Warne bagging 4/38 and chipping in with 34, stumped after sounding the bugle against the wily Keith Roscoe. But it would be the next two days that finally got his season jumping, a Worsley Cup first round match against Ramsbottom that has entered Lancashire League folklore. Accrington were defending a middling score of 166 and the opposition had reached 107/2 in reply, with 18 overs left, when the game was interrupted by rain and had to be finished off on the Monday evening. Inspired by Warne's 19-7-46-5 – including a final over that began with 10 to defend and went: leg-bye, missed stumping, missed stumping, slogged six, stumping, dot – Accrington got home by two runs.

Nevertheless, it would be a further month before Accrington won their first league game, the return fixture against eventual runners-up East Lancs. Warne picked up 4/45, another step in placating his doubters and detractors among the membership, another step in his understanding of the culture, as he explains in *No Spin*. "I hadn't realised how important this Lancashire League cricket was – it was more important than Test cricket in their world. The supporters got there really early and I remember thinking, 'Whoa, look at this lot!' In Bristol a few blokes came along for a beer but in Accy there were loads of people setting up their barbecues and stuff – there were people everywhere... The rules were simple: if you didn't perform they bagged you! Or worse, they didn't even bother to talk to you."

Despite the uptick in performance, Warne would have to wait until June 29 for his first league 'Michelle' five-for – 6/63 at Rishton – and, with it, the fabled collection tin, which "usually amounted to something between 20 and 40 quid", writes Warne, "and I'd always say, 'Let's put it on the bar'. I was told that the pros previous to me had kept the money in their pockets and headed back to their digs at the first opportunity and they loved that I hung around with them and spent it." Despite this landmark, Rishton's own Australian leg-spinning pro, Peter Sleep, edged the head-to-head – taking 6/24 and scoring 60 – as he would in the return fixture, with 100* and 4/32 to Warne's 4/58. Lessons were being absorbed.

If it took Warne a while to get to grips with things on the field, his off-field adaptation was rather speedier, centred around frequent visits to the town's main nightspot, Lar-de-dars, reputed to be the country's first million-pound nightclub. His tipple was the bright green melon liqueur Midori mixed with lemonade, lubricating him for another of his favourite passions. "He did well with the ladies," confirms Barker. "They liked him because he was fun. He'd say, 'This is the one I'm gonna marry, Barks. Next week it would be a different girl: 'No, this is the one'. There were six or seven who were going to be 'the one'."

A couple of years later, in the wake of the Gatting bamboozler, the tabloids started snuffling around town for scandal. "I phoned Shane to tell him some reporters had been in the Crown [a regular Warne haunt, next door to Accrington Stanley's stadium]," recalls Barker. The *News of the World* eventually published a kiss-and-tell. "The information that the press got hold of could only have come from someone who Shane confided in," he adds, "an Australian overseas player who got him in trouble. They didn't speak for a long time afterwards."

Barker is adamant there was nothing particularly untoward in Warne's off-field behaviour, although there was one occasion, early in the season, when his extra-curricular activities impinged upon his on-field responsibilities: he was late for the start of a game, the skipper administered a bollocking, and it never happened again. He knuckled down. Indeed, his Accrington teammates laud not only his well-documented competitiveness and generosity but also his enthusiasm and diligence at training, where he introduced professional drills and the then-novelty of stretching. Warne could invariably be found bowling for hours on end in the nets, even on non-training days, honing his craft with a group of Aussie professionals located in the north west. Some less porous than others.

Still, says Barker, there were ways in which he wasn't entirely the model pro. "He was a lot chubbier back then. He was carrying a bit of timber. He used to live off McDonald's. And his terrace house wasn't the cleanest or tidiest place you've ever seen. I wouldn't have fancied a cup of tea there. It was like *Men Behaving Badly*." Nor was the battered white Ford Fiesta provided by the club and used for those trips to Bristol on first-name terms with the vacuum cleaner, adds Barker. "It was full of fag packets, Mars bar wrappers and beer cans. A right state."

Untidy, horny, partial to a beer, not great in the kitchen – these are not particularly unusual attributes among 21-year-old men, and those protective instincts Barker had shown in dealing with the red-top knicker-sniffers were simply an extension of the paternalism he had felt a couple of years earlier, when he did everything he could to help his leg-spinning prodigy settle, even sourcing Warne's beloved Vegemite from Asda after unsuccessful missions to Tesco and Morrisons. And despite the unflattering early-season stats, Barker never lost faith in his bowling. He realised he had a gem on his hands, if not quite a future all-time great. The problem, he says, was that diabolical close-catching and even worse wicketkeeping failed to support Warne's emergent genius: "We dropped about 30 catches off him, if not more, and the amount of missed stumpings was unbelievable. It was also the 'Season of Byes' and I ended up virtually putting a long-stop in. We had one of the top keepers in the league at the time, Billy Rawstron, and Shane was making him look as though he'd never kept before." It was perhaps ironic, then, that when Warne played for the Lancashire League representative team against the Northern League in late August, Rawstron was picked as keeper.

Long before then, Accrington had resorted to the emergency measure of a code for his variations. "He used to scratch his backside for a leggie," chuckles Barker, "touch his boots for a googly, and flick his hair for a flipper. It was no use, though, partly because Shane kept forgetting to give the signal. Or he'd scratch his arse absent-mindedly, and Billy would be expecting a leggie only for the ball to spin down the leg-side. He ended up throwing his gloves down and said: 'I can't pick him!' He was quite agitated. It was painful. We went through three keepers that day."

These signalling issues issues notwithstanding, Warne followed up that maiden 'Michelle' at Rishton with 5/35 against Ramsbottom, for whom Jack Simpson once again made a half-century, one of only two amateur players to get twin fifties against Warne that summer. The other was Nelson's Ian Clarkson, an insurance salesman who scored 69 and 50, both not out, ably supporting another Aussie pro, Joe Scuderi, who made 121 and 52, also both unbeaten. Clarkson admits he did it without being able to pick Warne: "Joe told me I'd spot the googly because he drops his arm. His first googly, I never saw it. It was like a snake. But if he tossed it up I couldn't resist. We became quite friendly and he got us tickets for Old Trafford, the day he bowled the Gatting ball."

Warne's combined figures for the two Nelson games were a less than flash 20-0-119-0, yet one quality he could never be said to lack was self-belief, and so the game after being marmalised by Scuderi and Clarkson to the tune of 14-0-87-0, he somehow managed to parlay his way into opening the batting – this at a point in the season when he boasted 77 league runs at 8.55 – chipping in with 39 in Accrington's victory over Enfield, one of only two they managed before August. A few weeks later, he made his sole half-century, bunting 51 against eventual champions Haslingden to finish with 329 runs at 14.95, lower than his final Test average.

With the ball, Warne managed 73 wickets at 15.43, putting him sixth in the wicket charts, despite missing the last three games. Whether it was an unresponsive pitch or the pressure transmitted by chuntering members, Thorneyholme Road witnessed just 26 league wickets at 21 apiece from Warne. Away from home, his final six games, culminating in a spell of 19-9-27-6 at Lowerhouse, brought 30 at under 10 apiece. Yep, he could bowl.

There were only two more wins before Warne's early departure for an Australia 'A' tour of Zimbabwe, both against bottom side Colne, the only team below Accy in the final table, a major disappointment for a team that had finished fourth and second in the previous two years. Barker felt this was less a reflection of Warne's contribution than of "a squad in transition", and he was unequivocal when consulted about retaining the leggie for the following season. "I said he'd benefit enormously from having a year under his belt and that he'd play for Australia within 12 months, and people in the committee room laughed at me."

The club instead opted for Dipak Patel, the New Zealand off-spinner, although as it transpired Warne would not have been available. On the second day of the following year, four months and a day after his Accrington farewell, he made a Test debut at the SCG and after that ... well, it turned out fairly well for him. But he didn't forget his old comrades, says Barker. "Whenever he toured England, he'd always phone us up from the team hotel to meet him somewhere. We'd secretly take him into Accrington and no one knew. And he always paid for his own taxi back."

10

Shane Bond

at Furness CC

Pick the bowling attack for an all-time New Zealand Test XI and after you've inked in Sir Richard Hadlee, yet before you weigh up who to select from the fast-bowling battery that took the Kiwis to the inaugural World Test Championship in 2021, in goes the name of Shane Edward Bond, the late-bloomer from Christchurch whose flame burnt bright if not for long. What the injury-afflicted Bond lacked in international appearances, however, he more than made up for in high-grade devastation, picking up 87 wickets at 22.09 in 18 Tests (including four Player of the Match awards) at the otherworldly strike-rate of 38.75, second best among those to have bowled more than 2500 balls in the longest format.

He was equally effective in ODIs, allowing the Black Caps to throw punches back at their trans-Tasman tormentors, then in the midst of bullying their way to three straight World Cups. Bond took out Ricky Ponting in his first six ODIs against Australia, the last of which came in a spell of 6/23 at the 2003 World Cup, and he bagged another three five-fors and three four-fors in just 17 games against the old nemesis. It was hot, hot, hot. Indeed, another of the era's greats, Virender Sehwag, rated Bond the toughest bowler he faced in his career, doubtless because inswinging 150kph yorkers and rib-rattlers was a useful match-up to someone who generally stayed legside and carved merrily away through the off.

A pretty handy package, then, all the more so for the poor club players of the North Lancashire & District League – 15 of whose 16 clubs were, counter-intuitively, in Cumbria, after a re-drawing of the county lines in 1974 – when a 23-year-old Bond signed for Furness CC for the 1999 season. Not that they would have known much about him at the time, with Bond having just 12 first-class games and 36 wickets at an unremarkable 27.8 under his belt.

Indeed, the NLDL itself had no tradition of big-name overseas players, although clubs were obliged to engage a pro for each game, otherwise it was a £200 fine. Andre Nel had taken 102 wickets at 6.75 for champions Millom the previous year, although he was a 21-year-old pup still three years out from Test debut. Other than that, the hired help tended to comprise lesser lights from the subcontinent and Caribbean, along with aspiring state players from the Australian grade cricket circuit. And then along came Bond, like a storm blown in from the Irish Sea. Within weeks, his name would be on everyone's lips, while severely testing the punning capabilities of the headline writers at the *Barrow Evening Mail*.

Built on the steel and shipping industries, Barrow-in-Furness sits at the south-westerly tip of England's most north-westerly and picturesque county, hemmed into its eponymous peninsula by the Palaeozoic undulations of the Lake District, where Wordsworth once "wandered lonely as a cloud" and artists of all stripes are still drawn: poets, painters and, occasionally, pace bowlers. Despite its kernel of grand red-brick Victorian civic buildings, the town is not quite as lovely as the rest of Cumbria. In his autobiography, *Looking Back*, Bond writes: "Barrow was a curious place. Its dubious, perhaps apocryphal, claim to fame was that it was the easiest place to get laid in England. Tracey [his girlfriend, now wife] and I went out one night and all night long she was saying 'Oh … my … god!' Two abiding memories I have of the town are of pregnant teenagers and dog shit all over the footpaths." Even so, he would leave with fond memories of the place.

It wasn't Bond's first English club-cricket experience, having spent nine weeks in London four years earlier, playing unpaid for Wembley CC and working as a bricklayer's labourer during the week, before leaving early with a stress fracture of the back. Perhaps this is why Furness CC's chairman at the time, Robin Dunn, described the signing of Bond as "an absolute gamble", taken after five other candidates had fallen through. But then, it was probably time for a punt. It had been 19 long years since the club had won the league, 21 since they'd landed the Higson Cup. They were desperate for success.

To make matters worse, the 17 titles and 10 cups won by cross-town rivals Barrow – later Liam Livingstone's alma mater – made their neighbours the league's second most successful club (just behind Millom's 18 league and 10 cup wins). It was a long old time since Furness had held local bragging rights. And so, as a gruelling 30-game league campaign got underway on April 17 at Penrith, the players were eager to see how their chairman's 3am roulette spin looked in the flesh.

"I spoke to Robin Dunn before coming and asked what the temperature was like up there," recalls Bond, 23 years on from that debut. "He said, 'You're probably going to want to pack a long-sleeve jersey'. First game, there were actual snowflakes falling when we started and I remember thinking: 'Far out!'" Still, Bond took 4/34 and clubbed 70* in an eight-wicket win, one of eight half-centuries he would churn out in a surprisingly productive – and hugely aggressive – season with the bat. The impression he made on one teammate was instantaneous.

"Back at our club after the game, I was sitting with our chairman," recalls Alan Sippy, a former Furness pro and Ranji Trophy player with Mumbai (average 49.38) who five years earlier had compiled a league-record 2004 NLDL runs (at 100.2) and, in December 1988, made 127 alongside a 15-year-old debutant centurion by the name of Sachin Tendulkar. "Robin asked me, 'How's this new professional?' I said, 'Robin, we'll win the league'. He looked at me as if to say, 'Are you f**king mad?!' I said, 'Robin, believe me. We'll win the league. This guy's f**king good. This kind of pace is not what you see every day.' Even though the wicket was a little bit soft, I knew his speed through the air would be too much for the league cricketer. He was special. I knew it straight away."

Bond was simply happy to have made a solid start. "At first, you're just trying to make an impression," he recalls. "You're walking into the unknown. You have no idea what the standard is, and they had no idea who the hell I was. I was lucky that first game went well. I remember Alan said to me afterwards, 'We're going to win this league' and sort of going, 'Oh, okay'."

A seven-wicket win on Bond's home debut a week later was followed by three consecutive six-fors – total cost: 87 runs. The first came against Cleator, and provided the moment Furness skipper Marcus Fisher jumped on board the Giddy Optimism train. "We'd watched other teams have quick bowlers and us turn up at their ground and be intimidated," he says. "We always felt this was the missing piece in our armory. But because the signing was a gamble, we didn't know what was coming. The game at Cleator, he bowled a guy who always got runs against us: Ian Clark, [Surrey's] Jordan and [Durham's] Graham's dad. He just absolutely cleaned him up. That was when I thought, 'This guy is good. He's going to make the difference and help us win the league'."

To underscore the growing notion at Furness Park that the fresh-faced Cantabrian kid might deliver a long-awaited title, the third of that triptych of six-fors had come after Ulverston had knocked them over for 75. At the interval, Bond gave his teammates a pep-talk: "No sweat lads, let's go and sort them out." Sure enough, 36/4 became 36/9 and eventually 55 all out, Bond returning a pretty handy 15-6-19-6 to give Furness five wins from five and send a crackle of nervous chatter across Cumbrian cricket's jungle telegraph. Bond had 25 wickets from five games, all but three of which were bowled or lbw. In *Looking Back*, he writes: "I bowled two lengths – bouncers and yorkers. It was a fairly potent recipe when you're coming up against club players." True enough, although, as a YouTube clip of him detonating Adam Gilchrist's leg stump at 148kph would attest, his yorker was a fairly tidy ball against anyone.

The growing trepidation among NLDL batters was further finessed by a double-page splash in the *Evening Mail* that week, under the headline 'The Name's Bond' (picture captions: 'Live and Let Fly,' 'A View to a Thrill' and 'The Man with the Golden Ton,' though not 'Thunderball' or 'The Living Daylights'). There was a bog standard Q&A with Bond – Favourite food? Favourite bowler? – in which he observed, helpfully: "I think people in this league aren't used to playing quick bowling."

Below that was an effusive profile from Sippy, who took the opportunity for some none-too-subtle psy-ops (helped, it must be said, by a subeditor who capitalised the word FAST in the standfirst). Reflecting on Furness's decision to cut Bond's predecessor as pro, Indian one-cap wonder Margashayam Venkataramana, after he had taken an underwhelming 57 wickets, 'Zip' writes: "Sadly, [he] was not an outright match-winner and most importantly he was unable to exhort belief among his teammates. On the field, Venkat was like a dolphin, often splashing about and wanting to please. Bond on the other hand is like a shark, all fiery eyes, with a hint of repressed fury."

Shark or not, the doughty Cumbrian players were not simply about to roll over, and after a spell of 5/24 extended the winning sequence to six, Furness followed a Lancashire Cup exit with a first league defeat, to Carnforth. This wasn't going to be a procession, with both Barrow and reigning champions Millom – whose pro was Daryl Tuffey, Bond's great mate from Canterbury and a colleague when he made his Test debut in 2002 – in dogged pursuit. A losing draw against Vickerstown, making it three without a win, was not an ideal way to enter the home derby game on May Bank Holiday.

"Barrow was our toughest opponent, a very good side," says Sippy, as fiery and loquacious a character as his great mate Ravi Shastri. "They were always in the top three and were very cocky. It was a derby, so there were always fireworks. The Barrow members were saying, 'Who is this Bond?' We felt they thought they were better than us." Sippy was up for it, and made sure the pro was too.

Furness batted first, Sippy plundering 113 and Fisher 75 in a 187-run opening partnership on a typically bouncy Oxford Street surface as the home team posted 242/5. "It was one of the fastest wickets I'd played on at Furness," recalls Sippy. "As I was batting, I was thinking, 'What is Shane going to do on a wicket like this?'" The answer, in a word, was demolition.

With that famously dreamy run-up, Bond tore in down the bank and returned 11-4-24-7 as Barrow were routed for 55. Their Aussie pro, Justin Quint, who would compile 1674 league runs, suffered a cracked rib before steering Bond to slip for 3. Two more players left with finger injuries. Furness were jubilant, Barrow less so, and their skipper, Mike Hughes, wasn't particularly magnanimous in the press, observing that Bond "bowls at a reasonable pace" while intimating that wheels may yet come off: "Heads can drop and he can lose his appetite for it." The sort of interview you pin to the dressing-room wall.

At this point, a filmmaker might include a Busby Berkeley-style montage of flying stumps and joyous high-fives as Bond's bumpers-and-yorkers approach pushed Furness on through the heart of the season, but the truth is it wasn't so straightforward. A nine-wicket win over Duddon SC (Bond 4/47 and 65*) was followed by a frustrating abandonment with Furness well placed in the chase, at which point they lost Sippy – then averaging 99 – for two weekends as he took a holiday-cum-business trip to Malaysia. Next game, they were routed for 91 at home by Carlisle (Bond 8-0-33-0), whose veteran spinner Ronnie Kirk took 7/15 from 13.3 overs, ultimately propelling him to the NLDL average award.

The following Wednesday, they saw off the same opposition in a Higson Cup first-round replay, albeit with Bond having one eye on the TV – specifically, New Zealand's World Cup semi-final against Pakistan in Manchester, a nine-wicket rout chiefly remember for *that* Shoaib Akhtar yorker to Stephen Fleming, the Black Caps countering such heavy artillery with the pea-shooters of Gavin Larsen, Chris Harris, Nathan Astle and Craig MacMillan while the country's quickest bowler was terrorising clubbies 100 miles up the road. Not that Bond had any thoughts of a leftfield, Mike Whitney-style call-up from club cricket for the Test series in England that followed. "I wasn't in contention at all," he says. "I just wanted to go and enjoy a league cricket experience. Although I did watch a day of the Old Trafford Test."

The next round of the Higson Cup was the quarter-final against Vickerstown. "He really came to the fore that day," recalls Fisher. "The pitch was hard and quick, Alan was still away, and Shane bowled absolute lightning. I took a catch at slip, arms above my head at full stretch, and I was *easily* 25 yards back." Despite Bond's 9-4-28-5, the visitors still made over 200, yet Bond then slammed 94* as Furness romped into a semi-final against Millom – who also happened to be the next league fixture, a top-of-the-table clash that brought an escalation in Bond and Tuffey's banter war.

"Barrow might have had its shortcomings," writes Bond in *Looking Back*, "but it was like Paris compared to Millom, which shut on Wednesdays." This meant Tuffey usually took the 20-minute train ride into town to hang out, often shooting pool with his mate. Competitively. "I hated getting out to Daryl," continues Bond, "or have him hit me for four, absolutely hated it, and I know he felt the same way too." Notwithstanding this needle, the pair of them and Tracey took regular excursions together, including trips to Edinburgh, Loch Ness, Alton Towers theme park and into the Lakes.

Business is business, however, and come match day, it was Tuffey who landed the first blow, castling Bond for 7 en route to figures of 6/36. Sippy, straight off a 13-hour flight, made a duck, but Fisher chiselled out a crucial 66 as Furness were restricted to 156/9. In reply, Millom slipped to 43/5, all five to Bond, who failed to dislodge Tuffey on a hat-trick ball. Despite a courageous 45 from tailender Dominic Connor, Millom were eventually dismissed for 142, giving Furness a priceless 14-run win and a return to the top of the table. Eight days later, the Kiwi frenemies would lock horns again in the Higson semis, with Millom skipper Ian Sharp opting to praise Bond in the build-up, telling the *Evening Mail*: "I rate him very highly. He is a 110 percenter. He runs in hard, plays hard, and shakes your hand after the game."

Sippy's return from Malaysia meant an end to Shane and Tracey's short stint housesitting for him, and a move back to the tiny one-bedroom flat that had also been Sippy's digs back when he was club pro. "The flat was about 800 metres up the hill from the club," recalls Bond, "long enough to be a bit of a pain in the arse walking to training with your cricket gear. There was no shower, so you had to have a bath every time you wanted to clean yourself up. And we used to have to take our washing down to the laundromat."

Bond was by now past the 50-wicket mark, activating a £5-per-wicket bonus, money that was very welcome with he and Tracey saving up for a three-week whistle-stop coach trip around Europe at the end of the season. "Tracey was working in McDonald's on about £3.20 an hour, cash in hand, £120 a week," adds Bond, "which was pretty much what I was getting – around £3,500 for the season. So I did a few side jobs. I worked some shifts in Alan Sippy's car battery business, which cost me a few good t-shirts when I got acid on them, and I cut the grounds up at Furness. That took three to three-and-a-half hours, but it paid the electricity bill on our flat."

Heading into that semi-final on the back of a fortuitous winning draw against Carlisle, Furness seemed to have gained the upper hand after restricting Millom to 139/9 from their 45 overs. However, the chase was an almighty struggle, and 15 were still needed when last man Peter Lawson came to the crease. Bond was still out there, however, holding the fort and, amid the percolating pressure, he survived a dropped catch in the third-last over to finish with an unbeaten 62, his 17-year-old partner hitting the winning runs with a couple of balls to spare, sending teammates into raptures. Almost two decades without a trophy, and the double was still on.

Before facing holders Cleator in the final, attention switched back to the holy grail of that elusive NLDL title, starting with back-to-back games against Whitehaven. Neither of which was won.

"Second ball, he hit my opening partner, Peter Goldsbrough, on the helmet, almost knocking it off," recalls Whitehaven's Jonny Bruce, a strapping utilities meter-reader whose innings of 89 Sippy rates the best played by an amateur against Bond that summer. "I met him halfway down to see if he was okay, and he said: 'Ian Lucas [a clubmate] told me he was only medium pace, nothing to worry about!' Next ball, he got him caught behind. After that, facing Shane, it was just survive, survive. He was quick, although I did manage to put him into the houses a couple of times. I was usually a front-footer, so I suppose it was the adrenaline taking over."

A frustrating run of three draws was ended with a nervy one-wicket win at Duddon, backed up by victories over Workington and Penrith, the first of which saw Bond hit sixes from the first five balls of one Andrew Reed over before clothing a four through mid-wicket from the last. He then roared in to take a season's best 8/41, including a hat-trick, although opener Gary James valiantly held firm, carrying his bat for 91*, the top amateur score against Furness that year. Next up was the Higson Cup final.

"It was a great day," recalls Bond. "We got all dressed up and went out for a lunch beforehand. There was a pretty big crowd there too." Lunch digested, he continued his stellar cup form with the bat, top-scoring with 64 as Cleator were set a middling 196. Unfortunately, for once he was unable to back it up with the ball and went wicketless, Ian Clark this time having the measure of him as his 81 anchored the chase. A flurry of four late run outs gave Furness hope, but Cleator scrambled to victory, eight down, off the final ball of the game. It was a bitter disappointment, potentially devastating, but with ten league games left and a 12-point lead over Millom, Furness had to dust themselves down and stay optimistic – not easy when the first match of the run-in, at bottom side Dalton, was abandoned due to their lack of covers. Elsewhere, all their rivals won. Bummer.

By this stage, Bond had 76 league wickets and there was excited talk of him breaking the 73-year-old NLDL record of James Simm, who had taken 114 for Ulverston back in 1926. Wins over Cleator (Bond 5/56) and Vickerstown (3/31) either side of a winning-draw against Vickers SC (4/48) maintained Furness's 12-point lead over Millom as they headed into the August Bank Holiday derby game with Barrow.

Once again leading from the front, Bond cracked 74 in a healthy 221/7, then promptly knocked over the home team's top four in an opening burst of 4/22, with skipper Mike Hughes' stumps demolished first ball. *Reasonable pace*, indeed. However, with Barrow recovering to 113/4 and Bond set to return to the attack, the umpires took the players off for bad light. Meanwhile, Millom won, reducing the lead to six, which it remained after the following weekend's double-header, which saw Bond pass the 100-wicket mark, bagging 6/24 and 5/22 as Haverigg and Ulverston were routed for 53 and 74 respectively. Three to play, bums squeaking.

Prior to the penultimate weekend's double-header, Furness held a benefit night for their popular Kiwi pro: £2.50 entry for a race night, fancy dress (Bond in drag), with around £500 added to the kitty for that European coach trip and, just as importantly, anxiety gently lubricated into relaxation.

With ten points for a win, five for a winning draw (and a washout), two for a losing draw, plus three batting and three bowling bonus points, Furness felt they needed to win both games – against Carnforth and Lindal Moor, neither of whom were beaten in the outward stretch – to keep their noses ahead of Millom, opponents on what was shaping up as a final-day showdown. Carnforth were duly knocked over for 136, Bond taking 6/49 to move within five of the league record, but the game was in the balance with Furness at 71/5 when, once again, they were hauled off for bad light. With Millom picking up 13 points, the gap was now just a single point. Several pints were drunk at Furness that night: some glasses half-full, others half-empty.

The next day, however, Lindal turned up with ten men. Aiming for the 16-point win, Furness won the toss and batted, posting 226/7 with Bond clubbing 47 before readying himself for his most important spell of the season – and arguably the club's most important session for two decades – the spell that would ensure an advantage on that final weekend should September showers roll in off the Irish Sea. Charging in down the bank, Bond delivered to the tune of 11-5-10-6, securing maximum points and breaking that long-standing league record into the bargain. Millom, meanwhile, had gone off for bad light, their 10-point haul meaning the gap was now seven. Barrow were a further five points back and, with a few plot twists, could themselves win it on the final day.

The tension on that final Saturday was asphyxiating, albeit less so for reigning champions Millom, who had won seven titles in the previous ten seasons, including a run of six. Batting first, they reached 164/5 from 46 overs – a challenging chase with Tuffey and the pressures of both scoreboard and history to contend with – at which point the heavens indeed opened, and that sweet, sweet rain did not relent all evening. Furness were champions. Finally.

"The weather did us a favour," says Bond, who finished with 118 NLDL wickets at 9.53 and 774 runs at 38.7. "It was absolutely glorious."

Later, as the drinks flowed, an exuberant Sippy held forth for the *Evening Mail*: "This is for all the doubting Thomases who said we would choke it at the end. We have proved we have been the best team because we have beaten everyone. We have beaten Millom twice [including the cup]. And we didn't just beat Barrow, we murdered them."

For skipper Marcus Fisher it was especially gratifying. He had moved to London with work in early August, yet drove the 300 miles back north each weekend to see the job through. It turned out to be his last game for the club, a glorious memory enormously indebted to a professional he respected as much for the way he played the game as his outstanding abilities: "He was competitive but humble, and not arrogant at all about his standard compared to anyone else. And he was a very fair cricketer. He wouldn't appeal for things he didn't think were out. There were no bust-ups with opposition players, no moaning at umpires."

When Shane and Tracey returned from Europe, they stayed with Fisher in London before catching the flight home. Bond had been mulling over an offer to return to Furness for the 2000 season, but near the end of the trip he heard that his application to join the police had been accepted and, in November, he began the six months' training that put him out of the domestic first-class season back home. "I wanted to go back [to Furness]," he says. "I found the club environment great. You had the same guys sitting in the same seats every night. Alan and I spent a lot of time in there, drinking

Bacardi and cokes and talking nonsense. All the lads did. It was a real meeting point on Tuesday and Thursday nights. We'd hang out, play pool, talk crap. Then I'd wander back and have a Chinese feed. It was a lot of fun."

It was an unforgettable season, for both Furness and their Kiwi quick. A measure of how much it meant to Bond is that, even now, 24 years later, having played in World Cups and been part of multiple IPL-winning campaigns with Mumbai Indians, he can still vividly recollect details from some of the games – certain shots, certain deliveries, even pitch or weather conditions at one of the little Cumbrian grounds that charmed him. He still has a scrapbook full of press cuttings. Meanwhile, a measure of cricket's capacity as a social connector and forger of friendships is found in the fact that Bond is still in touch with many teammates and opponents from that season through Facebook – not least Sippy, who he sees regularly when over in Mumbai.

Shane Edward Bond came to Furness as an "absolute gamble" and left as a hero. He played hard but fair, making friends along the way. He inspired kids and made time for pensioners. He hit many towering sixes, set an almost certainly unbreakable league bowling record, and he helped a club's dreams come true. And, of course, he bowled very, very fast.

11

Courtney Walsh

at Tynedale CC

Welcome to the Courtney Walsh Room, ladies and gentlemen.

You're at the recently opened Museum of West Indian Pace-Bowling Terror, and have just removed the VR goggles in the Holding suite, where you relived the Boycott over in Bridgetown and the Brian Close battering at Old Trafford. You feel queasy. Eventually, though, you zap back into the thread of the tour guide's well-practised though seemingly spontaneous presentation:

...especially awkward was his height, and thus the steep bounce of his so-called 'throat balls'. Then there were his long, spidery fingers, which made the ball jag around at alarming angles, even from bouncer length, often following the batsman from his wide-of-the-crease delivery, as Robin Smith found out in Antigua in 1990.

By this stage – the guide now stepping forward toward a laptop – you feel as though you need to go outside for air. He presses PLAY.

This fiendish delivery came two balls before lunch, the culmination of a deliberate intimidatory barrage aimed at Smith after he had batted for over 10 hours in the previous Test. You will notice how the ball spits from the pitch as it thuds into Smith's unprotected jaw, which was fractured by the blow. The concerned West Indies players gather round. Smith indicates he's okay to continue. After all, there is only one ball before lunch: get through that, have a cup of tea, maybe a sandwich if you're still able to chew, and see how you feel. Meanwhile, the dead-eyed enforcer lopes back to his mark, turns, and rushes in...

He mutes himself now as the clip plays out. There are gasps of horror.

...and bowls another bumper. Of course he does. He's Courtney. "Just business, man." Smith grins. Walsh doesn't. As someone once wrote, "This was Guantánamo Bay cricket and they weren't quite done with him yet."

If you were a mechanic from Morpeth, accountant from Ashington or butcher from Benwell Hill who played a good level of recreational cricket back in 1983, then the sight of Courtney Walsh standing at the top of his mark was probably enough to acquaint you with both *heebies* and *jeebies*. There was not a whole lot of difference in height, skill-set or temperament between the fully developed shock/stock-bowling hybrid that routinely terrorised international batters and the 19-year-old who arrived to pro for Tynedale CC in Hexham in the Northumberland County League seven years before roughing up Robin Smith. The violent geometries were all there. And most of the speed.

Walsh had been recommended by his first West Indies captain, Clive Lloyd, to Tynedale's veteran left-arm spinner Ken Norton, 50 years old and in possession of 599 wickets across 220 games for Northumberland by the time the Jamaican arrived in the north east after signing in late March. Walsh had paid his own airfare, lodging with Mr and Mrs Nicholson on Duke's Road, a short walk west from Tynedale's Priors Flat ground, which sat below Hexham's handsome ancient heart, with its Victorian park and library nestled alongside a medieval market place overlooked by a 12th-century abbey. "There weren't too many six-foot six-inch Jamaicans in town back then," chuckles his teammate and junior by one year, Gary Cant.

The saving grace for local batters was that there were few hard-baked pitches for Walsh to slam it into – certainly not in the first couple of weeks, when the team's first eight games were all washed out without a ball being bowled. Four of those were the same fixture, the 20-over midweek AM Browne Cup against Sacriston, eventually played in June, but they also missed the opening three league games, subsequently rescheduled for July. "We had a hailstorm in the early season," recalls teammate David Murray, who took Courtney under his wing and showed him what Hexham and the wider Northumbrian region had to offer, from the nearby Hadrian's Wall to the castles and beaches of the coast. "He put his hand out and held these hailstones. He couldn't believe it. He'd never seen it before."

Tynedale finally got on the park on May 14, Walsh taking a match-winning five-for on home debut against Backworth and Cant doing his bit to add to the mental demands posed by the West Indian. "I was a bit of a wild boy as a youngster," he says, "but I'd reined it in to study for my A-levels. The night before the Backworth game, I'd been to a dinner at Tynedale Rugby Club and we'd all dyed our hair pink. So my first game with Courtney, I had shocking pink hair. Their opening batsman, Les Smith, said to me, 'Look, I'm having enough problems concentrating against this fella, do you mind putting a hat on?'"

Three days later, both Walsh and Norton took 5/17 to rout Backworth for 39 on home turf in the opening round of the Smith Print Cup, one of a clutch of competitions providing a midweek gallop for the emerging thoroughbred. "Courtney couldn't believe we played night matches till nine o'clock," says Murray. "He assumed it was one innings per night, being used to the sun setting early in Jamaica."

A strong early impression had been made, and word would quickly spread about the uncomfortable afternoon Walsh would likely provide. It wasn't only opposition players who were fretting about the big Jamaican, however. "Going back 40 years, your practice facilities weren't as good," muses Cant. "Trying to face Courtney on a wicket cut on the outfield by the scorebox without a helmet wasn't the healthiest thing in the world. It's incredible there were no serious injuries, really. He used to have to walk past my house on the way to the club. He'd knock on my door and my mam would answer. I'd say to her, 'Tell him I'm not in!' because I didn't want to go to practice."

The Tynedale team joined by Walsh were gunning for a third straight league title, plus a fourth consecutive triumph in the Alcan Trophy, the region's most lucrative cup competition. Comprising the top five teams from the previous season's Durham Senior, Tyneside Senior and Northumberland County leagues, the Alcan final was held in the upscale Newcastle suburb of Jesmond, home of County Club (since renamed Newcastle CC), a famous venue on the Minor Counties circuit and regular host to international touring teams – before or after enjoying a fabled *neet on the toon*.

The next two NCL games were won without much fuss (31 maidens from 46 completed overs would suggest Alnwick struggled with the champions' attack), before momentum was briefly slowed. Walsh took 5/28 in a winning draw against Percy Main, following on from

5/46 against Benwell Hill – whose pro, the future Northumberland skipper Mike Younger, employed the 'get 'em while you can' method in a 10-ball 25 featuring three fours and two sixes – but Tynedale had to hang on for a losing draw, which would turn out to be their worst result across the whole league campaign.

They also breezed past Whitburn in the quarter-final of the Alcan, having scraped to a four-run victory over Blaydon in the opening round thanks to the last-over run out of visiting Guyanese pro Clyde Butts, a future Test teammate of Walsh, for a hard-hitting 86. Things were going well. Tynedale even saw off Sacriston in the much-delayed AM Browne opener after a 30-mile Friday evening drive into the Durham heartlands – the sort of journey ideal for testing the sharpness of one's eyesight ahead of longer jaunts south – with 45-year-old second-teamer Bobby Wood, author-to-be of the club's centenary book in 1988, clubbing four sixes as he rolled back the years. Tynedale only got home by nine runs, however, with Sacriston's David Metcalf hooking Walsh out of the ground en route to a well-made 53, a shot duly slipped into the Jamaican's memory banks. It would be five days only before he was retrieving the file.

The game was the first round of the prestigious Tyneside Charity Bowl, the region's oldest knockout competition. It was the longest night of the year, but damp, and Tynedale skipper Edwin Bell, a proto-pinch-hitter, smote 86 as the home team racked up 151 from their allotted 22 overs. At which point, over to Courtney. "Bowling as fast as he has all season," reported the *Hexham Courant*, "the big West Indian returned a creditable 5/20." *Creditable!* Tough crowd!! The reporter also noted that "he was particularly fearsome against Metcalf" as Sacriston limped to 46/8. A hard lesson had been administered to local batters.

"Courtney *usually* had the attitude not to bounce club players, unless they were pros or very good Minor Counties players," says Cant. "He believed that if he couldn't hit the stumps or get them caught behind bowling at 85, 86mph or whatever, then he wasn't doing his job." This was one occasion on which the caveat implicit in that "usually" was exercised. But then, with Walsh, it was a fine line between a bona fide bumper and a bog-standard back-of-a-length number that leapt at your throat from the pitch like a rat scurrying up a drainpipe. Usually, though, he pitched it up, falling back on that trademark indefatigable accuracy. "He had a lovely fluent run-up," writes Wood in *A Tynedale Centenary*, "a high arm, great pace and from that height a most fearful lift. The fact that he had a vicious leg-cutter was, at league level, quite irrelevant. All that he needed at that pace was to bowl straight and that he invariably did."

That largely superfluous Walsh leg-cutter would later befuddle Nigel Wardropper, top-order batter with South Northumberland, County Club's neighbours from the equally well-heeled Newcastle suburb of Gosforth and the region's dominant club since the turn of the century, three times winning the national 45-over knockout and twice the T20. South North's 150th anniversary book recalls Wardropper "walking out to bat at five in the league game at Tynedale with only two fielders in front of the bat, the one at mid-off merely there to ferry the ball back to Courtney. Having experienced exceptional bounce in a midweek cup tie a few days before, Nigel decided to try the Brian Close approach and take it on the chest! This lasted all of one ball, much to the amusement of Michael Lishman at short leg." This was the day after the Sacriston jaunt, Walsh and his tip-top eyesight continuing his fine form with 6/36 in a four-wicket win, and Wardropper was no closer to fathoming it all out by the time Tynedale visited in September, when top-scorer Gavin Wake "became increasingly amused as Nigel played and missed at very rapid away seaming Walsh deliveries and by the end of the over was in tears!"

The pitch-it-up *modus operandi* adopted by Walsh for this level of cricket was helped by having the region's best wicketkeeper, Kevin Corby, to take the edges. Also that, at Priors Flat, there was good carry through to the cordon. "It was a small ground," says Corby, "and we'd be halfway back to the boundary or more, which was probably pretty intimidating. He was a lovely fella most of the time, but he meant business when he bowled. Even though he was only 19, he probably hit the gloves harder than anyone I kept wicket to, other than Imran Khan."

When Corby missed the odd midweek cup match due to his Northumberland duties, his deputy was Ian Dodds, a pain-oblivious, rugby-playing police sergeant with a penchant for keeping without the frippery of pads. Dodds might reasonably claim to be the only person ever to stand up to the wicket to the adult Walsh in a competitive match. On this occasion, *with* leg protection. Although not for very long. First, he had to persuade a batter who was insistent he would pull away unless Dodds moved back that he wasn't going anywhere, then Walsh came rushing in from off the sightscreen and launched another fireball. Unsurprisingly – and, all things considered, probably for the better – Dodds failed to get anything on it as it made its way speedily to the opposite sightscreen. At which point, he reverted to Plan A.

It was another midweek game, on the final day of June, that brought Tynedale's opening defeat of the season, the first leg of a double-header with Ashington – later home to Steve Harmison and Mark Wood, of course – games in which Courtney's chill was inadvisedly prodded. "We played them in a cup game up there on Thursday night," recalls Cant. "We were the two best teams in the area at the time. There was a decent crowd, quite hostile. Ashington was an old mining village who saw us as posh Tory farmers. Their pro was a guy called Jalal-ud-Din, a medium-pacer who'd played Test cricket for Pakistan, and they'd watered the wicket for him. There was no limit on how many overs you could bowl, and we only made 70 or 80 on this wet pitch with the rest of the outfield completely burned off."

Ashington's plan succeeded. They won by four wickets. "So for the Saturday," continues Cant, "Courtney told the groundsman he wanted the wicket as fast as possible. I opened the batting and Jalal-ud-Din hit me on the thigh-pad a couple of times in the first over. I walked up the wicket and said to Michael Lishman, 'If he can get bounce like that, what's Courtney going to do on it?'"

Already stewing on the pitch-doctoring chicanery of two nights earlier, Walsh's temper was further frayed by the manner of his dismissal, run out by Murray, who recalls it being "one of the few times Courtney made any runs. He was not a happy chappy. He hardly spoke to anyone at tea."

"Courtney took his batting seriously," adds Cant. "He went in about eight or nine and hit it a long way – when he did hit it, which wasn't very often. The game against Ashington, I don't think he even ate his tea. He just sat in the changing room, grumpy. As an opposition batter, that's probably the last thing you want. He opened the bowling down the hill that day and came tearing in. It was pretty scary."

Returning, then, to the question Cant posed of his opening partner – what is Courtney going to do on this? – the answer was that he would send down a spell of 7-3-15-9. Corby, Murray, Lishman, Cant and the rest of what became an extensive slip cordon were given the best seats in the house for an early airing of Total Walsh, hipsters catching an off-Broadway performance of a show that would run for 18 years. The worst seats in the house – fractionally too close to the action to attain the optimal perspective on things – were reserved for the Ashington batters, starting with Derek Wood, Mark's dad.

"He bowled quite quick," recalls Wood Sr. of his brief visit to the theatre, "but mainly it was his bounce. He angled everything in and cramped you for space. Obviously, that day it was a pretty helpful wicket. *Obviously!* It was at a time when the Windies lads had an aura about them. He bowled really well but I felt we should have dug in a bit more. We didn't get bowled out for 39 very often!"

"They had a guy called David 'Banty' Johnson, who came in at No.5," adds Cant. "He played fly-half for Gosforth, which became Newcastle Falcons, and was an England 'B' international. He managed to stay away from Courtney until near the end. When he did get down that end, he got in line alright, but this ball was just too quick for him and he got hit where he shouldn't have got hit. I've never seen a batsman lie on the field for so long."

"He was properly felled," chuckles Murray. "He managed to get himself sorted out but next ball he was virtually stood at square leg. He really didn't fancy it."

Only Terry Etwaroo, a nephew of Rohan Kanhai who had played for Guyana, offered any resistance, making the sole double-digit score as Walsh took the first eight wickets and was three times on a hat-trick. When Ian Darling took the ninth, Ashington keeper Si Hooks emerged. "He was a tiny fellow," says Cant. "As he's coming down the steps at 30-odd for 9, you could see he was terrified. The crowd were hushed, then somebody shouted, 'Just get in line, you'll be fine.' He turned around and said, 'It's alright for you lot, you're alive!'" Hooks nicked off to Walsh from the first ball he faced and Ashington had been eviscerated.

The next two weekends were league double-headers, with the first of those rescheduled games from the wet opening weeks. Walsh had a quiet time, taking ten wickets in four gallops as Tynedale picked up just one victory, against County Club, for whom skipper Ken Pearson – Northumberland's all-time leading run-scorer by almost 3,000 by the time he retired – made a measured 46: one for Walsh to file under 'possible recipient of chin music'. In among this, there were two victories in the AM Browne, Walsh finishing the first by bowling leg-spin and closing out the second by conceding seven runs in defence of eight, putting them into the semis. A quirk of the fixtures then threw up three games in six days against County Club, all at Priors Flat.

At the time, County Club's professional, as the name might suggest, was always whoever had the gig with Northumberland CCC. In 1983, that meant Pakistani batting all-rounder Wasim Raja, who was following in the recent footsteps of Mushtaq Mohammed and Dilip Doshi. A dashing left-hander with a Master's degree in politics, Wasim still had a dozen of his 57 Tests to play by this stage, and had proven himself more than comfortable against the West Indian pace battery, averaging 57.43 against them in 11 Tests, a figure bettered only by Greg Chappell during that era. Wasim would go on to average 59.75 for Northumberland that summer, while Pearson's 729 runs (at 48.6) were the third best in the competition. A formidable double-act. In the first game of the triptych, however, Tynedale routed them for 67, Walsh taking 6/46 in an eight-wicket win, including Wasim caught behind for 7 after Corby had spilled him moments before.

Twenty-four hours later, in the Alcan semi-final, Wasim began to find his range, carving his way to a round 50 with Pearson making 20-odd in support. The wiles of Ken Norton did for them both, and County Club spluttered to 124, which Tynedale knocked off for the loss of just three wickets, Cant notching a maiden first-team half-century as the first of four possible late-season cup finals was inked in. Things would be different on Thursday night, however.

Tynedale reached 43 without loss in the twelfth over of 20, yet failed to kick on and finished with a disappointing 81/4. There were no restrictions on bowlers, so it would be a diet of Walsh down the bank and AN Other from the bottom end, initially Norton, who took the first wicket with 11 on the board, bringing Wasim to the crease. "He hit a four, a six and a single," recalls Pearson, "but then had a bit of trouble with Courtney. He got another single away, and I faced the rest of the over. Courtney was going to bowl all the even overs, so I said to Wasim, 'I'll stay here and take him; you go up the other end and demolish whoever bowls.' And that's what we did: me ducking and diving, Wasim smashing the other end everywhere."

The pair added 74 in six overs, of which Pearson's contribution, expressed as a percentage, was zero. Wasim's 74* from 25 balls comprised 10 sixes, three fours and two singles. "I was in as much danger of being hit by him as Courtney," adds Pearson. And the innings was all the more impressive, recalls Cant, because "Wasim wasn't very well. He had sickness and diarrhoea, and nearly didn't play."

Two days later, Tynedale returned to winning ways with a 120-run trouncing of Backworth, Edwin Bell declaring with Walsh on 23*, thus denying him a tilt at his season's best of 28. He followed up with 4/36 – bringing his league and cup wicket tally to 96 by the end of July – as they kept their noses in front of Benwell Hill, who were soundly beaten the following Thursday evening in the AM Browne semis, Walsh taking 5/26. A day later, the teenager was knocking over Graham Gooch at Jesmond for a combined Northumberland and Durham side against an International XI also featuring Graeme Pollock, Clive Rice, Kapil Dev and David Gower. How the county selectors wished they could have picked him for the Minor Counties team. Wasim Raja's presence precluded that, so instead he trained his crosshairs on the doughty Northumbrian clubbies.

When the *Hexham Courant* was not documenting Walsh's exploits for Tynedale – run some word-cloud software through its reports that summer and "devastating" would figure prominently – it was reporting on the heatwave gripping England, with temperatures of 100F and electricity blackouts, melting tar, isolated thunderstorms and flooding in the Tyne valley. Still, with the sun on his back Walsh cranked that freakishly resilient body up for the season's sharp end. First, his 5/54 sealed an 86-run win against Morpeth. A week later, it was 5/46 at Alnwick, whose last man survived his final three balls to claim the draw, although a haul of 17 points kept Tynedale 29 ahead of Benwell Hill, who would head east along the A69 for the following Saturday's title decider.

In the interim, the club hosted a benefit match for Walsh, who invited a smattering of overseas players for his Select XI and, as captain, put himself up the order, hoiking a couple of enormous sixes before acquainting himself with the rum punch. "He really fitted in superbly well," says Murray, "and everyone loved him." One of the few photos that exists of Walsh's spell at Tynedale shows him sitting among a throng of kids at a summer coaching session, their eyes all drawn to this exotic superhero about whom they had heard their parents speak in awed tones.

While sharing some of this awe, his teammates remember 'Cuddy' – a nickname earned as a youngster, deriving from the Jamaican slang for workhorse – being laidback around the club and a joker in the dressing rooms, run outs notwithstanding. "There was one story I told him that he loved, going back to when I was 13 or 14," recalls Cant. "Obviously my surname can be a problem, depending on your accent, and we were playing a game one day when the opposition's scorer, who was on his own – a public schoolboy, a real Jacob Rees-Mogg-type – shouted out: 'Bowler's name?' The umpire shouted back: 'Cant!' This scorer nearly fell off his chair. He asked again; the umpire shouted back even louder, thinking he hadn't heard. This happened once more before he gave up, although you can imagine what he wrote in the scorebook! This really made Courtney laugh and throughout the season you'd see him and he'd just shout, 'Bowler's name?!'"

For all the off-field joviality, there were few on-field laughs to be had when Walsh had the cherry in hand, although Cant recalls one such instance. "He went for a return catch and got hit where you shouldn't get hit, but he didn't seem to show much reaction to it. When we got back in the dressing room, we saw that he had his box on. 'Courtney, man, what you doing bowling in a box?' He said he always did it, because he'd been hit there when he was younger. I'm not sure whether he had one on when he took his 500th Test wicket, mind!"

As it turned out, there wasn't a whole lot of mirth for Benwell Hill in that title showdown: invited to bat first, they were blitzed for just 69, Walsh the workhorse bowling 19 overs unchanged for 3/36, while Ian Darling, who would finish third in the league averages, picked up 6/31. The runs were knocked off for the loss of one wicket, Cant unbeaten on 29, and with the first of a possible three cup finals the following day – the AM Browne against Eppleton at Blaydon – he and Walsh made their regular trip to the neighbouring village of Corbridge to unwind.

"At the time, there was one nightclub in Hexham, called Dontino's, and Courtney had gone on and on about wanting to go," recalls Cant. "So that night before the cup final, I said we'd go, even though the captain, Edwin Bell, was quite strict about preparing properly. I'd got one of the more sensible lads, Richard Byerley, to promise to drive us around. Back then, you'd go to the nightclub after the pubs shut, 11:30 to 2am, so I told Courtney we'd go to Dontino's for an hour. In those days, going to a nightclub in Hexham, a Tory stronghold in the countryside, with a six-foot six-inch West Indian – he's going to stand out. Let's just say there were a lot of ladies interested in him and leave it there. I stayed with him till about one o'clock, when he said words to the effect of 'Canty, can you f*** off.' By that stage, I was quite happy to do that."

Subsequent gaps in the timeline will have to be painted in by the imagination, but Cant shuffled home, hit the hay and "never thought about it until I hear a knock on the door about 9:30am. I still lived at home, and I can hear the chairman, Frank Charlton, talking to my mother. Next thing, he's up the stairs and standing in my bedroom. 'Where is he?' 'What you on about?' 'Where's Courtney?' 'I don't know,' I says. 'I got him safely home about 12 o'clock.' I guess Mike Nicholson had phoned Frank with the news that Courtney hadn't been home. Bear in mind no one had mobile phones in those days and we're meeting to go to this final in an hour's time. Next thing I know, the captain's on the phone, going mad at me. To this day, I don't know where he'd been, but he turned up 10 minutes before we left with a big smile on his face."

The AM Browne was a 35-over game, once more without bowling restrictions. Overnight rain – heavy enough to muffle all but the most energetic bedroom fumblings – had produced a sticky dog, and Eppleton duly inserted upon winning the toss. The first ball of the game saw Bell caught at short leg off Trinidadian professional Rangy Nanan (whose first Test wicket had been Wasim Raja, stumped, in what turned out to be his only game). Nanan bowled unchanged, taking 5/56, figures dented by four sixes from Paul Pickworth, whose 48 would win him the Player of the Match award. Defending 116 in front of a sizeable crowd and perhaps still feeling the afterglow of the previous evening, Walsh returned figures of 16.2-7-17-4, including the big wicket of Nanan, as Tynedale won by 30 to secure the campaign's first trophy.

Seven days later – during which they won the Mallinson Denny semi-final up at Alnwick, Walsh going wicketless after a day on the beach – Tynedale doubled the silverware count, demolishing Horden by 78 runs at Jesmond on August bank holiday weekend to land that fourth straight Alcan Trophy and pocket a very welcome cheque for £500. Kings of the North East.

A day later, and Walsh was pushing off the sightscreen at Priors Flat to the tune of 8/31 in a 122-run win against Tynemouth that left them on the brink of securing their NCL three-peat with three games left. The following Saturday, in a tight game at South Northumberland, the deal was duly sealed, Tynedale scrapping to 126/7 before Walsh whittled through 25-10-46-4 as the home team came up 20 short. South North's historian, Duncan Stephen, back then the first team's No.4 batter, recalls the challenge being as steep as the bowler's trajectory. "His run-up didn't seem to be quick but the ball whistled through, and the bounce and movement were very tricky. I was caught off the gloves in the first game and at short-leg in the second." Join the club.

Rain denied Bell's team a champions' parade on home turf against Blyth, but 24 hours later they were back up to Ashington for a third cup final, the Mallinson Denny, played under scowling September skies. Tynedale chiselled out 129/5 from their 30 overs, then ran through the home team for 102, Walsh contributing 15-4-23-4 as a fourth trophy of a phenomenal season was bagged. And if Ashington weren't already sick of the sight of him, six days later Walsh was back in town, signing off with 7/54 in a 24-run win that meant Tynedale had gone through the league campaign undefeated and which left the Jamaican top of both league wicket charts and averages, with 86 at 8.97, including 10 five-wicket hauls.

It was a lively end-of-season do that night, after which, having verbally agreed to return to Hexham the following summer, Walsh said his see-you-soons, this time making it safely back to the Nicholsons on Dukes Road. His teammates knew it was goodbye, however, with the club already having been approached by three counties. Rumour has it there weren't too many disappointed batters in the North East when Walsh was included in the West Indies' 1984 touring party. Three years later, however, another 19-year-old Caribbean speedster turned up at Tynedale.

Ian Bishop has a much smaller room than Walsh at the Museum of West Indian Pace-Bowling Terror – look, that's him bowling at the other end when Robin Smith has his jaw broken in 1990, before his stress fractures, sending down hypersonic missiles that have Tony Greig in the comm box purring, "I take back everything I said about this bloke; he's *quick*" – and he would take just 31 league wickets at 23 for Tynedale. "I think he struggled with the weather," says Cant. "He was a fish out of water."

Walsh had played 13 of his 132 Tests by the time Bishop arrived in Hexham, although he had been an unused squad member in the 5-0 'blackwash' of 1984, busy taking notes as Andy Lloyd's Test career was ended after 10 minutes. He eventually made a debut at the WACA 14 months after that curtain call at Ashington. The following winter, with England touring the Caribbean, he invited David Murray out to Jamaica for three weeks.

"Near the end of Courtney's season with us," recalls Murray, who has remained in touch down the years, "we were playing a midweek match up in Alnwick, which is 50 miles away in north Northumberland. It was a day off work for me, so I took Courtney over to my parents' house for lunch, then up to Bamburgh Castle, where we went for a walk on the beach. I told him it was one of the nicest beaches in the North East. Anyway, while I was out in Jamaica, he took me to Hellfire Beach one day, just outside Kingston. We walked out on it and he says, 'Now *this* is what you call a beach, man. Hot sand!'"

Cant would later catch up with him, too, swinging over to Lord's while studying in London to watch Walsh bowl a few dozen of the 44,210 balls he would end up sending down for Gloucestershire. "I just dropped in mid-afternoon without telling him," he says. "He didn't know I was there, so I went to find him at the close of play, and there was a queue of kids waiting for autographs. He's got his head down, signing these autographs, and hasn't seen me. I get to the front of the queue and hand him a piece of paper that just says 'BOWLER'S NAME?' on it. He reads it, looks up, and starts laughing. 'You idiot Canty, man!' Then he says: 'BOWLER'S NAME?!'"

Not a question the Northumberland County League batters needed to ask in that long-ago summer of 1983.

PART II

1

Matt Hayden and Mark Taylor
at Greenmount CC

When the Australian selectors announced the touring party for the 1993 Ashes, the newsletter of one cricket club in Lancashire was moved to proclaim: "Want to open the batting for Australia? Come and play for Greenmount!" At least, that's according to Matthew Hayden's autobiography, *Standing My Ground*. The club's historians are unable to corroborate this, suggesting it was either poetic licence or a wind-up to which Hayden fell prey. What is true is that the big Queenslander had spent the previous summer in Greenmount, a village north of Bury, with fellow tourist Mark Taylor the paid man there in 1988.

Both these illustrious left-handed opening batters broke records for Greenmount, both finished top of the Bolton League (BCL) batting averages, both made good friends and left deep impressions, yet it is unlikely the two of them ever shot the breeze about it over a couple of coldies. In Test careers that overlapped by five years – Taylor winning 104 caps, Hayden 103, two of only 14 men to rack up 100 Tests in the baggy green – they played just six matches together. Hayden intimates in his book that this may have had something to do with an incident between them while he was playing for Australia 'A' in a quadrangular one-day series, when he defended a teammate by sniping at Taylor: "You've got one crap shot, a little pull over mid-wicket, and you're putting the crowd to sleep. Shut up and bat." Probably not the greatest career move, given 'Tubby' was Australia's Test and ODI captain at the time.

Back in the early months of 1988, however, Taylor's cricket was on a downward trajectory. He'd averaged 53 in his debut Sheffield Shield campaign, a solid 43 the next – when Channel 9's *Today* programme mistakenly invited him on to discuss his Test selection (it was New South Wales' other Taylor, Peter, who had been picked) – but he endured a poor third season, averaging a meagre 25. Having just completed a degree in surveying, he even wondered whether his future might lie outside the game. So, in an effort to reboot things, he accepted Greenmount's offer of £3,000 for the season and headed to Lancashire with his girlfriend, now wife, Judi. It would turn out to be the perfect marriage of club and pro.

Greenmount had started life as an adjunct to a congregational school, and the church's aversion to the noise of mowers and the ensuing unkempt outfield led to the Bolton & District Cricket Association rejecting their application in 1930, the year the ambitious BCL clubs had split from it. They mooched around the lower leagues, before eventually joining the BCL in 1984, reaching the final delivery of that season's Hamer Cup final, the league knockout, with five runs to defend, at which point the sub-pro and soon-to-be Australian Test spinner Murray Bennett was launched out of the ground. They had just about recovered from the trauma by 1987, when, with Franklyn Stephenson as pro, they led the table for almost the entire season before losing on the final afternoon to Farnworth Social Circle, who themselves won the title and duly cavorted in front of them.

All of which meant Taylor came into a team desperate for success, with a degree of confidence in their ability, but no track record in – and perhaps some trepidation about – taking the final step. He also found a team that practised in somewhat shambolic fashion and, prompted by big-hitting batter John Ashworth declaring that nets were "fookin' rubbish", he immediately set about organising training along NSW lines. "Mark really shook us up as a club," says teammate Gary Chadwick. "He showed, even at 23, that he was a leader. He knew as pro he had to come in and lead not just the team but the club. He took us to another level."

Greenmount started with a tie and two wins, Taylor contributing 13, 21 and 45* before making 90 out of 145 in defeat to Farnworth. They would only lose once more in the first half of the season as the runs began to flow for Taylor: 131 against Kearsley, sharing a club record stand of 248 with Andy Williams (who later that summer skippered England under-17s), 111 against Farnworth SC a week later, and another hundred against Walkden as Greenmount reached halfway in pole position.

They were helped by 50 wickets for the overseas amateur, Patrick Farhart, now best known for his stints as physiotherapist for India and the Delhi Capitals, but back then bowling inswing off the wrong foot for the St George Club in Sydney's southern suburbs. He and Taylor didn't know each other before arriving, but hit it off immediately, taking regular midweek sightseeing jaunts with Judi and embedding themselves in the life of the club. "Pat was great," reflects Chadwick. "As soon as he knew we were batting, he would go and do slow laps of the ground, chatting to all the members about what they'd been up to. He remembered everyone's name. And Judi would always come along, even when we went watching other teams play on Sundays if we didn't have a game."

With Farhart and Taylor more than covering Stephenson's all-round contribution from the previous summer, Greenmount would lose just one more game all season, a narrow Lancashire Cup quarter-final defeat to Bootle at the end of a fallow July for Taylor in which his top score was a disappointing 32. Even so, despite this lean trot and his negligible contribution with the ball, Taylor was always influencing things, recalls then 16-year-old all-rounder Phil Heaton: "His cricket brain was so far ahead of anything we'd seen at the club. He picked things up in an instant and fixed them straight away."

However, if Greenmount were to slay the ghosts of the previous September's last-day stumble, they would need to turn draws into outright wins. They would also need, in the face of old habits, to sustain the professionalism instilled by the pro, a culture that was given a test during a mid-July visit to second-placed Westhoughton.

"It hammered down all morning," recalls Heaton, who travelled to the game with a "very keyed up" Taylor, for whom it was a chance to take a significant step toward the title. "We got there and a couple of our senior players thought, 'There's no chance. We're going to have a couple of pints'. Mark saw this and never said anything, but you could tell he wasn't happy. Within a couple of hours, the sun came out, they started mopping the ground and eventually the umpires said it was fit to start. A couple of our lads had had three or four pints by this time, so Mark starts going absolutely berserk at them: 'You're a disgrace. You're going to throw the league away.' Then it started raining again before we could start."

"He just ripped into us," adds Dave Mason, the team's left-arm spinner. "Both barrels. 'I've not come all this effin' way to play in teams that aren't taking it seriously.' Everybody was taken aback. There hadn't been a cross word said until then and it really had the desired effect. The dressing room went quiet. Nobody knew what to say. We went into the clubhouse and, me being a smart-arse, I said, 'Would it be okay if we bought you a beer?' He just smiled and started laughing. The ice was broken again."

August saw a return to form for Taylor, with 114 against Farnsworth SC followed by a top-scoring 33 against Heaton and a battle with Indian Test off-spinner Arshad Ayub, who finished top of the league's bowling averages. The bank-holiday double-header brought an abandonment, then a nervy game against Astley Bridge in which, with the finish line in sight, the old wounds appeared to be opening up. Batting first, Greenmount had struggled to 101/6 with 10 overs left, at which point Neville Neville – the late father of 13-year-old Gary and 11-year-old Phil, future Greenmount first-teamers and Manchester United and England full-backs – smote eight sixes in the final five overs to help secure a winning draw.

A week later, Taylor made 108* as Greenmount chased down Eagley's 144, which meant the club's maiden Bolton League title could be wrapped up on the penultimate weekend against a Tonge side that had trounced them earlier in the campaign. The favour was duly returned, with the visitors rolled for 73 and Taylor making an unbeaten 35 in an eight-wicket romp. When Westhoughton's result came through, Neville Neville went to collect the trophy and the team threw themselves into their celebrations.

They were still going by Tuesday night, when Taylor accompanied a friend of Chadwick's to watch Bury FC at Wrexham. "They busted a gut to get back to the club for a drink, 60-odd miles," Chadwick recalls, "only for the barmaid to refuse to serve them. Mark went absolutely ballistic. Needless to say, they managed to get themselves a pint when it was explained he was club pro."

Friday night, the team reconvened for a celebratory pub-crawl through the neighbouring village of Tottington, all of which left them rather bedraggled when they arrived at Walkden for the victory lap. Taylor was soon shaken from his hangover, however, recalls Heaton. "That last game, we picked the batting order out of a hat. Patrick drew number four and made late-40s, which he said was his best ever score. Mark drew number eight or nine and he wasn't having it. He just said, 'No chance, I'm going for the league record!' and opened the batting."

Taylor duly signed off with 119, a record sixth BCL hundred of the campaign, while Farhart took the three wickets he needed for 100 across all competitions. Taylor's aggregate of 1,283 runs (at 64.15) was the fourth best in BCL history, though just short of the tally of both his opening partner on Test debut four months later, Geoff Marsh (1,334 runs for Little Lever in 1984), and the man who stood alongside him in that great slips cordon, Mark Waugh (1,359 runs for Egerton in 1985). The following summer, Taylor plundered 839 Ashes runs, which remains the third highest aggregate in any Test series. "He definitely got his mojo back," observes Mason. It was mission accomplished.

After this breakthrough season for the club, Greenmount stuck with the Australian template, engaging Jamie Siddons the following year, Wayne N Phillips the year after (who indeed opened the batting with Mark Taylor in his solitary Test) and Dean Waugh in 1991, but it wasn't until Hayden's arrival in 1992 that they again struck gold. He had just topped the run charts in his debut Sheffield Shield campaign, and came over with state under-19s teammate Chris Holding, the overseas amateur, the pair living together next door to club stalwart Tony Horrocks, whose wife Glenys ensured they were well looked after.

Hayden's first competitive game on English soil actually came as sub-pro for Bacup in the neighbouring Lancashire League. Deputising for Roger Harper, he took 4/47 with seamers that Greenmount teammates would uniformly describe as "terrible, though not as bad as Mark's bowling", and followed up with 73, adding 101 for the first wicket with someone by the name of Mark Taylor, who he ran out for 44, which may or may not have been an omen. His keenness for a game even saw him turn out for the BCL representative XI in their annual Trinity Cup match with the Bolton Association. Hayden top-scored with 69 in a one-run win.

Still, Greenmount lost their first two BCL games, Hayden upstaged in the early part of the season by Jon Harvey, a colleague of Heaton's with the MCC Young Cricketers, whose first five innings were 36, 41, 122*, 63 and then 132* as he and Hayden chased down 259 without loss, the pro chipping in with 117*, his only score over 55 in his first

11 knocks. Not that Hayden was struggling – he made 27, 50, 55, 24, 30, 117*, 35, 39, 34, 55 and 44 – although this was exactly the sort of thing that frustrated him. "I always found scores under 10 easy to reconcile because they were essentially no result," he writes in *Standing My Ground*. "For me, the scores that niggled most weren't the outright failures but the half-results."

That's a whole lotta niggle, then, and to compound matters nine of his 10 dismissals were caught, which might suggest a man too eager to go into that famous bullying mode, the big front dog and pummelled straight drives. "I've never seen a batsman hit the stumps at the bowler's end as often as he did," says Heaton. "One time, he smashed one back and the stump ended halfway to the pavilion." And yet, Hayden didn't hit a single six across those games, which doesn't exactly scream of an attempt to dominate. Perhaps it was a simple case of professional caution and gradual adaptation from the bone-hard Queensland pitches to the softer Lancashire offerings. When it did click, though, Hayden certainly made hay, averaging 173 over the next 11 games. Another man on a mission.

"We used to take him to the local hostelry on a Friday night," says Chadwick, "and he would only drink water. Absolutely nothing was going to get in the way of his cricket. He couldn't believe that us lot, who'd worked all week, would be having eight, nine, 10 pints."

"He was so single-mindedly obsessed with the goal of playing cricket for Australia," adds Heaton, "even though he wasn't as close to it as Mark was when he was with us. He was so fit. He was running up hills every day. He was going to the gym every day. He was totally obsessed with making himself a better player."

Some of which may well have rubbed off on Gary and Phil Neville, footballers who maximised relatively earthly gifts to collect 85 and 59 England caps respectively. Having become the youngest player to represent Lancashire second XI in May, aged just 15, Phil opened the Greenmount batting with Hayden for four matches in June. He also captained England under-15s in both football and cricket that year, with his Lancashire under-15s teammate Andrew Flintoff, who failed to make the national squad, later asserting that the younger Neville "could have been England's Sachin Tendulkar".

Gary was no slouch either. In the middle of Hayden's mid-season purple patch, he and the Queenslander added 236 for the third wicket in a tight Hamer Cup semi-final win against Astley Bridge, a now famous press clipping from the *Bury Times* showing them stood in front of the scoreboard, Hayden with 140* and Neville with 110*, an impressive effort given that half the overs were bowled by Ian Harvey, later to play 72 ODIs for Australia. Even so, with the Bridge cruising at 200/2 in pursuit of 279, and ex-Greenmount pro Brendon McArdle unbeaten on a hundred, it needed an umpiring intervention to get them home. "It was going miles down leg," says Mark Stewart, Greenmount's spearhead, "and I was a bit embarrassed it were given."

It was the last game of cricket Neville ever played, with Sir Alex Ferguson – eyes and ears everywhere – pulling the plug on things lest there were any injuries (apparently, he had plans for his Class of '92). The following Saturday, *sans* Nevilles and with a cup final appearance already banked, Hayden and Greenmount pulled off an astonishing win at home to Westhoughton that strengthened their BCL title push.

On and off amid regular showers, the visitors eked out 166 from their 50 overs. Greenmount started their reply at 7:34pm, leaving a maximum 17 overs to chase, light permitting. Heaton recalls a divergence of opinion as to how things should be approached. "Derek Kay, a senior player, said: 'There's no point going for these. We'll get nowhere near.' Hayden just turned round and said, 'Watch this'."

Hayden's opening partner, Harvey, remembers it slightly differently: "He said, 'We'll bat four overs, then make a decision'." They were 18 without loss at decision time, and the remaining 149 were biffed off in 11.5 overs of carnage, despite the visitors' pro, Frans Cronje (brother of), exaggeratedly lengthening his run-up to slow things down. Harvey finished unbeaten on 87, Hayden on 75. "He said to me at one stage, 'There's no way you're getting your hundred here'," says Harvey, "and just milked the strike for the last 20 runs. Pure quality."

Heading into August joint-top with Heaton – whose pro Maninder Singh would finish first in the BCL bowling averages, although his club were less than enamoured when he departed for the Indian pre-season with five games to go – Greenmount suffered a crucial three-run defeat at Farnworth, for whom Chetan Sharma sent down

18.3-6-39-6, including the big wicket of Hayden, caught behind for 11 in pursuit of a sub-par 122. The following week brought a contentious draw with Little Lever, the players taken off for bad light with Greenmount needing 28 runs from 20 balls, five wickets in hand, and Hayden happy to trade verbals throughout an innings of 90. "If he wanted to say anything to the opposition," says Heaton, "he never thought twice about it. He just stuck his chest out and walked straight up to them."

"I never saw him have a go at other pros," adds Chadwick. "There seemed to be an unwritten code of respect there. But if any of what we used to call 'Billy Shitfighters' started sledging him, then they'd get it. Matthew really did know how to put them back in their box."

The rest of the month was a washout – incredibly, just three of 35 BCL fixtures were played to a conclusion – although Greenmount were able to squeeze in their Hamer Cup final, at which, with 55 overs to chase Egerton's 224/3, the stage was set for Hayden. He promptly made his lowest score of the season, caught by Keith Hornby's one-handed diving catch at mid-off for 2. "He hit it like a tracer bullet," says Heaton. "It was a once-in-a-lifetime catch. I was lying down in the dressing room, and Matty came in and absolutely dismantled the place. He was not happy." (Some sub-10 scores aren't so easy to reconcile, it seems.) Jon Harvey carried the fight with 113, but Greenmount could only muster 193, and were well beaten.

By the time the rains relented in September, Greenmount were outsiders in a four-horse race for the title. They slipped badly at the first hurdle, dismissed for 84 as Egerton inflicted a third defeat of the season. A win the following day gave them a mathematical chance on the last afternoon, but another defeat left the calculations moot, and they wound up in a creditable if disappointing fourth place, sneaking into the Lancashire Cup qualification spots. Hayden signed off with 59, giving him 1,438 runs at 75.68, beating Taylor on both counts (which may or may not have pleased him), albeit not in terms of hundreds or trophies. "Matt was absolutely dedicated," says Stewart, who would retire as the league's all-time leading wicket-taker, "and you just knew he was going to do really well. It was like bowling to a brick wall in the nets, he was that good."

In their different ways, both men left a huge impression on Greenmount, the club's story interwoven with that of these two legends – two of the Australia's all-time top 10 Test run-makers, compilers of the country's highest and joint-third highest individual scores – just as Hayden and Taylor's stories are interwoven with that of Greenmount. Indeed, Taylor recorded a video message for the club's 150th anniversary in 2017 ("making a point to big up his own bowling, and the fact that he got the Kearsley pro out," says Mason), and when he was ambushed by Nine Network's *This Is Your Life* crew during the Brisbane Ashes Test in 1998, his valedictory series, he was more than a little surprised to see Mason walk out as the final guest.

"I got a phone call from Neville Neville, who wasn't able to go," recalls Mason. "He asked if I'd go instead, all expenses paid. I thought it was a wind-up at first, but I flew out to Brisbane with my wife and son and we stayed in a fantastic hotel, the same one as the England team. Some guests, like Ian Botham, were able to pre-record their messages for Mark, but I couldn't as it was a live broadcast. I've never been as nervous in my life. My claim to fame is I made the final cut of the show, whereas Botham didn't."

As for Hayden, 14 years after his Bolton League adventure he was lying on his back at the MCG nets, doing stretching exercises, when he heard an "Oi!" from the viewing gallery and looked up to see Phil Heaton. They went for a few beers at close of play (Hayden made 153 in an innings victory), reminiscing, among other things, about kit. "When Matt and Chris Holding left," Heaton recalls, "they headed down to the markets at Cheetham Hill and bought a load of clothes to take home with them. He said to me, 'I need a bag for it all. Can I have your cricket bag?' I said, 'Okay, but I want your cricket kit then'. He said, 'Fine, you can have it', and gave me his bat, pads, even his Queensland helmet – the lot. I wore that helmet for the next 15 years!"

The year after Heaton acquired his new maroon lid, Greenmount engaged Jon Harvey as pro, but in 1994 went back down the Australian route, signing New South Welshman Richard Chee Quee. He had a decent season – 1,415 runs at 54 – yet failed to go on and open the Test batting for Australia, which he may have considered a flagrant case of false advertising.

2

Mark Waugh
at Egerton CC

It would be fair to say that, heading into the 1985 season, Egerton CC – founder members of the Bolton League yet without a league title in 55 years of trying – were quite happy with their winter's recruitment, which had begun with them contacting stalwart Lancashire off-spinner 'Flat' Jack Simmons in search of a replacement for the previous year's pro: the 21-year-old Salim Malik, already a veteran of 16 Tests during a truncated season at Longworth Road that yielded 702 runs at 54 with a best of 152*.

BCL rules permitted both an overseas pro and overseas amateur, and Simmons had come back with two options for the paid role: 20-year-old Victorian batter Jamie Siddons or a promising 19-year-old all-rounder from New South Wales who had just made 71 at No.8 in a one-wicket Sheffield Shield final victory against Queensland. In the end, the sage committee men of Egerton took the second option, Stephen Rodger Waugh, swayed by his bowling ability and the fact that the package included an overseas amateur of a similar age who Waugh knew very well from the NSW set-up and as a teammate at Bankstown in Sydney Grade cricket. His twin brother, Mark.

The pair arrived in early April – Steve eight months from a Test debut, Mark still almost six years from the first of his 128 Test caps – and were billeted in the Bradshaw home of Peter and Iris Greenhalgh, a couple of miles down the road from the village of Egerton. "I think they answered an ad in the local paper," recalls 'Junior' Waugh. "Their daughter, Karen, went out with a guy called Billy who played for Farnworth. Peter and Iris were beautiful people who treated myself and Stephen like we were their sons. We were spoilt rotten: no washing, no cooking, everything taken care of. They looked after us better than could be expected, to be honest."

Although the teenage twins were still greenhorns – Mark was yet to make his first-class debut – there was cautious optimism at

Egerton that they might be able to challenge the league's big guns, recalls opening batter Dave Sumner: "I remember Rod Tucker, now an ICC umpire, who was pro at Farnworth, saying: 'Well that's it, job done. Egerton will win the league with those two.' That was before we'd bowled a ball."

A week prior to the start of the league campaign, Egerton played a pre-season friendly at Atherton – a name the twins would grow accustomed to inflicting pain upon – of the neighbouring (or overlapping) Bolton & District Cricket Association, the league from which the dozen founding clubs of the BCL had split in 1930, since expanded to 14. It was a chance for the squad to get to know their new overseas players, to have a hit and a bowl, get the cobwebs out of their systems. Opening the batting in icy April conditions, Mark made a measured 120, while Steve, at first drop, added a more destructive unbeaten 90. The brothers then shared all 10 Atherton wickets and big dreams started to form. Alas, it was the only game they would play together for the club, as forces far beyond the West Pennine moors snuffed out Egerton's season of Total Waugh before it ever really got going.

The day after the brothers had stepped off a gruelling 30-hour economy-class flight to the UK, a lawyer representing Kerry Packer – owner of the domestic broadcast rights for Australia's Test and ODI cricket – knocked on the Greenhalghs' door with a three-year contract for Steve to sign, the fall-out from the Australian Cricket Board's discovery that seven of the 17-man party they had selected for the upcoming Ashes trip had already committed to the rebel tour of South Africa that November. Murray Bennett changed his mind, while Graeme Wood, Wayne Phillips and Dirk Wellham were successfully offered inducements by Packer to reverse their decision, although it required an emergency meeting of Allan Border's squad to welcome them back, having initially refused. There would be no U-turn from Terry Alderman, Steve Rixon and Rod McCurdy, however, and they were duly replaced in the Ashes squad by Carl Rackemann, Ray Phillips and John Maguire. It then emerged that Rackemann and Maguire had signed up for the South Africa trip as well, so Jeff Thomson and Dave Gilbert were called up instead.

Gilbert was that year's recipient of the ACB's Esso Scholarship, and had been slated for a year with Essex second XI. When he was drafted into the Ashes party, Steve Waugh was sent to Essex to replace him, spending the summer playing for the county's reserves and club cricket for Ilford, but not before putting ink to Packer's contract, confirming he would not be going to South Africa. "I'm thinking, what are you talking about? I don't want to go on the rebel tour, I just want to play for Australia," Waugh later told *Australian Financial Review*. "She just said, 'Here's the contract. Can you sign it?' I looked at it. I'd never seen a contract before. I said, 'What's the catch?' She said, 'No catch, just commit to playing for Australia and you get $15,000 a year for each of the next three years'. I said, 'Where's the pen?' I'd had $100 in the bank in Australia when I left. It was no decision."

All of which goes to show that, of all the consequences of Apartheid, many of them grotesque, one of the least well known is how a Lancashire village of around a thousand people was denied a summer of watching SR and ME Waugh get stuck into the local bowling. They would have to wait for later Ashes series for that.

The upshot of Steve's departure was that Mark was promoted to pro – "Stephen and I were going to split the pro money anyway," he says – while Egerton engaged the 21-year-old Western Australia opener Mark McPhee as overseas amateur. McPhee, who would perish in a car crash in 1999 at the age of 35, was coming off a debut Sheffield Shield campaign in which he averaged 44.36, including what would remain his career-best score of 135 against South Australia at the WACA.

A gregarious soul who contributed 666 runs at 33.3 for Egerton, 'Jock' McPhee lodged with first-team captain, Pete Moss, a dentist who had promised Mark Waugh a new set of crowns for his teeth if he passed 1,000 runs. Not that this offer necessarily protected the skipper from his young Aussie's exuberance, recalls Steve Dickinson, a youngster of 14 at the time whose father, Ken, batted No.11 and bowled left-arm spin for the first team. "Pete Moss came into bat in a practise session in this silver metal helmet. This was before helmets had really come out. Mark just said, 'I'm going to knock his head off here, lads. He bowled him a bouncer and dented the side of this lid. Pete proper lost it and stomped off."

The precise ins and outs of Junior Waugh's Bolton League season may have fallen victim to the pre-digital perils of a lost scorebook, but the broad contours and a smattering of detail have survived the fall into cultural oblivion. First off, having been promoted to pro, he began with a duck at Heaton – in whose second team that day lined up a 14-year-old Ronnie Irani, later to become good friends with Waugh at Essex – although he would take a century off them in the return game (as would McPhee), one of five he churned out that summer, alongside seven half-centuries. Keen mathematicians will note that these scores alone edge Waugh quite close to free dentistry.

The BCL handbook's 'Review of the Year' from 1985 reports – over and above the penmanship news that "off the field, Eagley's Geoff Cleworth took his twelfth scorebook award" – that the "year will be largely remembered for its distinct lack of temperature, no lack of rain, and postponements galore!" None of which would have made batting any easier at Egerton, sitting as it did on a considerable incline that funnelled water down to the square and created the ideal environment for that hardy species of club cricketer, *dobberus parsimonia*. "I remember the ground clearly," says Waugh wistfully, "it had such a big slope. It was like there were two tiers on it."

Waugh quickly worked out what to do with the 63mph accuracy merchants and their keeper-up, ring-field asphyxiation devices, says Ian 'Taddy' Taylor, Egerton's tearaway opening bowler: "He treated the dibbly-dobblers like spinners. He just used his feet to them and hit them over the top." Not that he underestimated them, or didn't do it all with an element of professional calculation.

"Early season, he would just hit it in the 'V' for the first 10 or 15 overs," says Steve Dickinson. "A few of us were thinking, 'Flippin' 'eck, get on with it, you boring sod,' you know? 'It's club cricket, this.' But then he would just go into overdrive and was absolute class. He could hit a ball wherever he wanted. It's a large ground, Egerton, and there's some poplar trees at the bottom of it. He hit a six one day and may God strike me dead, it was still going up when it went over the poplars."

Of course, barracking slow-scoring 'boring sods' or otherwise underperforming pros was not something the avid watchers of Lancashire's hard-bitten club cricket ever felt unduly sheepish about. Ten penn'orths were frequently and vociferously proffered, as Westhoughton's professional that year, Dilip Vengsarkar – already a veteran of 76 Tests and a future world No.1-ranked batsman – soon discovered after three ducks in succession. Being the birthplace of former Manchester City and England midfielder and later toilet roll tycoon, Franny Lee, in whose factory a young Peter Kay had worked, Westhoughton wasn't short of wiseacres. "As getten a pen, lad?" asked one old wag of the Indian star, who, flummoxed, patted his pockets for a writing implement. "Nah, lad: a *pen*. To keep thee ducks in."

One of those ducks came at home against Egerton, caught and bowled second ball by Waugh, who took 5/44 to follow 79 out of 147 all out as the visitors won by 33 runs. Vengsarkar's season would finish early when he jetted off for India's tour of Sri Lanka, by which time he had scored 802 runs at 47.17 to finish fourth in the averages, helping Westhoughton finish third.

Waugh, meanwhile, got through a lot of hard yakka with the ball – "I bowled pretty much half the overs every week," he recalls. "I was six foot when I got there and five feet four when I left" – and he finished with 59 wickets (the same number he took in Test cricket) at 17.88, with 17 men above him in the averages, 10 in the wicket charts. "It would have been double that amount if the keeper and slips could have caught the chances! I reckon I was too quick for them," he quips. "It's a pity he couldn't field slip to himself," says Ken Dickinson. "Everything that went in the air, he caught. It was incredible."

Of course, when it comes to discussion of cricket's greatest ever catchers, Waugh is usually in the thick of the conversation, and this higher-plane fielding was just one of the ways he embedded himself in the locals' affections, to the extent that he soon became barrack-proof. Not that it would have bothered him anyway, recalls Sumner: "You'd always get barracking from the sides if you weren't getting on with it. Mark would say, 'Just ignore them, mate'. I spent a lot of time batting with him and it's no coincidence that was my best ever season in terms of runs [535]. He was so relaxed and it just rubbed off. It made you play better. Freer. There was no, 'Okay, that was a shit shot, Dave'. It was, 'Don't worry about it'. Encouragement."

Indeed, Waugh was a generally laid-back presence around the club, attending practice twice a week, enjoying a romantic dalliance with one of Sumner's wife's nursing friends, and sticking around on match days to partake of the ritual libations, even being thrown a 20th birthday party on the first weekend in June. "Personally, I wasn't a big drinker," he says. "But you've got to fit in with the team, don't you? There was a pretty big drinking culture. I would have drunk a little bit but it wasn't my cup of tea. But you fit in with what's going on and I certainly enjoyed it."

"He'd have a drink," adds Sumner, "although two or three pints as opposed to the six or seven others would have. He kept an appropriate distance, for want of a better phrase, from getting too involved in all that. I think he recognised he was being paid to do a sporting job and he had to be physically ready. He got the balance right."

In August, Junior made the 12-mile trip down to Old Trafford to watch the drawn Ashes Test, but otherwise didn't venture too far from Bolton. "I was young and naïve and I hadn't been away from home that much, so it was all a bit of an eye-opener. I was with Stephen to begin with, but you're pretty nervous when you first get there. Obviously, you don't know anyone. They were a really friendly club, though, and made me feel welcome very quickly. Away from the cricket, I just hung around the house during the day, played a bit of golf, and went to the odd pub with other Australian cricketers who were playing around the leagues."

His compatriots in the Bolton League that year included Greg Shipperd at Heaton, another who went on the rebel tour that winter and who finished second in the BCL batting averages, with 898 runs at a tick under 50. And there was Rod Tucker – a fellow Sydneysider, and a year older than Waugh – who contributed 913 runs at 35.11 and 73 wickets at 13.01 for reigning champions Farnworth as their duel with cross-town rivals Farnworth Social Circle went to the very last ball of the season.

Unable to take the wicket they needed, it was instead the Social Circle team spearheaded by Bajan quick Roddy Estwick's 116 wickets at 12.17 that landed their first BCL title, Farnworth settling for the Hamer Cup. Estwick had been sharing the new ball with Joel Garner and Wayne Daniel in the previous winter's Shell Shield, and wasn't necessarily someone the Egerton amateurs looked forward to facing, Waugh recalls, inadvertently alighting upon a key reason his teammates were weekend cricketers whereas he went on to be inducted into the Australian Cricket Hall of Fame: "I remember the other guys would panic about who they were going to play against the week after if it was a fast bowler, like Rod Estwick. I didn't know much about him, but it was nothing to me. I loved it."

Besides Vengsarkar, the other two pros in the league with Test caps were also Indians. Kearsley's paid man was Mohinder Amarnath, Player of the Match in the World Cup final two years earlier, in which he sent down a spell of 7-0-12-3 at considerably less pace than Estwick. Sketchy details of their game with Egerton have survived thanks to Mike Latham, then a 24-year-old accountant from nearby Leigh who later became cricket chairman of Cumberland CCC, chairman of Leigh Centurions RLFC and a presenter with BBC Radio Lancashire. Back then, he was a cricket-loving ground-hopper with a camera, and he captured Waugh launching the Indian's slow-mediums boundarywards en route to 67, Egerton's non-barracking supporters sheltering from Lancashire's July chill in their *Sweeney*-era cars.

The following Saturday, Tonge were the visitors to Longworth Road, their attack spearheaded by a 19-year-old Chetan Sharma who had already won four of his 23 Test caps. The previous year, Sharma had been overseas amateur at Morecambe, where Ravi Shastri was pro, and he too would leave early for that Sri Lanka tour, but not before his batting – later good enough for an ODI hundred against England – had contributed 695 runs at 46.33, finishing fifth in the averages. There were also 89 wickets at 11.75 in the main job – the third biggest bag at the fourth best average – to help his club to a fourth-place finish and the final qualification spot for the prestigious Lancashire Cup.

Having made a season's best 140* at Tonge earlier in the season, Waugh would have fancied a few more. "That 140 was his finest and undoubtedly best paced innings," recalls club secretary Mike Hall. "He drove Sharma and the opposition to distraction with ultra-sound defence, perfectly glides for ones and twos, and the occasional crisp strike to the boundary. It was a superb demonstration, from a 19-year-old, of balancing risk and relentlessly wearing an experienced attack down. In fact, his batting ability shone through in every innings. He was always superbly organised at the crease, an impeccable judge of length, always in perfect position for brutal yet well-placed cut shots and advancing down the wicket to the spinners."

A wise old man of 20 by the time of the Tonge return, Waugh fell for just 5 as Sharma's 7/43 hustled Egerton out for 147, McPhee making 66 before nicking behind to the 17-year-old Warren Hegg (not the only budding county gloveman to feature in the league that summer, as future Derbyshire stalwart Karl Krikken's 15 catches and 18 stumpings for Astley Bridge saw the 16-year-old become the first junior ever to win a senior BCL award). Tonge slipped to 55/4 in response, but Sharma's unbeaten 56 shepherded them home.

For Waugh it was a minor blip in a hugely impressive canter past the thousand-run, dentistry-securing milestone, so much so that he attracted plenty of suitors among Egerton's BCL rivals. "Other clubs were trying very hard to secure his services," recalls Sumner. "Neville Neville, Gary and Phil's dad, was really hunting him down for Greenmount."

In the end, Waugh amassed 1,359 runs – almost 300 more than the next best – at an average-topping 54.36, a phenomenal effort in a team that finished in 10th position, fifth from bottom. It was the third highest aggregate in BCL history, bettering the 1,334 runs that future Test colleague Geoff Marsh had collected for Little Lever the previous year, although Marsh was himself some way behind the league-record 1,535 runs churned out that same season for champions Farnworth by Rod Bower, Waugh's teammate at Bankstown. Bower's record would in turn be eclipsed in 1989 by Astley Bridge's Australian professional, also well known to Mark Waugh – namely, Dean Waugh, who certainly let his older brother know all about it, says Junior: "Yeah, he did mention he made more runs than me a few times. Dean could also drink a fair bit more than me, too."

Waugh's efforts may not have won him the BCL Professional of the Year prize – that went to Parvez Mir, the Pakistani all-rounder who played in the 1975 World Cup and who amassed 1,068 runs for Walkden, including a league record 219*, to go with 74 wickets – but it did lead to a new and improved contract at Egerton for 1986. In the end, however, he was awarded the ACB's Esso Scholarship, and spent the year with the MCC Young Cricketers, "pushing the covers on and off at Lord's", a ground he would adorn with an Ashes century 15 years later.

The future may have taken Waugh to the pinnacle of the game and 372 appearances for his country, but one small corner of Lancashire remained in his thoughts. "The Greenhalghs looked after me so well," he says, "and I kept in touch with Pete and Iris for quite a few years when I was playing for Australia." Nor did his former teammates slip entirely from his mind. "I bumped into him at a Lashings game at Farnworth," recalls Ian Taylor. "I'd gone over to the dressing room. He said, 'Alright Taddy, how are you, mate?' It was as though he'd never been away. That summed him up. He wanted to let people know he knew who I was."

Junior also popped in at Heaton with Ronnie Irani when Essex were playing at Old Trafford, while Steve Dickinson remembers Waugh returning to Longworth Road bearing swag: "Even when he played at Essex he would come up to the club occasionally in his sponsored Vauxhall Carlton full of Slazenger cricket gear and give it away. He used to let everyone know when he was coming up and people would go and get bats, gloves and all sorts. I used to feel a bit let down because I was a left-handed batter!"

Over the years that followed Waugh's run-laden season at Egerton, his diehard England-supporting former colleagues would have experienced acute cognitive dissonance, hoping against hope for an England Ashes win at the same time as wanting their old Australian mate to make some runs – Mark, that is; Steve could fail – and perhaps wondering whether that distant summer had played a small part in it all. "Looking back at the experience of being the overseas professional," says Waugh, "there was always that pressure for you to perform every week. I did pretty well – probably better than they expected, to be honest – and I have very fond memories of it. In a lot of ways, it was a really good grounding for future years."

It may be a stretch to claim that the major components of Mark Waugh's distinctively elegant game were shaped in Bolton League cricket, but it's undeniably true that, thanks to his prodigious batting feats, a couple of his teeth were.

3

VVS Laxman

at Pudsey St Lawrence CC and Hanging Heaton CC

June 22, 1996, a balmy late Saturday afternoon at Lord's, and Sourav Ganguly carves Dominic Cork through cover and off down the slope to bring up three figures in his debut Test innings. The second member of India's great batting quintet of the 2000s was in place, with the third – now saluting his fellow debutant's landmark – ready to join him the following day. Meanwhile, 180 miles north in Idle, a village long swallowed up by Bradford's northern suburbs, a fourth member of that quintet was playing for Pudsey Congs in the Bradford League, edging the left-arm swing of Ian Dewhirst to slip for a duck. A former colleague of Darren Gough and Michael Vaughan in Yorkshire Young Cricketers, Dewhirst cannot recall the dismissal, "although if my teammates say he was caught at slip then I'm going to tell you I set him up with three inswingers then shaped one away", he yorkshires.

Vangipurapu Venkata Sai Laxman was in his second season of Bradford League cricket and in the middle of a lean trot that yielded just 106 runs in seven knocks, one of which was 61. The following week, he was caught and bowled by Yorkshire Bank's Carl Smith for a single. The previous year, as a fresh-faced 20-year-old, he had been professional at Hanging Heaton, scoring 619 runs at a disappointing 29.48, although the team had landed the league title. While Rahul Dravid and Ganguly were lording it at Lord's, Laxman was nursing an average in English club cricket of barely 30.

The story of Laxman's Bradford League adventure starts with an innings of 28 for India under-19s at Headingley, against an England under-19s team skippered by Vaughan, with Marcus Trescothick his vice-captain. Looking on that day was Solly Adam, who arrived in West Yorkshire from Karachi as a boy in the early 1960s and by then had built a small business empire comprising a sports shop in the town of Dewsbury, six petrol stations, and a mini-market, Pick 'n' Pay. Preferring to think of himself as a facilitator rather than an agent,

162

Adam had arranged for several Indian and Pakistani cricketers to experience English league cricket, including Abdul Qadir and Imran Khan. He was also instrumental in Sachin Tendulkar becoming Yorkshire's first ever overseas player in 1992 – the year the latter's schoolmate, Vinod Kambli, had played under Adam's captaincy at Spen Victoria – with the 'Little Master' lodging with Adam before moving into a bungalow up the road.

Having been impressed by Laxman's cameo, Adam spoke first with Hanging Heaton's cricket chairman, Brian Wilkinson, and then with the India under-19s manager, Sandeep Patil. Laxman visited the club, signing up during the Youth Test at Edgbaston a week later. He was following in the footsteps of Indian batting legend, Dilip Vengsarkar, who, as Hanging Heaton's 1987 overseas pro, found the going equally tough in averaging 36.77.

"Playing junior grade cricket in India," Laxman reflects, "my coaches always said I should have one or two seasons in England, just to get exposure to different conditions. They always recommended the Bradford League. They felt it was the toughest in England, because most players in most squads got paid whereas in other leagues only the professional was paid and most of the others were amateurs."

Laxman moved into a three-bedroom town house on the Leeds Road, five minutes from the club. "In India, everything is taken care of by our parents," he says, "whether it's cooking, cleaning the house, washing the clothes. I had to take care of everything: cooking my food, taking my clothes to the laundry, mopping the floor. It made me more independent and self-reliant, which was one of the reasons my coaches and family advised me to go."

Not that Laxman was throwing dinner parties. "Even though my mother gave me a recipe book," he adds, "all I used to live on was baked beans on toast and cereals. In the second year, I learned how to make tarka dhal, aloo jeera and mixed vegetables with paneer, but in the first year, I used to go to Solly Adam's house in Dewsbury for lunch. In the evenings, my teammate Ismail Dawood – who was contracted to Yorkshire, and actually made a hundred for England under-19s in that Headingley match – his mother used to cook food for me for the entire week and his father would drop it off at my house. So Solly Adam and Ismael Dawood's mother basically fed me for five months!" Elite self-reliance.

If the off-field adaptation was difficult, it was equally tough on the field, Laxman recalls: "When you're in India, you have an excellent support system. Your parents are always encouraging you; your coaches are always motivating you. When you're struggling, there are various people who will help you try and find the reasons why you're not performing. But there in England I had to look after everything myself. I started to take responsibility for every decision I made and each action I took. Ultimately, I came to know myself much better as a person and understand my game much better. That first year was a huge change and it helped me a lot in my career."

Away from the domestic chores, his routine involved fitness work with teammate John Carruthers at Dewsbury Sports Centre, or mornings running laps of the Hanging Heaton ground, with training on Tuesdays and Thursdays, and coaching the juniors a couple of evenings a week, which invariably finished with them bowling at him deep into the gloaming. Dan Busfield, now head of the Leeds Rhinos RLFC Foundation, recalls "bowling all day at him in the nets in the school holidays, for literally hours, and VVS always saying 'two more minutes'," while James McNair adds: "Long after the nets were done he'd stand over where the covers were kept and get us to bowl to him again!" Even so, playing weekends only left plenty of hours to fill, so he took a part-time job.

When Laxman strode from the field unbeaten on 275 at the end of the fourth day of the middle Test of the 2001 Border-Gavaskar Trophy series, few in the Eden Gardens crowd would have known that less than six years earlier he was working for £3 an hour at a West Yorkshire petrol station owned by Manish Patel, who became a lifelong friend. But then there are many roads to cricketing immortality – in this case, the greatest Test innings played by an Indian, in one of the greatest games ever – and punching 20 gallons of unleaded, a Twix and a can of Fanta into the till is just one of them. "It really taught me the value of money and hard work," he says, "and Manish is still like a brother to me."

Laxman's unglamorous job was a breeze compared to the situation faced by Mohammad Kaif four years later, when he arrived in Bradford to discover the club he was supposed to play for had signed another overseas player. Visa in hand and desperate to experience English conditions, he offered his services to Lightcliffe, free of charge – the league's minimum wage was £1,500 – working in Pick 'n' Pay to make ends meet. However, the nine o'clock finishes meant he was unable to practise, so Adam found him a job in a takeaway pizza parlour, while six Lightcliffe members chipped in £5 per week apiece to supplement his income. Kaif scored 1,139 runs at 81.35 and the £30 payment was upped just enough for him to be able to quit his job.

Although Hanging Heaton won the league with Laxman, the pro finished the season as only their third highest run-scorer. "I enjoyed it and was well looked after," he says, "especially by Simon Purdy, the captain, 'Ishy' Dawood and John Carruthers, who had told me all about bowling to Sachin and Vinod Kambli in the Spen Victoria nets in 1992. But it was a tough learning experience for me as a youngster. First, the wicket there was very slow and didn't suit my style of batting. Second, I learnt that as a professional you're supposed to perform each and every match. If I didn't score runs on a Saturday, the way the members used to treat me for the next week would be totally different than if I had performed. I never realised what it meant to be a professional. Whether you like it or not, everyone expects your performance. That's the reason you're there."

Following this five-month field trip in West Yorkshire, Laxman returned to his regular coursework at the University of Ranji Trophy, signing off the campaign for Hyderabad with a magna-cum-laude run of scores: 79, 130, 196, 51 and 203*. Doubtless the news would have been well received at Pudsey Congs, with whom he had agreed to play the 1996 season.

Laxman's recollection is that he made a few runs against them for Hanging Heaton and skipper Phil Carrick approached him in the bar. Congs' then chairman, now president, Derrick Reason adds an important detail. "During the match at Hanging Heaton, Phil was bowling his left-arm spin to VVS, who nicked one to the wicketkeeper. The umpire never heard it and VVS didn't walk, so after the game Phil made a point of talking to VVS. That's where their relationship started."

The 43-year-old Carrick had enjoyed a 24-year career at Yorkshire, taking 1,081 first-class wickets and scoring over 10,000 runs. He skippered the county for the final three years of the 1980s, succeeding David Bairstow, and was an affable man who knew the game inside out. His influence on the 21-year-old Hyderabadi would be profound, a paternal presence away from the cricket and a professorial one on match days.

"Those five months at Pudsey Congs were the best period of learning in my career before I played for India," Laxman says. "Phil and his wife Ellie made me feel like part of their family. After living in a three-bedroom house the year before, which was a lot to look after, I asked if I could stay in a one-bedroom apartment. So for one week I stayed with Phil on his farm, and because I was a vegetarian, for the entire week the whole family ate only vegetarian meals. That gave me a feeling of trust and the relationship started from that moment and really grew through the season."

Carrick's deep knowledge of the game was one of the major draws of Congs, Laxman asserts. "Phil persuaded me I had the potential to play international cricket for a long time. He had played a lot of cricket with greats like Geoffrey Boycott, so I felt he would be able to help me a lot. Every chat with Phil was enriching. I became more knowledgeable about the game – how to address various situations, how to tackle opposition bowlers – and that experience really helped me to perform well the next season in India. But every chat was always about becoming an international cricketer, not just a first-class player."

There were other quality cricketers in that Congs team, too. Laxman's opening partner was Colin Chapman, a wicketkeeper who collected a smattering of Yorkshire appearances over an eight-year stretch with the county and scored 841 Bradford League runs in 1996. Future three-time ICC Umpire of the Year, Richard Kettleborough, batted at first drop, averaging 59.22. And then there was a 19-year-old blond-haired pace-bowling tyro, Matthew Hoggard.

"Hoggy was a very good friend of mine," Laxman says. "Phil always used to make sure that whenever Hoggy came back to Pudsey from his Yorkshire second XI match, he had to call me and we would go to the club and have a net session, with fielding and fitness too. It's so strange that it was only me and Hoggy, on the astroturf wickets at the bottom of the ground. Then his dog used to go and fetch the ball. It was me, Hoggy and his dog!"

In his autobiography, *Welcome to my World*, Hoggard writes: "After one game when [Laxman] had scored a few runs and I'd taken a couple of wickets, we were chatting to Ferg [Carrick, after 'Carrickfergus' of the famous folk song] in the clubhouse. 'One day,' Ferg said, 'you two will play against each other in Test match cricket.' We just laughed at him and told him not to be so daft." As it turned out, they faced each other eight times, and it took Hoggard until the final one of those Tests to dismiss 'Lax': lbw first ball en route to 6/57 and a Player of the Match award in Nagpur. Laxman was dropped for the next game.

Ten years earlier, he had started his season at Congs well, with 97 at Saltaire and 105* at Yeadon in the first two away games, sandwiching a score of 4 against Windhill. Their pro, John 'The Dentist' Maynard, had played for Leeward Islands and would later represent Nevis in the ill-starred Stanford Series, a man who acquired his nickname, fairly unsurprisingly, on account of a penchant for rearranging batters' pearly whites. Even so, Laxman would look forward to his dental appointment in the second half of the season, pulling and hooking his way to a hundred – the middle one of a trio of consecutive tons, with Saltaire and Yeadon again suffering – but not before enduring that mid-season slump, fixed with no little help from Carrick.

"Phil saw I was struggling for rhythm so he got me some nets and matches with the Yorkshire Academy," Laxman recalls. "He also made a subtle change in my grip. And he got me some games as part of Peter Hartley's benefit season, too, playing alongside the likes of Martyn Moxon and David Byas. So I almost felt part of the Yorkshire dressing room. I made a couple of fifties and didn't look back."

Indeed he didn't. The second half of the season brought 849 runs at 94.33, with scores of 79, 67 (against Bowling Old Lane, whose pro, Mohammad Yousuf, would replace Laxman at Congs in 1997, averaging 58 in 13 games), 31, 102*, 114, 104*, 62, 79, 27, 66*, 30, 95* and 60 in the final game, away at Yorkshire Bank. Congs had started the final match in second place, and with leaders Hanging Heaton failing to win, they had a golden opportunity to give VVS a second straight league title. They were unable to take ten wickets for the outright win, however, and third-placed East Bierley came up on the rails to snatch the spoils.

Nevertheless, Laxman finished with 1253 runs at 65.95, winning the Bradford League Player of the Season award. He also sent down 244 overs of workmanlike off-spin – he had bowled just 17 wicketless overs of medium pace for Hanging Heaton – picking up 30 wickets at 23.20 to support Carrick's 82 victims. Less than 10 weeks later he was making his Test debut, scoring a half-century against the Proteas in Ahmedabad, before heading off on the return tour to South Africa.

Embarking upon an international cricket voyage did not mean severing those bonds with his past, though. On New Year's Day, as he prepared for his first overseas Test in Cape Town, he faxed seasonal salutations to Derrick Reason, whom he would later invite to his wedding, in February 2004. He maintained correspondence with Carrick, too, up until his premature death from leukaemia at the age of 47 in January 2000, nine days after Laxman's maiden Test hundred in Sydney and, heartbreakingly, a couple of years before the latter's first Test duel with Hoggard in Mohali.

"Phil would write me messages, telling me I was doing well," recalls Laxman, an evident fondness laced with equally palpable sadness, even 20 years on. "Or he would pick up on weaknesses, like in West Indies in 1997. Then suddenly the greetings cards and letters stopped coming and I wondered what was happening. It was only when I was in Australia in the 1999/2000 series, and I met an old clubmate there, Mark Ross, and asked how everyone was doing and why Phil had stopped writing, that I found out he had cancer and passed away. Phil didn't say anything to me about it. The last I'd heard, he had started umpiring."

It was a tragedy for all three that Carrick was unable to see his two protégés carve their distinctive lines across the international stage: Laxman flipping fourth-stump balls through mid-wicket and, if the mood took him, steering leg-stump balls through extra cover; Hoggard sending down those leg-stump deliveries, until three-quarters of the way down the pitch they were suddenly something else entirely. But he would surely have beamed with quiet pride at his Pudsey starlets ending up with 201 Test caps: exactly a third for Hoggard, two thirds for Laxman.

When Laxman was next in England, on India's 2002 tour, Reason and club president Michael Knight drove up to the Indians' Hollins Hall Hotel and took him back to Congs to unveil a commemorative plaque on the clubhouse wall dedicated to Carrick, his "great mentor and friend". That same week, VVS took Tendulkar, Ganguly and several other players tired of hotel food over to the Patels' house in Dewsbury for authentic Indian cuisine. And 10 years later, a few months after his friend's retirement, Manish Patel sought his consent to found the VVS Laxman Cricket Club, entering it into the serious-but-not-*that*-serious Bradford Mutual Sunday League.

The curtain came down on Laxman's illustrious international career in 2012, six months after his old Congs teammate Kettleborough had umpired him in Dominica – his third Test, the ground's first, and Laxman's 123rd. He has retained links with West Yorkshire into retirement, however, visiting Solly Adam's wife after her leg amputation and dropping in at both his clubs while commentating on the 2019 World Cup, a pilgrimage to the places where some of the pieces of his batting fell into place.

Historians, physicists, economists, evolutionary scientists, cricket coaches – all of them grapple with causality. In some cases, this means going all the way back to the great 'uncaused cause' (about which there are distinct schools of thought); in others, it means isolating what is significant and discarding the rest. Who can deny that when Laxman scratched out a fresh guard on the fourth morning of that Kolkata epic and glanced up to see his team four down and still in arrears, a not insignificant part of what enabled him to believe the perilous mountain path to victory was navigable was embedded in those two summers of self-reliance, of nous absorbed on the pitches and in the dressing rooms of West Yorkshire?

4

Kevin Pietersen

at Cannock CC

There is a certain category of sporting superstar – Mike Tyson, Ronnie O'Sullivan, John McEnroe, José Mourinho, Cristiano Ronaldo, Lance Armstrong – whose careers seem best apprehended through the lens of a rudimentary psychoanalysis, a search for what made them tick (in the sense of both machine and bomb). Kevin Pietersen is one such, the questions usually centring on the extent of the Venn diagram overlap between 'compulsively disruptive individualist' and 'brash batting maverick', on how much the latter depended on the former (in his case, maybe quite a lot, but Tendulkar, Gilchrist, de Villiers, Root and many other lavishly gifted batters suggest it is far from a necessity). It's a thin line, indeed, between (KP)genius and *doos*.

At the centre of the Pietersen psychodrama, played out in various contexts across his professional career, is "a very strong sense of entitlement (unreasonable expectations of especially favourable treatment or automatic compliance with his or her expectations)", which happens to be the fifth of the nine key facets of Narcissistic Personality Disorder outlined in the American Psychiatric Association's *Diagnostic and Statistical Manual of Mental Disorders* [DSM]. Which is not to say KP has NPD – such a verdict is the province of trained clinicians, usually requiring direct access to the subject – only that he seemed to find it very difficult when people said no to him (being described as *somebody who won't take no for an answer* is not always a virtue), and perhaps as a consequence felt most comfortable surrounded by those who told him what he wanted to hear, who pandered to that monumentally needy ego.

A vivid recent model of all this has of course been provided by the ill-starred tenures of Donald Trump and Boris Johnson (a politician Pietersen admires) in their respective countries' highest office – in particular, the difficulty of recognising any social or even legal norms limiting their behaviour, but also the lust for admiration, the lack of empathy and so forth, all while seemingly becoming enraged at the merest slight. The Pietersen who emerges from 2014's *KP: The Autobiography* – an excruciating screed, a 300-page blindspot, an agenda bender in which there is no axe he fails to grind – is a similarly unsteady mix of the insensitive and hypersensitive, someone thick- and thin-skinned in all the wrong places, a man who complained of being bullied while welcoming debutant James Taylor with a whispering campaign to coaches and colleagues about his suitability for selection.

Which, again, is not to say there were no wrongs ever done to him – we are dealing with the opacity of dressing-room relationships, after all, which are woven from perceptions and thus as mysterious as Cheese dreams, as delicate as a Flower's petal – although it is not difficult to imagine how KP's bespoke blend of (apparent) self-assurance and his need for pecking-order affirmation, for confirmation of his specialness, was for a long while easily indulged with tactical praise (we need his runs, so I will exhale this smoke where the sun don't shine), but less easily stomached when it became something closer to pedestal-seeking. How could worker-drones such as Anderson, Swann, Cook and Broad possibly understand what it was like being KP in that dressing room?

Anyway, returning briefly to the DSM, the third facet of NPD indicates a person who "believes that he or she is 'special' and unique and can only be understood by, or should associate with, other special or high-status people (or institutions)". Again, it is difficult to comment on this with much authority, although perhaps it might be worth asking some of the characters from *KP: The Autobiography* from whom he sought occasional counsel: James Corden, Frank Lampard (with whom he "had become friendly"), "my friend" Piers Morgan, or perhaps the various *buddies* from his youth, none of whom were quite close enough, it seemed, to edge out Darren Gough from the best man's job at his wedding.

Yes, to access the cricket you need to go in via the psychodynamics, the abacus of grievances, the interplay between that hard carapace of a seemingly cast-iron self-belief ("I've always been a confident bloke," he writes in his first autobiography, 2007's *Crossing the Boundary*, in the unconvincing, over-compensatory manner of someone trumpeting their own sense of humour or Alpha-male status) and the fragility of that personal ecosystem. Getting to the bottom of this high-achieving, high-maintenance enigma is indeed the work of a professional. Nevertheless, many of the elements that coloured the later patterns of dressing-room commotion and combustion – the ancients say that where there is smoke, there is often fire – which later played out at Notts and Hampshire and England were present and correct during the summer he spent at Cannock of the Birmingham League. Proto-Kev.

Albeit with a twist, because the 19-year-old South African who arrived in south Staffordshire in April 2000 primarily saw himself as an off-spinner. He had taken 4/141 for KwaZulu-Natal against Nasser Hussain's England XI that winter, also scoring 61* from 57 balls, then returned 136.2-36-375-10 across four Supersport Series matches (in which he batted at No.10) prior to being omitted, as he saw it, "on political grounds". Thus, his principal and regularly aired beef at Cannock concerned the amount of overs he was being given: 21.3 in the league by the middle of June.

The club already had two battle-hardened and contrasting left-arm spinners in Guy Bulpitt, a former England swimmer who speared the ball in from height, and the more guileful skipper Laurie Potter, veteran of 13 seasons' first-class cricket with Kent and Leicestershire before taking up a teaching post in 1994 and overseeing Cannock's meteoric rise through the cricketing pyramid, one that briefly intersected with Pietersen's own astonishing rise into one of the greatest players of his generation. Not that he appreciated how things were playing out at the time.

"He came as an off-spinner to a club with two established spinners in the team, two league guns," says Bulpitt, by then Staffordshire's first-choice spinner and later good enough to return 30-0-106-5 in three List-A outings against heavy-hitting county sides in Warwickshire, Surrey and Lancashire. "It wasn't a great signing. It created friction, as he always wanted to bowl. Kevin was there for himself, to develop himself as a cricketer. He wanted opportunity in front of other people and to the detriment of other people. If he'd been the second spinner somewhere he'd have bowled more overs. He was at the wrong club. Laurie would often bowl Kev before himself, which wasn't ideal for the team."

The person responsible for signing Pietersen was chairman Jamie Fleet, who was at the forefront of the club's 1990s odyssey from the backwaters of the Staffordshire Club Championship to the sharp end of the Birmingham League. He had been a first-team player when the old ground was sold for £1m and the spanking new £1.7m facility at 'Four Crosses' opened in 1991, a couple of miles south-west of the town and a couple of KP slog-sweeps from Watling Street, the famous Roman road that runs from Dover to Holyhead (since re-branded as the A5). There were two cricket pitches, two astroturf hockey pitches for the Men's National League champions of 1996, '98 and '99, tennis courts, a bowling green, and a two-storey clubhouse with squash courts, function room, two bars and an apartment, extended by the time Pietersen arrived to include a restaurant and fitness suite, all manned by a full-time receptionist and bar manager, his teammate Greg Wright. "When I first arrived in the Staffordshire town," wrote Pietersen in 2007, "I was immediately impressed with the facilities at the club but…" (We will get to the 'but'.)

By the time Potter signed in 1994, Cannock had stepped into the more competitive Willis Corroon League, winning it in 1997 – perfect timing, given the following year's formation of the country's first ECB Premier League, to which they were duly promoted. They topped Division One of the BDPCL in 1998, then finished runners-up to Walsall in 1999, at which point they searched for a pro that might help an already strong team go one better. "The idea with the overseas players," says Potter, "was to get young guys who were hungry, who had a bit of bite about them and wanted to do well."

"A few years earlier we'd had Doug Watson, the Natal opener, for two seasons, a top professional who would do anything for anybody," adds Fleet. "He slept in a caravan at the club for a year. I got in touch with Doug and asked if there was anyone he could recommend. He said, 'There's a guy in the next hotel room'. He went and spoke to Kevin, who I spoke with that night, and everything was agreed."

Prior to finalising terms with Cannock, Pietersen had spoken to Hussain about his desire to play some cricket in England: "He thought I meant club cricket and gave me the number of his brother Mel, who played for Fives & Heronians in the Essex League. But I had bigger aspirations than that. I was thinking of county cricket, perhaps at that stage as a non-overseas player because of my British passport."

This ambition – the positive sense of not being able to take no for an answer – would of course propel Pietersen to the sport's loftiest heights. But for now, with the England captain unable to parachute someone with 253 first-class runs at 23 and 23 first-class wickets at 33 straight into the county game, Cannock it had to be, and those caveated first impressions: "I was immediately impressed with the facilities at the club but when they took me to my residence I found I was staying in a single room above a squash court. For me, a person who had always led an outdoor life, it was quite a shock. Totally not what I had expected. But I had to make do with that and I can honestly say I never had any real periods of self-doubt or ever questioned what I was doing there or whether I would be better off at home."

Potter's recollections are that his new South African recruit was initially in the old dressing rooms at the far end of the pitch, but had been swiftly upgraded to the main clubhouse after the skipper relayed his complaints to the chairman, and also that he would have been aware of this arrangement from the outset. For his part, Fleet, in whose home Pietersen stayed for a couple of weeks and whose wife routinely attended to his laundry, clarifies that the apartment was not directly above a squash court but at the other side of the building: "He might have heard people playing squash at 9pm but certainly not at 6am."

Doug Watson had stayed uncomplainingly in a caravan, but Pietersen "had to make do" with digs that, for Bulpitt, were way beyond what could reasonably be expected for a relatively cheap and inexperienced overseas player. "The flat was nice. Two bedrooms, living room, bathroom, kitchen. It had a cleaner going in. You could walk into the clubhouse and get food. There probably isn't a better gig in club cricket than that. What he said about that is madness."

For the first month and a half, the high-maintenance pro spent a fair bit of time in his low-maintenance flat as four of the opening seven league fixtures were abandoned, three without a ball being bowled, with only half a game possible against Walsall, Pietersen falling lbw for 12 to Australian Dominic Thornely, a future Hampshire teammate.

In among these showers, Pietersen was not only not bowling as much as he would have liked, there were also only glimpses of his emergent batting pyrotechnics, mainly due to the productivity of two guns above him in the order. Potter scored 118 and Warwickshire's Anurag Singh 66 as 249/2 were posted in the winning draw with Coventry & North Warwickshire, to which Pietersen contributed a cameo unbeaten 25, although he did have the pleasure of dismissing an 18-year-old Ian Bell, bowled for 7, as he picked up 2/48. A week later, Potter made 73 and Singh 67 as Cannock posted 243/9 against Old Hill, Pietersen chipping in with a sprightly 29 before being bowled by Jonathan Wright's off-spin, with whom he had earlier had a ding-dong.

"He nicked one down to third man and it was going for a three," Wright recalls. "He shoulder-barged me as he ran the first and I got a bit over-the-top angry about that. He definitely instigated it. But I stayed at Cannock till about 2am with David Banks and KP. He didn't have a bar shift that night. He was a complete arsehole on the pitch, but good company off it."

With Potter having plenty of strong bowling options, Pietersen was only given five of the 53 overs as Old Hill hung on at 149/8. Cannock's new-ball attack comprised Paul Thomas, a lively 6'5" paceman who bounced back from a savaging at the hands of Brian Lara to take 5/70 against the West Indians on first-class debut for Worcestershire five years earlier, and the 22-year-old 6'8" left-arm swing bowler Geoff Crook, who debuted for Staffordshire later that year. Back-up medium-pace was usually provided by Paul Greenfield, a policeman who became one of Pietersen's best mates at the club.

Given that Potter, Crook and Greenfield would finish the season occupying the top three spots in the league averages, with Bulpitt sixth and Thomas there as a shock option, it wasn't entirely unreasonable that Pietersen should find his bowling allotment so skimpy. "Kev believed the world should be bent to the needs of Kev," says Potter. "He was supremely confident, outwardly at least, and maybe a bit delusional in some areas – his bowling, specifically – but he knew where he wanted to get to."

Cannock picked up a first win on May Bank Holiday, Pietersen top-scoring with 51 as they posted 200/9, his first half-century in the league, but again his lesser-spotted twirlers were given just 2.3 overs in Barnt Green's reply, taking 2/0 in a 126-run victory. The following week's abandonment against Wolverhampton meant that, by June 10 and the visit of bottom of the table Smethwick – decimated by in-fighting and a subsequent exodus after Wasim Akram's stint the previous year – he had sent down just those 21.3 league overs, a number he failed to increase as Smethwick were winkled out for 145 in the final over of their allotment.

These frustrations nevertheless had the inadvertent by-product of nudging him into the KP Zone. By the time he had reached a 56-ball half-century, Cannock required 19 to win off as many overs, at which point the visiting skipper, Steve McDonald, decided to give his own under-used off-breaks an airing. "They were cruising to victory," recalls Smethwick keeper Adam Binks. "Pietersen watched Steve bowl a warm-up delivery to mid-off then turned round to me and said, 'The game finishes this over'. He then hit four sixes off the next five balls and just walked straight off." Talk talked, walk walked.

As with so much of Pietersen's audacious later *oeuvre*, a good chunk of it fuelled by the sense of being spurned or slighted, this fusillade had not emerged out of thin air. "He trained hard," explains Stuart Burrows, an 18-year-old who had signed for Cannock that year, "and he pushed me, as a youngster, to train hard, too. He would often ask spinners to bowl at him on the square so he could practise trying to hit them into the hockey pitches."

What, then, could be more satisfying than transferring this rigorously practised range-hitting into a match situation? Would he glide off after this explosive vignette into the warm acclaim and plaudits of teammates increasingly aware that they had a major talent on their hands? No, of course he wouldn't.

"He won the game then walked off in the wrong direction, towards his flat at the other end of the clubhouse," recalls Bulpitt. "He was still stewing about not having bowled. He took his frustration out in his batting, so you could argue Potts' decision not to bowl him made him into the cricketer he became!"

The apocryphal story with Pietersen is that Potter told him categorically that he didn't rate his bowling, then said "but you're a helluva batsman and you're going up to No.4". The more prosaic truth is that the transformation – manifestly vindicated by history – simply unfolded in the service of Cannock's needs, considerations that never really entered Pietersen's head. "We were just a stepping-stone

176

for Kev," observes Potter. At this stage, he was still in his own mind a bowler who batted, and one who was supremely determined to make a career out of cricket, be that in South Africa (still not entirely off the table at this point) or England, and everything else was subservient to this goal.

Again: "I can honestly say I never had any real periods of self-doubt or ever questioned what I was doing there or whether I would be better off at home" – the final phrase of which is not necessarily how Laurie Potter remembers it. "I used to get phone calls on a Friday night, Kev saying 'If you're not going to bowl me more I'm going home.' I would tell him I was captain and I do what is right for the team. 'If it's right for you to bowl, you will bowl.' Looking back, I was surprised by how often I didn't bowl, and that was basically to give Kev a go, to try and keep him happy. He obviously had ability with the ball at that stage, but he wasn't doing as good a job as Bully and I were. He turned it big, but didn't have the consistency. I felt he could be more successful for us as a batter."

By sublime coincidence, 2000 was the year Harry Enfield's absurdly stroppy teenager, Kevin Patterson, received a movie-length platform for his huffing and sulking, *Kevin and Perry Go Large*. Meanwhile, having gone large against Smethwick, the still-teenage Kevin Pietersen's mood was improved somewhat by an invitation to bowl at Edgbaston in the lead-up to England's series-opening Test against West Indies, who had seven lefties in their top eight to be exploited (the visitors won by an innings).

Two days' tweaking in the tank converged neatly with Potter deciding to cave to his young batter's demands and give him a good bowl on a sun-baked pitch at Kidderminster. He responded with 11-1-63-0 as the home team racked up 254/8, of which 141 were scored by young Worcestershire keeper Jamie Pipe, Potter's 5/33 from 12 dragging back what could have been a monster total. He and Bulpitt picked up 7/94 off 31 overs, although Pietersen was still unamused to be withdrawn from the attack. It was almost as though he had *a very strong sense of entitlement* and *unreasonable expectations of especially favourable treatment or automatic compliance with his or her expectations.*

"KP was bowling to a 7/2 legside field and went for about 14 in one over," recalls Bulpitt, "Pipe just standing back and whacking it through the offside. Potts said, 'I think we need to change this. What do you think, Kev?' And Kev went, 'Yeah, I think you're right. I need another player over'. He meant from off to leg! He says, 'Yeah, I'll bowl a tighter line. I need an 8/1 field.' Potts just said, 'Well, I think you better come off then'."

Pietersen's outspokenness about his bowling frustrations – be that delusion or just Kev *telling it like it is* – were by now starting to grate with teammates, chief among them wicketkeeper Mark Humphries, Potter's meaty, no-nonsense lieutenant, chirping away in a thick West Bromwich accent. That week, 'Humpty' had played his 91st game for Staffordshire, at Cannock, and had been first-choice gloveman for the Minor Counties XI through the 1990s, taking part in giant-killings against the 1992 Pakistanis and 1995 West Indians. "Humpty was the most team-oriented player I ever played with," reflects Bulpitt, "so he'd have struggled the most with KP, who was all about himself. They were never going to get on."

Tits were being trodden on by the boy from Pietermaritzburg. "There was a bit of conflict," admits Humphries. "He'd got one thing in his mind, and that was himself. I was more about the team. That was the conflict. I think Laurie did well to accommodate him as much as he did."

If all this seems to prefigure the unravelling of KP's England career, with Humphries as a sort of Prior precursor and Bulpitt, no shrinking violet on the field, perhaps cast as the ebullient Swann, then Potter would be something of a Strauss figure, attempting to manage the incipient irritation toward this fellow the club had employed to help them – this player who, even with the team fighting at the top of the table and his performances vindicating the allocation of overs, was causing a stir.

"He was alright most of the time, Kev," says Potter. "But I did spend a lot of time managing other players' attitudes toward him. He wasn't universally popular. Me and Humpty often spoke long into the night: 'How are we going to sort the bloke out?' Kev had the potential to annoy, but we needed to see the bigger picture, so I would try and mediate, to make sure that didn't get in the way of the job we wanted to do, because I knew what was going to be best for the team. He didn't have the consistency of Bully and I as a bowler, but what he did have was the ability to strike the ball and devastate bowling attacks, certainly against that quality. He went on to prove he could do it against any quality."

Kidderminster's 254 was the only time Cannock conceded 200 all year. Nevertheless, with Potter's 104 leading the charge, they chased down the runs and went top of the table. Pietersen contributed a brisk 57, Humphries 37*, a partnership without too much love lost. "He kept telling me to do this and do that," recalls Humphries, "and I told him in no uncertain terms that I knew how to play the game, thanks. I suppose that was part of the ego thing." (When Pietersen deployed his usual charm and sensitivity in *Crossing the Boundary* to describe "those horrible Black Country accents I had such trouble understanding," it may have been Humphries he had in mind.)

A couple of days later, Pietersen turned 20 years old. Between matches, he was "making do" with his fully serviced flat, free food on tap, washing picked up. He would call Laurie in Leicester to discuss his bowling. He would head out some days with the team's opening batter, Jason Revill, a delivery driver, usually nodding off in the passenger seat. He did some coaching at the school where Jamie Fleet's wife taught, topping up his income, as he would with extra bar shifts, although this also caused him some angst: "People looked after me and I didn't have much to moan about," he writes in *Crossing the Boundary*, "but I did run into some trouble when I wasn't paid what I reckoned I was owed for the work I did behind the bar. I still haven't been paid that money now!"

Fleet says these issues were the bar manager's concern, describing them as "throwaway comments" with "very little substance to them". However, one Friday, with Fleet in Spain and the pro not having been paid, Potter did field a call from an upset Pietersen who was talking about not playing the following day's game. Potter arranged a cash sub and the storm was averted.

Aside from all this, he would practise as often and as hard as he could, heading up to Trent Bridge a couple of times to work with Clive Rice and occasionally popping down to see his Natal teammate Wade Wingfield, pro at newly promoted Harborne, the next opponents, whose skipper, Richard Cox, recalls how Pietersen "became a Harborne socialite, even coming for throwdowns with Wade at Harborne instead of being at Cannock". Indeed, KP spent

179

the Friday night before the match down in Birmingham, hitting some balls then hitting Harborne High Street.

"Kev talked cricket 24/7 and by now knew the lie of the land at Harborne," says Cox. "During a banter-type conversation he mentioned he was going to hit me over the trees and into the Knots Ground, our second pitch. I replied, 'Well you won't, Kev, because I don't bowl that end, mate'. 'Well someone's getting it. You're all bang-average, china.' Later he said, 'And something else you need to know: tomorrow I will get my first league hundred and smash you clowns out of the game. You won't get near us.' I replied, 'Well you won't Kev, because I'm going to win the toss and bat first'."

And lo, it came to pass. Cox won the toss and batted first, leading from the front with 102 of Harborne's 199/9 (initially 98, but he persuaded umpire Billy Smith at tea that one set of four leg-byes had come off the bat), before then being dismissed by Pietersen who, with Potter unable to bowl, returned a season's best 19-2-65-4. In reply, Cannock slipped to 53/3, at which point Pietersen and Humphries added an unbroken 147 in 22 overs, the latter unbeaten on 51, KP slamming an 88-ball 107* containing 12 fours and five sixes, one of which not only cleared the Knots Ground but landed in the Bishop of Birmingham's garden on its far side, one of the biggest hits ever seen at the ground. Talk talked, walk walked. Fireworks. Carnage. Bragging rights. Cannock top of the table. But was he happy?

"It was an unbelievable hundred," recalls Bulpitt. "It was a quick deck, and Wingfield was probably bowling mid-80s mph. Kev just whacked him. Even after doing that and winning the game, he wasn't interested in the batting. All he was saying was, 'My coach wants me to bowl more. I need to bowl more'."

These thoughts were aired not only inside the dressing room but also in front of the pavilion, where some of the Harborne players were milling about – comrades from the previous evening's revelry, perhaps sympathetic ears as the lager loosened his tongue – and Tony Leighton of the *Sunday Mercury* was waiting for a word. "There was a big row at Harborne," confirms Humphries. "If he sulked on the pitch [about not bowling], he sulked. But after that game he had a big moan that he should be bowling more. He was very vocal about it. It was a lot more than sulking. There was media there, and he had a bit of a barney with Potts outside the dressing room."

At some stage, it all starts to get a little much. You admire the willingness to go toe-to-toe, you are delighted that these extraordinary batting powers are being put to the service of your team, but you still grow tired of the soap opera, the tantrums, the inability to see beyond his own needs and wants, the transfiguration of anyone opposing them into an Enemy. As for Potter, he told Leighton: "Once he gets into a rhythm when he's batting, there's no stopping him … I believe he can go a long way, and I certainly feel it would be worth a county taking a look at him." What a bastard!

Little did Cannock know, as they moved into July and the guts of their title challenge, that they had already seen the high point of Pietersen's season. He left Harborne that night with an average of 89; over the rest of the campaign it would be just 21.66, although he did start with a blitzkrieg 45 in a rain-reduced game at West Bromwich Dartmouth, the club at which, five years earlier, his future nemesis Andy Flower had become only the ninth man in 107 BDCL seasons to register 1,000 runs. Pietersen smote his second ball for an enormous six over the conifers at the back of the car park and on to the adjoining golf course, and at one stage WBD skipper Paul Swainson simply told his fielders to "spread out". With Potter scoring 51 and Singh 79, both at a brisk clip, Cannock were able to put time back into the game, declaring at 205/5 from just 25 overs and leaving their opponents 40 to chase. That they crawled to 51/5, with opener Chris Abbey finishing unbeaten on 29 – Pietersen given eight overs (0/3) to Bulpitt's two (1/0) – perhaps indicates the general feeling toward the Cannock *arrivistes*.

Pietersen headed off to Devon that week to join a South African school's cricket tour, and the quirks of the scheduling meant that he came back to the return fixture against Harborne, who were bowled out for 134 after 59 overs of grind on a slow turner – KP 1/58 from 21 overs, Bulpitt 7/22 from 14, Potter not bowling. In reply, Cannock could only muster 84/9, Pietersen registering his first golden duck on English soil.

"Wade had spoken to him on the Friday," recalls Harborne seamer Andrew Bryan, "and KP had told him to put the fielders in different postcodes. It was overcast and doing a bit. I got Potter early, always a big wicket, and KP came in. Confidence and respect is a fine line, from both batter and bowler. It didn't matter: off stump knocked back, pitching middle and doing enough. There was a look of disbelief from KP. I saw him on his way with 'Don't use all the hot water', meaning his early shower. Ironically, this was the game that sent us down that season, as the umpires took the strangest decision to come off for bad light with 10 overs left. KP had already left the ground by then. I believe he was supposed to work the bar that evening but had just disappeared. Not his greatest day."

It seems plausible to suggest that the need to massage Pietersen's ego, to keep him sweet for his match-winning batting capabilities, was now harming Cannock's prospects. How many might Harborne have made had Potter sent down 21 overs and KP none? It was like going on holiday to Tuscany and eating in McDonald's to keep the kids happy. Not that Pietersen couldn't bowl; only that the tactical waters were being muddied where they might otherwise not have been in the company of a less volubly self-centred person – one for whom the club was there solely to serve him and his ambitions, even if meritocracy was compromised. It was a marriage made for Kevin.

Pietersen would again bowl more overs than Potter and Bulpitt in the next game, against Halesowen, whose pro was also a South African spinner. Eight years later and six miles east, in a game famous for Paul Collingwood's career-saving hundred, Graeme Smith's epic fourth-innings 154* and a tearful resignation from Michael Vaughan that led to KP's brief tenure as England captain, Paul Harris reeled in the big fish by playing on his ego and inducing a "dumbslog millionaire" hoik that was caught at long on with the game in the balance. "Go on KP," said Harris at Edgbaston in 2008. "You're everyone's hero, you're winning the Test; get there with a six, Big Boy!"

Cannock began their pursuit of 161 by losing Potter and Singh cheaply, yet Harris would not snare his man on this occasion as the delivery van double-act of Revell and Pietersen, with 47 and 49 respectively, seemed to have sealed things. However, a clatter of wickets left the last pair, Greenfield and Bulpitt, to inch them nervily over the line, the sort of win that has teams believing it might just be their year, the sort of win that unites a dressing room, that provides a bonding buzz for the hired-gun outsider. Usually.

Cannock backed this up with a nine-wicket romp over West Brom to move 25 points clear at the top of the table. Pietersen sent down

10-0-48-1 as the visitors were rolled for 144 (Potter and Bulpitt's combined figures were 9/65 off 36). He was not required to bat, as Potter, Revell and Singh each registered forties, and then shot straight off after the match as he was heading back to South Africa for a week to discuss his future with Natal, badgering a lift into Birmingham from WBD's Worcestershire-contracted left-arm spinner and future CEO Matt Rawnsley.

"I had a sponsored car, which he obviously noticed," recalls Rawnsley. "He asked me for a lift to New Street station, which is nowhere near on the way from Cannock to Worcester, but I said yes, because none of the Cannock lads were going to do it. The whole drive to Birmingham he told me how terrible first-class cricket was and how he was going to play for England one day. We pulled up outside the station and he got out without a word of thanks. I just laughed at the bizarre situation. Little did I know that in a few years' time I'd be watching his kit thrown off the balcony at Trent Bridge from another dressing room that hated him."

Returning from South Africa late on Friday night, Pietersen sent down a commendable 3/48 as Coventry & North Warwicks were held to 148/6 from 37 overs in yet another weather-truncated match. In reply, Cannock capitulated to 93 all out, their first defeat of the season, Pietersen caught by the sizeable mitts of legendary Coventry City goalkeeper Steve Ogrizovic at slip from the bowling of *Test Match Special*'s Charlie Dagnall, who finished with 8/51. The defeat had trimmed Cannock's lead to nine points over Walsall as they headed into August, with Old Hill, their next opponents, a further 16 back.

The Old Hill game was a spiky affair, two teams with their fair share of salty seadogs disinclined to take backwards steps. Geoff Crook, back after a six-week absence with a broken arm, took three prize early wickets to leave the home side in trouble at 11/4, before Pakistani leg-spinning all-rounder Riaz Sheikh's 55 instigated a recovery. Pietersen's three wicketless overs cost 16, but with Bulpitt and Potter combining for 6/85 from 32 overs, Cannock's chase would be a sub-par 158.

At 65/5, however, with the cream of the batting back in the hutch – Pete Burgoyne snaring Potter, Singh, Revell and Humphries while KP was trapped lbw by Sheikh's flipper for a duck, to the crowing delight of the fielding team – this target looked a long way off. At which point Pietersen's bar manager, Wright, and 18-year-old protégé Burrows – two of his *buddies*, thus meriting unconditional support – added 94 to steer Cannock to a huge win. "All through the innings," Burrows recalls, "KP was shouting encouragement, and ran me a bat out when mine broke, although I don't think he was happy I chose Anurag Singh's instead of his. As soon as we hit the winning runs, he rushed on as one of the first to congratulate us and grabbed me, saying 'This is why I have pushed you so hard, to do things like this'. Still one of my finest cricket memories."

It is tempting to wonder whether charging on to the pitch had as much to do with the opportunity to celebrate in the opposition's face as any spontaneous outpouring of comradely joy, while one might also raise an eyebrow at a young player's breakthrough Premier League innings immediately being arrogated to his own training-session influence. Cynical, perhaps, but the world of human motive is murky and ambivalent, perhaps especially to the bodies it sweeps along through life. Even so, the idea that Pietersen was suddenly all aboard the Cannock train was somewhat shot out of the water over the next two weekends, beginning with the top-of-the-table clash at home to Walsall, during which he told Potter he would not be able to bowl.

Earlier, Cannock had been dismissed for 194, Potter and Revell taking the score to 95 without loss before they were pegged back by six wickets for Chris Boroughs, including Pietersen for 18, who then sat with a towel on his neck and announced he was injured. With Thomas unavailable, and Boroughs and Thornely's half-centuries putting Walsall in the driving seat, this might have been inconvenient. However, four wickets apiece for the two left-arm spinners induced a collapse of 16/6 in nine overs as Cannock ran out winners and took their lead at the top to 25 points over Stratford. No dramas.

At least, not until midweek, when Pietersen trialled for Warwickshire second XI in a three-day game against Surrey at Leamington and bowled 21 overs in the match, picking up 2/70, as well as bludgeoning 92, the game's top score. Suddenly, the Cannock players smelt a rat. "He might have been struggling with injury," says Bulpitt, "but he'd protected himself on the Saturday so he could play in midweek for Warwickshire. He wanted a contract. That upset people more than the other things he did."

The final day of the game, a Friday, was washed out, denying Pietersen the chance to make a further impression on the Warwickshire hierarchy (Jamie Spires, a teammate in that game, says the main impression he left on coach Steve Perryman was that he was "a prat"). That night, however, Pietersen declared himself unfit for Cannock's trip to second place Stratford – a blow, although perhaps he might come down to Shakespeare country and support his teammates' quest for a maiden Birmingham League title?.

In a harbinger of the day he sat glued to Delhi's IPL final eliminator while involved in a Test match against West Indies, Pietersen spent the day watching Harborne play at Kidderminster, later throwing shapes at Wade Wingfield's leaving party. "What are you doing here?" asked Cox. "Injured, china." Harborne's scorer and webmaster at the time, Claire Easter, recalls how, as the season unfolded and Pietersen's grievances increased, she unwittingly "took on the big sister role" for their frequent visitor, "and didn't get the bullshit when there was no one else around to perform to", although "time has meant I've only ever referred to him as the most unpopular player in the most unpopular team on the circuit."

And that was that: no one at Cannock saw Pietersen again (other than on TV). The following week, after cold-calling the Warwickshire CEO Dennis Amiss for a meeting to push his case, he flew back to South Africa and then on to Perth with the Natal squad, having amassed 485 BDCL runs at 48.5 in 13 visits to the crease (Ian Bell scored 465 in the same number of innings), finishing fourth in the divisional averages.

While KP had been goofing around taking selfies with his buddies from Harborne, Cannock waited two-and-a-half hours to get underway, lost the toss, and were torpedoed for 40 by Stratford, losing by seven wickets. Wheelnuts were coming loose. Without Pietersen or Singh for the final four games, the clubbies would have to dig deep.

They began with a late-starting, early-finishing abandonment at home to Barnt Green. Meanwhile, Walsall dodged the rain to pick up a win that moved them level on points at the top. A week later, Potter's 52 and 4/44 were not enough to force the win over national club champions Wolverhampton and Stratford took advantage to move three points clear. The penultimate round took Cannock to already relegated Smethwick, who they bowled out for 79, knocking the runs off in 11 overs. Meanwhile, Stratford recovered from 37/5 to chase down Halesowen's 210, maintaining their three-point lead, while Walsall also beat WBD to sit just five behind the leaders, whom they would meet on the final afternoon while Cannock hosted Kidderminster. There was no good luck telegram from Perth.

On a stodgy track at HQ, Cannock posted a competitive 162 thanks to Potter's third half-century in four down the stretch, while Paul Thomas, unable to bowl due to a knee injury and repurposed for the KP-sized hole in the enforcer niche, made a crucial 63. Meanwhile, Walsall had set Stratford an imposing 239 and would have been hopeful that Kidderminster could knock off or block out. In the end, Stratford pulled up well short on 151/7, while early wickets for Crook and a spell of 12.4-5-14-4 from Potter – who finished the campaign with 32 wickets at 9.34 to Pietersen's 16 at 25.31 – saw Cannock to a 74-run win and an historic triumph.

"We wrote the Kev situation off," says Potter. "We just said, 'Fine, we can still do it'. If it was a choice between Kev going early or Bully and Humpty going early, I'd choose Kev every time. He wasn't always giving to the team, whereas they were. Kev was giving to Kev." There was no congratulatory message from Perth.

The rest of Pietersen's journey is well known, starting with Amiss passing up the opportunity to sign him, the pre-season tour to Western Australia that turned out to be his last cricket for Natal, the contract with Nottinghamshire, and on via several dropped jaws into cricketing immortality. While at Notts, he played a couple of club games for Bridon, pummelling an 86-ball 127* in one, and he appeared as a deputy pro for Todmorden in the Lancashire League's knockout where Nelson's Jonathan Finch had the tell-my-grandkids moment, dismissing him for 7. There was also a winter playing first grade for Sydney University CC, where, he says, the format of alternate batting weekends taught him to put a high price on his wicket. That being said, teammates remember someone who, at times, batted with the fury of an infantryman who had been up all night then sent out of the trenches the next morning with nothing but strong stimulants and a sense of righteousness to sustain him. They won a first title for 92 years.

186

The ever-present cloud of drama dragged around by their embryonic batting genius was the low point of the high point of Cannock CC's journey, one that soon took a turn for the worse. Potter played two more seasons, and two years after that they were relegated, passing through the Birmingham League's second, third and fourth tiers and back out into the wilds of the Staffordshire Club Championship. In 2019, the Chase Park site went into receivership after the Irish bank that had initially supplied the loan sold their debt to some venture capitalists, who immediately demanded £250,000. Despite never having defaulted on their repayments, they were forced out and moved to a new ground in town. The site was secured at auction by a businessman who failed to complete the purchase after being frustrated by planning regulations. However, after around 1,000 days of moss growth on the hockey pitches and tennis courts and cricket squares, a sale finally went through and cricket is due to return there in 2023. If that sounds like the seeds of a revival, there seems little prospect of Pietersen boosting it with a sprinkling of his celebrity, much less any visible reminders of the part he played in the most glorious chapter in the club's history.

"There's no memorabilia of KP at the club," says Bulpitt. "Absolutely nothing about him there. It's a sad indictment. One of England's great modern players and nothing there to commemorate it. It sums up the fact that he was never really part of the club."

"It was a shame how it finished with Kev," adds Potter, "because what a great story it would have been if he'd left saying 'I won the Birmingham League' with a dressing room that he remained friends with, instead of leaving under a cloud."

The formation of this particular cloud was later outlined in a typical Pietersen *mea non culpa*, a justification of the rancour: "As far as I'm concerned, Cannock didn't honour their agreement with me […] It makes me smile now when people at Cannock contact me or my agent to ask for signed shirts or stuff like that. They could have been a lot more straight and forthcoming with me during my time there."

But then, getting autographs from him wasn't necessarily all that straightforward, as Barnt Green's Simon Froggatt found out a few years later when Pietersen, by then a star, declined to put pen to his eight-year-old son's bat on the grounds that he was contractually forbidden from signing those that weren't made by his sponsor, Woodworm – not necessarily the most maverick thing to have done – immediately after which the Woodworm-sponsored Andrew Flintoff came along and obliged. The transactional nature of this episode stands in contrast to the generosity and common touch of Pietersen's fellow individualist and good friend Shane Warne, about whom there are many stories of him sitting for hours scrawling his moniker for wide-eyed kids – which, to return to the question posed at the outset, goes to show the maverick streak can fit a number of personalities.

Consider the career of Ben Stokes – a similarly competitive clutch player as Pietersen, equally capable of the audacious under pressure – whose radically imaginative and aggressive vision of the game has ripped up the Test captaincy manual, all the while emboldening his charges through a palpable empathy. Before this revolution, however, Stokes spent five years dutifully adhering to Joe Root's more conservative vision of things, and all without any disruptive histrionics or endless chafing against management, humbly serving the cause. Not every maverick is a *doos*.

Where the parents of many ambitious young overseas players remark how, fortified by their experiences, their offspring had 'left a boy and came home a man', Pietersen left a bowler and came home (briefly) a batter. Potter's assessment and deployment of his talents was both astute and unequivocally vindicated. He explicitly told the press that counties should be looking at his batting. And yet Pietersen's overriding takeaway was one of bitterness. "I didn't get the feeling he had much respect for me at all," Potter reflects. "As far as he was concerned, I was just someone controlling his Saturday afternoons. I haven't seen him since, so there was never any clearing of the air. His time at Cannock, in his own mind, isn't particularly happy. I think it had a major influence on him, if I'm honest."

How easy would it have been for Pietersen, a superstar from the moment his 158 at The Oval prized the Ashes from Australia's grasp, to have acknowledged that Potter, who tried to accommodate his desire to bowl as much as possible, sometimes to the detriment of the team's needs, was essentially right about his cricket – if not in a phone call then certainly when he committed his story to print? *My captain was among the first to see the potential in my batting.*

Instead, there is this cursory gloss: "I did have some disagreements with people at the club over the direction in which my cricket was going."

And so Pietersen's abiding memory of his summer in Staffordshire is this: "It was character-building. By the end of my time at Cannock I hated the place. My experiences coping with my little room in this little town and my dispute over not getting paid what I believe was owed to me for my bar work definitely contributed to who I am. Some people said I wouldn't be able to cope in Pakistan when I toured there with England because there weren't any flash restaurants or nightclubs. Well, there weren't too many of those in Cannock either and I coped."

Not too many restaurants, no. But should Pietersen ever return, there is now one alongside the A5, a mistimed forehand from the tennis courts at the bottom of the Four Crosses ground. Its name is Ego at Tumbledown Farm.

5

AB de Villiers (wk)

at Carrickfergus CC

When Bobby Robson replaced the legendary Johan Cruyff as coach of FC Barcelona in 1996 – taking on one of the most intensely pressurised jobs in football – he was told by the club's president that a team in transition badly needed a striker, and was asked whether he knew of one. There is a 19-year-old kid at PSV Eindhoven, replied Robson. Señor Núñez duly took out the *blaugrana* chequebook and paid a then world-record fee of £13.2m for Ronaldo Luís Nazário de Lima, making Robson acutely aware that his job depended on the Brazilian scoring goals. *O Fenômeno* struck 47 times in 49 games and won the FIFA World Player of the Year award, which still wasn't enough to prevent Robson being given a 'lateral promotion' to Director of Football as Louis van Gaal replaced him as head coach.

A similar, if slightly scaled-down predicament faced the Carrickfergus CC committee in the winter of 2003/04. The club – founded in 1868 but without a permanent home until 1988 – had just earned promotion to the top division of Northern Irish cricket for the first time in its history. A pro was needed, an overseas player – not permitted in the lower tiers if they had played first-class cricket – to give the team an edge, to allow them to be competitive against the established sides of Ulster cricket (although it is fair to say the club's budget didn't extend to breaking any world records).

Step forward club stalwart Roger Bell, who earlier that summer had been watching Sky Sports when a sprightly young lad in the South African under-19s team made 143 against his English counterparts at Arundel before being dismissed by Liam Plunkett. Bell floated the player's name to the committee and, after brief deliberation, they made the appropriate calls.

It was a gamble – dipping into the young-pup Southern Hemisphere market can be perilous – and the club's short-term future depended on one Abraham Benjamin de Villiers – just seven first-class appearances into his career, averaging an unspectacular 33.7 – making a few runs. You probably don't need a spoiler alert at this point before being told that he turned out to be quite useful. A little bit handy. Not the worst. But in the spring of 2004 Carrickfergus were more interested in what he could do for them in the here-and-now, or the there-and-then: namely, not allowing one of the oldest clubs in Ireland to embarrass itself on its maiden top-flight voyage.

De Villiers was due to arrive on the morning of Carrick's third game of the season, May Bank Holiday Monday, but after a delay in his flight's layover in Germany, and another transit through London, there was still no sign of him as Ryan Eagleson prepared to toss with the Belfast Harlequins skipper. Just then, word reached the team that the flight had finally touched down at Belfast International, and so the new pro's name was hastily inked on to the teamsheet in the hope that he might be able to bat at number five or six.

However, after a pedal-to-the-metal lift from the airport off Bell – and a 54-run opening partnership in 16 overs – AB arrived at the ground, padded up, and strode out at first drop, joining the man in whose house he would lodge for what turned out to be a 12-week stint on the Emerald Isle. Barry Cooper was a New Zealander who first went to Ulster as a replacement overseas player and settled there after landing a job as a quantity surveyor. He had recently bought the house from Roger Bell, "and part of the deal was I had to put up the overseas pro," he says, deadly serious.

"The first time I met him was literally when he walked out to bat," continues Cooper. "It was like, 'OK, hi. How you doing? I'm Barry.' It was a stinker of a wicket, wet, doing a fair bit, and slow going. I said, 'I know you've probably never played on a wicket like this in your life. I know you're going to want to impress. But you're just not going to be able to play the shots that you're used to playing. Let's just see how we go here.' He spooned a few up and was nearly caught at mid-off in his first few balls. But he adapted."

De Villiers would end up with a debut 82 from 85 balls, working his way up through those now familiar gears. "Their overseas pro was Ijaz Ahmed Jr, who played a couple of Test matches for Pakistan," recalls Cooper, who would himself bat through for an unbeaten 87. "He came on with his off-spin and I said to AB, 'This guy is going to be near impossible to get away. It's a tough wicket and he's not going to bowl any bad balls. We'll nurdle him, and if we can get 20 off his 10 we'll worry about the rest later.' AB obviously took that as a bit of a challenge and in his first over skipped down the wicket and stuck him back over his head for six. Twice. That was the first time I remember thinking to myself: this boy's a bit special."

Although de Villiers ending up spending just shy of three months in Northern Ireland, his Carrick teammates would only see him bat a further nine times, starting the following Saturday with a visit to North Down and a breezy 44 in an emphatic defeat to the champions of the previous three seasons. The following day's Ulster Cup first round match saw a coach trip to Donemana CC in the town of Strabane, nestled right up against the western border with the Republic of Ireland.

"This proved a real eye-opener for the young AB," recalls teammate Ally McCalmont. "He slept for almost the entire hour's bus journey, only waking as we drove into the ground. Greeted with a 25-metre boundary one side and a 25-metre hill on the other, he couldn't believe we would be playing on such a ground, and when some of the home side opened the pavilion shutters and stumbled out of the bar, after clearly a heavy Saturday night session, he was visibly taken aback. A few hours later though, AB had been dismissed for 18 and been pumped all around 'The Holm', going for 74 off his eight overs. It definitely gave him a different perspective."

Partly due to the weather and partly to his ineligibility for both the NCU Challenge Cup and the island-wide Irish Senior Cup (Carrick conceded the highest total in that year's competition, 346/6 vs Leinster), de Villiers would not get back on the park for over a month. This gave him plenty of time to kill in the sleepy fishing port, 11 miles up the northern shore of Lough Belfast, which funnels seaborne voyagers down into the capital's docks, where the ill-starred *Titanic* was built. Famous for the eponymous Irish folk song covered by Van Morrison and Bryan Ferry, among others, Carrickfergus wasn't obviously endowed with ways for a young visitor, just turned 20, to keep boredom at bay. "At that age, he wouldn't have been too interested in what I believe is the oldest Norman castle in Ireland," deadpans Cooper.

Instead, he went to the gym and occasionally trod the fairways – Cooper remembers him as a very good golfer, not quite scratch as the infamous meme about his sporting prowess has it, but chuckles at the memory of AB "fluffing his very first tee shot 50 yards down the fairway" (McCalmont notes also that, despite his skills with an oval ball, "like every South African we've ever had, he struggled kicking a football in a straight line from A to B"). He also did some under-14s coaching in Belfast alongside the Harlequins wicket-keeper, a then 18-year-old Gary Wilson, who racked up almost 200 international appearances for Ireland. And he spent hours at home strumming his beloved guitar – Cooper still has a tape of AB's favourite band, South African acoustic rockers Just Jinjer – as he endeavoured to adapt to life away from Pretoria.

"I was quite nervous and scared of being so far away from home," recalls de Villiers. "This was the first time I was planning to stay overseas for longer than a month. It was pretty tough to get used to being on my own, many miles away from home."

It proved something of a crash course in domesticity and self-reliance. "I think I frustrated Barry at times," he adds, "but I learnt over time and think I eventually pulled my weight in the house. He was the perfect roommate and I learnt some really good life lessons staying with him."

Cooper has only good things to say about his South African lodger, even though "he didn't know the difference between a washing machine and an oven when he got here. He wasn't a womaniser – he flew his girlfriend in at one point – and he wasn't a raker, so there wasn't too much drinking or many big nights out."

Not that AB was a choirboy, exactly. He has admitted to being "a bit of a washout" who would "eat pepper steak pies at 3am after a big night out" while at university (where, unlike close friend Faf du Plessis, he was not in the first XI). He had debuted for Titans since then, the penny of professionalism having dropped, although he fully understood the necessity of involving himself in the team's bonding rituals, says McCalmont: "He would always join the lads on nights out in Belfast after a game, win or lose. One such night we had too many travelling back in the car, so our overseas professional was consigned to a 20-minute journey stuffed in the boot."

"He was a professional cricketer," adds Cooper. "Very polite and well-reared and well-behaved. He looked after himself. But there was one night when he forgot his key to the house and ended up climbing up the drainpipe and through the window instead of rapping the front door, all because he didn't want to wake me up. He was bleeding all over my curtains from a cut to the hand, but it wasn't serious and didn't prevent him playing cricket or anything."

Eventually, AB got back out on the park, taking out his frustrations with a 30-ball 55 against Lisburn. Skipper Eagleson – part of the Northern Ireland team that had beaten Bangladesh in the sole Commonwealth Games cricket tournament, in Malaysia in 1998 – top-scored with 78. Yet Carrick lost, as they did the following Saturday against Lurgan, despite AB crashing 108 from 93 balls, having moved up to open the batting with his housemate, who by now was thoroughly impressed, if not by his lodger's cooking skills then certainly by his batting ability.

"The thing is that he was never slogging," says Cooper. "It never looked like he was taking a risk, even when he came down the wicket and hit a six, you know. It wasn't how most people come down the wicket and hit a six. Ally McCalmont, who likes a wager, said: 'I wonder what odds we can get on him playing for South Africa?' Even then, you thought it's probably not going to happen because loads of South Africans come over and dominate then barely play for a franchise, never mind international cricket. Looking back now, you realise that what we were watching was pretty awesome."

Even so, with more bad weather around, it was a further three weeks before AB was back in the pads. And he still hadn't made a home debut, two months after arriving.

The next game was at Waringstown, top dogs of Northern Irish cricket with 30 top-flight league titles (14 in 20 years across the 1970s and 80s), 26 NCU Challenge Cups (second to North Down), and twice as many Irish Senior Cups as any other club on the island of Ireland. Nevertheless, Carrick recorded their first league win since de Villiers had stepped off the plane, 68 days earlier. He only made 13 himself – "that was when his girlfriend had flown in to visit," observes McCalmont wryly – while Cooper made a hundred and Eagleson a third straight 60-plus score.

In an effort to make up some of the washed-out fixtures, the Northern Cricket Union mandated double-header weekends, and so AB's long awaited home debut came the day after the Waringstown win, against Bangor, the eventual champions. Again Carrick chose to chase upon winning the toss, yet Bangor amassed a mammoth 366 from their 50 overs, with Johnny Hewitt exploiting the short straight boundaries to score a daddy-hundred 182. When de Villiers fell for 89 from 92 balls, a stiff chase became an impossible one and they crashed to a 165-run defeat. Despite 391 runs in six innings from their pro, Carrick were in a relegation dogfight. Then things got worse.

"We were sitting in the living room at Barry's when the phone rang," recalls McCalmont. "It was passed to AB and he took the call calmly, not saying much for around 10 or 15 minutes, then politely said 'thank you' and hung up. He had gone pale. Naturally, we asked what it was about. He explained it was the South Africa 'A' selectors and that he'd been picked to represent them for the first time, in Zimbabwe. He said, 'What am I going to do?' We didn't understand what the issue was. 'I have a contract with Carrickfergus.' Both me and Barry started laughing, but he was deadly serious. The fact that he even for a second thought that he could turn down South Africa 'A' out of loyalty to this small club he'd only just joined spoke volumes. It goes without saying that his mind was set straight almost immediately when we talked it through."

Three matches remained for AB to make his mark; three matches to leave behind something special for the club he was reluctantly departing, albeit for the next big step on his fast-tracked trajectory; three matches for a budding genius – who would later crack a 31-ball ODI hundred and sweep nonchalant sixes off the pre-eminent pace bowler of the age (a mate who made his first-class and Test debuts in the same games, for the same teams) – to do something befitting his outlandish talents. Over those final three matches for Carrickfergus, when his thoughts could have been forgiven for drifting toward the bright lights of international cricket approaching fast from the horizon, Abraham Benjamin de Villiers would average 503.

And he started with a measly 62, albeit collected from a sprightly 57 balls in defeat to Downpatrick: Carrick's fifth loss in six. The following day, at home to derby rivals Cliftonville, he exploded. Facing exactly half of Carrick's 300-ball allotment – 24 of which he stroked to the boundary, 11 he smote over it – de Villiers made an unbeaten 233, over 75 per cent of the team total of 308 and the highest score in the history of Northern Irish cricket. Already a fairly strong front-runner for Player of the Match, he then had a go at keeping wicket before turning in a season's best spell of 10-1-28-3 in a much needed victory. "I was trusted with the new ball as a bowler," he says, "which was quite refreshing and very enjoyable. I think it took some of the pressure off of my batting." Indeed.

The final chapter of de Villiers' truncated spell as a league cricketer was a trip to Instonians CC in south Belfast. "When the covers came off," recalls McCalmont, "there was more green on the wicket than a table at the Crucible and we politely asked the opposition skipper if their f***ing lawn-mower was broke. His reply was that they wouldn't be going for 233. And he was right…"

In the opposing ranks was Andrew White, who later played alongside Eoin Morgan, Boyd Rankin and the O'Brien brothers in Ireland's famous 2007 World Cup victory over Pakistan in Jamaica. "There had been a bit of rain around," he says, "and so we put them in because it was damp. There was even moisture on the outfield. I vividly remember him hitting a front-foot square drive and the ball skimming across the surface with a bit of moisture spray behind it as it travelled to the fence at a fairly serious rate of knots."

Truth was, recalls Cooper, AB had been slow to get going: "I remember getting to 20 while he was scratching around, barely off the mark. Then he just took off. I got out in the 40s and I remember thinking 'I'm almost glad I got out then' because he was in the 90s and was about to get his hundred before I got my fifty, and that was with a 20-run head start! I said to the captain, 'You know what's going to happen here, don't you?' We both knew he was going to get a second double-hundred."

Put down in his 60s – "a tough chance, with the keeper stood up," says White – he duly powered on to three figures, then 150, then the double-hundred. No one had previously achieved it in top-flight Northern Irish cricket; AB de Villiers had done it twice in seven days. "It just got to the stage where he was really, really difficult to bowl to," White continues, with more than a little understatement. "No one else really got any runs [Cooper's 47 off 93 was the only other double-figure score], but he was so good, he had all the shots, and he found it quite easy to manipulate the strike. No matter what we tried to do in terms of field settings, he always had an answer. And it was never brutal. It was always done with the minimum of fuss, the minimum of effort. He just made it look really, really easy."

On a pitch the colour of the Emerald Isle itself, AB had made 208* from 161 balls, with 16 fours and seven sixes, bringing his final tally to 912 runs at 114 in all cricket, with 894 runs from nine league outings at an eye-watering 127.71. The consensus was that Roger Bell had sniffed out a good'un. "It took me some time but by that stage I really just felt settled in," says de Villiers. "I felt like I was part of the club and that I had my own special place in Carrick. Once you get that feeling in any set-up, you can then just focus on being yourself and performing to your full potential. It was the perfect way to sign off."

Having said his farewells, de Villiers made 91 and 84 in the first SA 'A' outing in Zimbabwe, sweeping him ever on toward his (and Dale Steyn's) Test debut on December 17 that year, against England in Port Elizabeth. Meanwhile, Carrickfergus staved off the drop, winning seven of their 18 games, including a final-day relegation decider with Harlequins, who fell through the trapdoor. By the time Carrick's next campaign rolled around, de Villiers had 11 Test caps to his name and almost a thousand runs at 53.7, with three hundreds, including 178 and 114 in his two most recent games. He was no longer on the club-pro market. Roger Bell renewed his Sky subscription.

Andrew White bumped into de Villiers when Ireland met South Africa at the 2007 World Cup – "a nice moment for those of us who played against him locally in the league to see up close how far he had progressed" (he was out in the first over for a duck, sadly/happily) – while Carrick hung on in the Premier League until 2012. They bounced back from relegation at the second attempt, though, winning an all-Ireland cup in 2014 and being named the island-wide 'Irish Cricket Club of the Year' despite being in the second tier of the Northern Irish structure. They have grown up, put down solid foundations and, where possible, remain in touch with the South African virtuoso who lit up the club for those three short months. Indeed, a couple of his teammates caught up with AB in the summer of 2019 when he dropped in at the Open Championship at Portrush, just beyond the Giant's Causeway along Ulster's Atlantic coast.

De Villiers' was a truly great career. He was an outlandish talent, an utterly box-office trailblazer and bona fide superstar, and yet palpably down to earth. And he hasn't forgotten the part a wee club in Northern Ireland played in his star-spangled journey. "I learnt about taking ownership and responsibility for my own success and happiness there. I learnt to stand up for myself and realised no one was going to do everything for me. There's a time in one's life where you need to start thinking for yourself and I certainly learnt that there. I will forever be grateful to the Carrickfergus club, for the friendships and special memories. I truly miss the place and hope to return sometime soon. Life happens quickly, my kids are growing up too, but I'm sure I'll soon get the chance to return."

When he does, there will be a spare bed at Barry Cooper's house. And, of course, a spare set of keys under the wheelie bin.

6

Steve Waugh (c)

at Nelson CC

November 1988, a hot Brisbane Saturday at the Gabba. West Indies, having rolled the home team for 167, have ambled to 135/0 on day two when Steve Waugh – playing his first Test against the Caribbean machine, his 22nd overall, and still without a century to his name – lands a couple of punches, nicking off Desmond Haynes and Carl Hooper. At 162/3, out sways the West Indies' captain, Vivian Richards, playing his 100th Test. Waugh, future Professor Emeritus of Mental Disintegration at the University of Baggy Green, is pumped, and greets the Master Blaster with a series of I-don't-give-a-shit-who-you-are-mate bumpers, on the pedestrian side of medium pace but dripping with attitude.

This was the thick of Waugh's short-lived phase as a bona fide all-rounder – the period of Bill Lawry's giddy assertion that he was "surely the best all-rounder in the world right now" and Ian Chappell's timeless retort: "Mate, he isn't even the best all-rounder in his family" – and one of the bouncers even caused Viv a flicker of concern. But it was the follow-up, a back-of-the-hand slower ball, that discombobulated the great man, Waugh missing his length by several metres and causing Richards, who had lost the flight path, to avert his purple-capped head, the ball hitting him square between those middleweight's shoulder blades.

Waugh's response to his borderline beamer was to bellow an appeal at the umpire, look bewildered when it wasn't upheld, and decline even a cursory apology to the now bristling legend at the other end: precisely the attitude that would lead Australia to knock Windies off their perch seven-and-a-bit years later. On this occasion, though, Viv made a 78-ball 68 and West Indies won by nine wickets.

In a certain corner of East Lancashire, the young Aussie upstart's stoush with King Viv would not have come as much of a shock. In fact, it was déjà vu, reprising a confrontation from 16 months earlier when Richards had become the most glamorous overseas pro in the history of a league synonymous with glamorous overseas pros and 'Tugga' Waugh was a 21-year-old fresh off a home Ashes defeat to Mike Gatting's team. Even better than front-row seats, the players of Rishton and Nelson were actually on the stage as Waugh bowled Richards a bouncer that put him on his backside, that famous purple cap almost dislodging the bails.

"That was Steve," says Marcus Phelan, Nelson batter and brother of long-serving former Manchester United assistant coach Mike. "Off the pitch he was very quiet, shy almost, but on the pitch the fire came out of him. He was very aggressive, a different personality altogether." His teammate, wicket-keeper Michael Bradley, concurs: "On the field he was in people's faces, but off the field he was an introvert with a really dry sense of humour. He's not the kind of guy who sits and chats with you for 30, 40 minutes but he's really good at the one-liners. He wasn't super-serious, unlike a few pros we had. He liked a laugh. But he wouldn't do big speeches or anything. He wasn't the great orator, even though he obviously became a great leader for Australia."

It was Waugh's second summer in England. In 1985, he had initially signed for Egerton in the Bolton League, with brother Mark as overseas amateur, but after making 90-odd in a pre-season friendly he was offered the Australian Cricket Board's Esso Scholarship, turning out for Essex second XI and under-25s, for whom he made 200* in a 55-over game the day after turning 20 (suggesting a remarkable ability either to shake off a hangover or avoid them in the first place). On weekends, he played for Ilford in the Paladin Plastics Essex Cricket League alongside a 17-year-old Nasser Hussain. A couple of weeks after blazing that double century, he took a 28-ball hundred off Chingford in the prestigious regional knockout, the Bertie Joel Cup.

The cricket in Lancashire was both drizzlier and grizzlier – more Shane Meadows than Sam Mendes – and there were a few decent pros around besides the two chaps who'd finish their Test careers with an aggregate of 19,467 runs at 50.7 from 289 games. Nelson had won more titles than any other Lancashire League club, and their past professionals included Learie Constantine – chief architect of seven titles in nine seasons – Ray Lindwall,

Sarfraz Nawaz, Larry Gomes and Kapil Dev. They were reigning champions, too, a campaign in which South African seamer turned coach and commentator Eric Simons was the paid man. Simons had missed the final match, however – a playoff with Todmorden after Nelson had failed to take the point they needed from their final game – because he had booked what he thought was a post-season holiday to the Greek islands and his wife insisted it would not be cancelled. Neal Radford deputised, a first title in 17 years was secured, and the Nelson players met Simons at Manchester Airport the following day to give him his championship medal while he waited for his connecting flight.

Not that expectation (or history, or reputation) was anything to cow Steve Waugh, even as a 21-year-old, and so when Viv strolled out in front of a large crowd at Rishton that July afternoon as though he owned the place, the Australian gave him one up the proverbial snot-box. In his autobiography, *Out of My Comfort Zone*, Waugh describes "the serious bouncer I let rip that ended up hitting him right between the eyes," a version of events that is disputed by Richards' partner, David Wilson: "He swayed backwards, did Viv, like a boxer evading a punch, but it did put him on the seat of his pants and his cap fell off, almost on to the stumps. It was a real effort-ball. I'm thinking: crikey, this guy's military medium and he's just done that to the best player that's ever lived, apart from Bradman. It was a surreal moment."

Nevertheless, Richards went on to make 79 before being caught by Phelan, a former professional goalkeeper at Burnley and Bury, who ran 20 yards round the mid-wicket boundary and took a one-handed diving catch in his 'wrong' hand inches from the turf. It was so good that Viv even took a detour to congratulate him before leaving the field, and later told him in the bar it was the best catch that had ever dismissed him. "That made me feel 10 foot tall," says Phelan. Teammate Paul Garaghty, on holiday that day, still has the catch on an old VHS tape, local TV station Granada having showed brief highlights on a news report. Different times.

Chasing Rishton's 205/6, Waugh made a grafting 54 before being undone by Colin Kuhn, a Zimbabwean swing bowler who drove buses in Blackburn: three outswingers followed by an inswinger, to which no shot was offered, ball thudding into front pad. All over, red rover. Nelson lost by 36, a dent in their title aspirations, but Richards and Waugh would lock horns again three weeks later.

* * *

Waugh had signed for Nelson after a visit to Australia by the club's chairman, Ken Hartley, who spoke with Bobby Simpson and Don Bradman, among others, both of whom enthusiastically recommended the young Sydneysider. Upon arrival, Waugh and his fiancée Lynette were whisked to a 'Meet the Pro' night in the clubhouse, attended by local dignitaries. It was only a short stroll from Nelson's Seedhill ground back to the two-up, two-down terraced house on Ball Street, Steve and Lynette's digs for the summer.

In his autobiography, Waugh describes getting "a bit of a shock" when he first saw a house that was "not more than four metres wide", although "the real concern for Lynette and me was the seven different latches and accompanying bolts that covered the door. This wasn't exactly a reassuring sight, and when all our washing was stolen from the clothesline in the back courtyard two days later we knew the neighbourhood wasn't about to throw a party to welcome us. Having to put pound coins into an archaic gas heater to thaw us out quickly went from having novelty value to being a pain in the butt when we ran out of coins and had to sit frozen in front of a TV."

"It was in a poor part of town, a really dark and dismal place, and the house was in a pretty poor state of disrepair," confirms Bradley. "My missus had our first son that summer, so Steve and Lynette would come round to our house and sit with Julie while I was out at work. They also went out on day trips to Wales, the Lake District, York, Blackpool, and the four of us went to Paris for Steve's birthday [June 2]. We all drove down to Dover and got on the ferry in my Austin Maestro."

On the field, the season began with defeat to Enfield, Waugh taking 1/93 and scoring 38 at No.4. Above him were two of the four Lancashire League players he singled out for praise in a late-season interview with the *Nelson Leader*. Skipper Ian Clarkson was a destructive opening batter who would finish third in the league's run charts for the season (42 behind Waugh, 89 behind Richards), while 'Carrots' Garaghty, then running the family butchers business, would provide the new pro with both quality cuts of meat and something of a shock when Waugh discovered he used a four-pound cricket bat.

Nelson also lost their second home game, against Todmorden, who knocked off the runs from the last ball of the match, Waugh making just 19. Between those defeats, they won at Lowerhouse, the pro managing only 13 this time, either side of a break for snow. "It totally covered the ground," says Garaghty. "Me and Steve came off and he started taking his pads off. 'Flipping heck, end of another game,' he says. I said, 'What you on about? See that big hill there? Once the clouds clear from Pendle Hill we'll be back on in half an hour.' And we were."

Garaghty justified keeping the future world No.1 batter at second-drop by making 96 in that Lowerhouse game. No-one has made more Lancashire League runs without scoring a hundred than his 13,123 (from 548 innings at almost 30), and his heart-breaking dismissal – caught by a full-length diving catch in front of the sightscreen – saw Nelson fold from 161/5 to 161 all out with 72 balls unused. Even so, Waugh – definitely the best all-rounder in the Nelson first team – took 7/58 to get the campaign up and running.

In mid-May, Tugga headed down to Taunton to play for Somerset against the touring Pakistanis, a workout against a 20-year-old Wasim Akram sharpening him up for the return fixture against Lowerhouse. (The Lancashire League doesn't operate symmetrical half seasons, but blocs organised around local holidays and rivalries; players also had to live or work within six miles of the club, which were fined £200 for not playing a pro.) Waugh was finally moved up to No.3 – "it wouldn't have been because Steve moaned," says the demoted Garaghty, "because he just got on with it" – and he made 103* in a comfortable win, his sole hundred of the campaign. "Three times he skipped down to hit our left-arm spinner Dave Whalley for effortless, flat straight sixes onto the adjoining speedway track," recalls Stan Heaton (who had taken the catch that denied Garaghty his ton), "which caused delays while a ladder was found to climb the 12-foot wall."

This was the first of a run of seven wins in eight games leading into that first Rishton encounter, by which time Nelson sat within three points of the leaders, Rawtenstall. With four points for a win, a bonus for dismissing the opposition, none for a defeat and one for an abandonment, they were nicely poised to defend their title.

Nelson's muscle-flexing mini-run had included a two-wicket win against Rawtenstall, Waugh adding 62* to figures of 4/81 as he steered his team home. However, he had been impressed by the visitors' left-arm spinner, Keith Roscoe, who had also dismissed him in Nelson's first-round Worsley Cup exit. "I've only ever taken seven catches in the Worsley Cup," says Roscoe, "and four of them were in that game: all caught and bowled. I usually catch about one in three! He just bunted it back and I nearly made an arse of it. I ended up catching it between my legs, sat on the floor, and he didn't even hit it that hard." The following summer, Waugh recommended the 25-year-old to Somerset. Roscoe trialled strongly, but regime change in Taunton meant a return to both the family's racing pigeon accessories firm and his Lancashire League bread and butter, where he was still playing first-team cricket 35 years later, top of the league's all-time wicket charts.

Another Nelson highlight was a career-best 130 for Ian Clarkson as they avenged the earlier defeat to Todmorden, whose pro, future South African opening bowler Fanie de Villiers, returned figures of 4-1-35-0. "De Villiers literally pulled out a white handkerchief," recalls Phelan, "waved it in the air and said, 'I surrender. I can't bowl at this guy any more' and took himself off. No word of a lie."

By the end of July, Waugh had only passed 40 in four knocks out of 13, failing to reach 25 in eight of those innings, a sign both of the strength of the league – eight current or future Test players among the pros – and the difficulty of the pitches. He had bowled an awful lot of overs, though – all bar 19 from one end, taking 45 wickets at 18.18 – and, in *Out of My Comfort Zone*, he describes how he "would pay the price when fractures in my back revealed themselves the following year".

Keeping the engine oiled with some high-quality midweek cricket, the last two months of the campaign saw Waugh average 68.5 with the bat. In the lead-up to the Rishton sequel, he played two one-dayers up in Newcastle alongside Allan Border, Malcolm Marshall and Gordon Greenidge for the Rest of the World team preparing for the MCC Bicentenary match at Lord's, invitation to which IVA

Richards declined in order to honour his contract with Rishton. Their return match at Nelson proved to be a humdinger. With the memory of being dumped on his backside three weeks earlier still fresh, Viv had brought his gameface.

"It was a really wet wicket," recalls Garaghty, "and Viv walked out to bat with training shoes on. I said, 'Viv, you're going to slip over. Go and put some studs on.' He says, 'Don't worry about me, man. I'll be fine.' His first scoring shot was a six over mid-wicket off our opening bowler, Peter Cockell!"

"I was an inswing bowler, mainly," adds Cockell. "The groundsman had put us on the edge of the square – against the best batsman in the world! – and I was defending the short legside boundary. Probably not the right end for me to be on, you would think…"

The Antiguan maestro anchored the Rishton innings, scoring 103 out of 199, Waugh returning 0/52 off 12. Clarkson fell in the second over of the reply, but Howard Lonsdale, Garaghty and Phelan all made 20-odd in support of Waugh. With seven balls left, six were needed, six wickets in hand. Kuhn dismissed Chris Hartley from his final ball, however, Viv taking the catch before stepping up to bowl the final over – seamers, because of the damp conditions – with Waugh on strike for a classic superstar-pro toe-to-toe.

Rishton's veteran 'keeper Frank Martindale came up the stumps and Richards began with two dots. Third ball, Waugh advanced, trying to win it in one hit, but the ball popped a touch and a smart piece of work from Martindale did the rest, Waugh falling for 93. Three singles from the final three balls meant defeat for Nelson by two runs. Rishton – Viv especially – were jubilant.

A week later, Nelson were beaten by high-flying Haslingden, whose pro was everyone's favourite Zimbabwean chicken farmer, Eddo Brandes. Between those two defeats, Waugh had made the first of four County Championship appearances for Somerset, for whom he would play the full season the following summer. Drafted in as injury cover for Martin Crowe, he scored 340 runs at 113.33 – twice his final Lancashire League average – returning from an unbeaten 71 against Hampshire to be clean bowled for the first and only time that year, for just 9, Haslingden's Alan Barnes, a post office counter clerk, succeeding where Malcolm Marshall had failed. "It was a straight yorker," says Barnes. "The umpire reckoned it slanted in. I don't know about that but he had travelled up late on Friday night so probably wasn't in the best of nick." Well, yes and no.

By the middle of August, Nelson still had 10 fixtures to be played, including some rescheduled games. The final five weekends were therefore all league double-headers. Crunch time. It began well, with wins over Church and Burnley (who, incredibly, had just one point on the board heading into August), Waugh making 52 and 80, both unbeaten.

He followed up with 111* at The Oval against Sylvester Clarke's Surrey, in what he described as "the most ferocious and awkward spell I ever encountered", but was prevented by rain from carrying the form into the following Saturday's Lancashire League game against second-placed Rawtenstall. On the Sunday, however, Nelson got a huge break, beating Colne in the local derby – Waugh contributing just 5, Clarkson making his third ton of the campaign – as the other six fixtures succumbed to the weather.

With six to play, they sat just five points behind leaders Haslingden, who would tie against rock-bottom Burnley in their next outing, taking two points while Nelson were hosting second-bottom East Lancs. The visitors from Blackburn had just two wins all season, yet posted a testing 157/5 on a damp pitch. With the pressure on, Waugh made 87, edging to the keeper on the Aussie bogey number off compatriot Dave Gilbert, the man who had shared the new ball with Craig McDermott on Waugh's Test debut, and Nelson came up nine runs short.

If that was a body blow, the following day's two-run defeat at Ramsbottom was a haymaker that left their title hopes on the canvas. Rammy's 40-year-old opening bowler, Brian Fielding, who spent his working weeks visiting far-flung factories selling industrial felts for paper-making machinery, had a good deal more joy than ST Clarke, nicking off Waugh second ball for his only duck of the summer. "It was back of a length, just outside off, seamed away and bounced a touch; he pushed at it defensively but edged through to Jack Simpson behind the wicket. When you look at the career he went on to have, it was a nice scalp to take. But then a spongey one at Acre Bottom was a little bit different to a rock-hard pitch at The Oval..."

It was a fatal setback, but they remained in third spot and, this being Lancashire, runners-up earned you a trophy. On the Saturday, with both the teams above them washed out, Nelson managed to beat Church – Waugh following his 137* against Courtney Walsh's Gloucestershire in the week with 60* – but the entire Sunday fixture list was again lost to inclement weather. As was the following Saturday's schedule, barring one match. Nelson had been due to play joint-leaders Haslingden, and the abandonment put a mathematical end to their chances.

Nevertheless, the rain cleared for the final Sunday (mercifully for neighbours, and co-leaders, Rawtenstall and Haslingden, who would otherwise have ended the season with four consecutive abandonments and been left to contest a playoff). While Haslingden were clinching the title, Waugh's last outing for Nelson was a nail-biting one-run victory over Accrington, for whom the Lancashire seamer Ian Austin was sub-pro-ing. Bully's opposite number wasn't taking things easy, the hard edge and white-line fever remaining as strong as ever.

"I remember Steve Waugh being a complete arsehole," says Austin, who made 66 to Waugh's 25. "I came in to bat and the first nine deliveries he bowled at me – every one was a bumper; every one went about a foot-and-a-half over the top of my head. He just stood there and abused the shit out of me. Next ball I ran down the wicket and flat-batted him for a one-bounce four. He never said a word to me after that. Anyway, I went in the bar afterwards, as I always did, and went over to him. 'Are you having a drink?' He just turned around and blanked me."

Nelson had finished third, Waugh scoring 851 runs at 56.73 – not a million miles above his Test average – while bagging 69 victims at 19.36, to put him second on the wicket charts, above de Villiers (7th), Brandes (8th) and, yes, Viv Richards (11th).

He wasn't quite done yet with English league cricket, turning out in three Birmingham League games for Smethwick in May 1988, scoring 2, 124 and a match-winning 135* against Coventry & North Warwickshire. James While walked out in that game with 15 required from 13 balls, and took a single off his first. "Between overs, Steve says to me, 'Right mate, you've got to block the next over off this fella…' It was Rob Grant, one of the top seamers in the league. Sharp. 'If he gets me out, we'll lose. I will take 12 runs off any three deliveries the fat c**t at the other end bowls me.' It was Geoff Edmunds, Shropshire's left-arm spinner. Anyway, to say I blocked out six would be wrong: I played and missed at three of them, and pushed one through cover for two. But I survived. And lo and behold, Steve then hit the first three balls of Edmunds' over for four. A brilliant lesson in backing yourself and thinking about the right way to win a game."

Nor was Tugga done with his mates up in Nelson. He remained in touch with Michael Bradley, who was willing on his mate when he bowled the clutch penultimate over in the World Cup final a few months later – against England! – and who travelled out to stay with Steve for two weeks at Christmas in 1990. "He was playing the one-dayers against India but wasn't in the Test side. I sat in the back of the car, with Mark and Steve in the front, all the way into the SCG. It was fascinating. It was a 45-minute trip and they didn't say a lot to each other. Mark was a bit of a lad – girls, gambling – but Steve was very much focused on cricket."

Waugh has been back to the former mill town on a handful of occasions, too, most recently in 2013. With the old two-up, two-down on Ball Street unavailable on Air BnB, he and Lynette, along with their three children, spent three days chez Bradley, during which the legend of a then-record 168 Test appearances, two-time World Cup winner and captain of one of the game's greatest ever sides enjoyed a few coldies with his old teammates in the Nelson clubhouse. Prior to that, in 1999, he scored World Cup tickets for Clarkson, who watched Waugh's iconic, granite-hewn hundred at Headingley against South Africa. And in 2005, doing a promotional tour for *Out of My Comfort Zone*, he called an old friend from across the time zones.

"I was working in a paper mill, doing a night shift," recalls Garaghty. "We'd sold the butchers by then. About three in the morning, my boss came to me and said there's a phone call for you. I said, 'No one calls me at work.' He says, 'It's a guy called Steve Waugh. From Australia.' Steve was being interviewed on the radio about his book, so I ended up talking for three or four minutes on Australian radio about his time with us at Nelson. I said, 'He was a great teammate, a great player, but I was just taking my forklift truck driving licence and if you don't mind you've gone and interrupted me.'"

7

Shahid Afridi

at Little Stoke CC and Leek CC

If ever there was going to be a 'Shahid Afridi Rule', a regulatory change named after the archetypal law-unto-himself, then you'd imagine it would be in honour of some misdemeanour or other: Thou Shall Not Pirouette on a Length; Thou Shall Not Bite the Ball; that sort of thing. But no, the player perhaps least associated with the establishment of norms in the entire history of cricket managed, during a half-season sub-pro-ing in the North Staffordshire & South Cheshire League, to lend his name, colloquially at least, to an entirely mundane piece of legislation that nonetheless fundamentally changed the way its clubs operated.

In June 2003, still only 23 and already a seven-year veteran of international cricket, Afridi and his burgeoning celebrity turned up for a two-week stint at Little Stoke, deputising for Justin Kemp who was at Worcestershire deputising for Andrew Hall who was with South Africa. He began with a boom-boom at Checkley, although earlier in the day, says Rob Haydon, Little Stoke's opening bat and chief drumbeater, "We had to beg him to bowl leg-spin. He came on bowling seamers!" He returned 19-3-35-3 as the hosts grafted their way to 202/9, and then the party started, Afridi smearing eight sixes and 10 fours in a 70-ball 112 that melted down a potentially tricky chase into a seven-wicket stroll. It would be comfortably the slowest of his three NSSCL centuries.

Nick Hunt's darted off-breaks caught the tail-end of the storm, his 3.2 overs disappearing for 39. "He had a huge entourage with him," he recalls, "10 or 15 people sat on the banking, and he kept chatting to them between balls, and vice versa. Most off-putting. I blame them for my figures. He was probably telling them how far he was going to launch the next one. I think he may have hit one all the way to the village."

Word of Afridi's presence was soon crackling through the local Pakistani community. Stafford's Sean Connolly recalls dropping into his local kebab house on the eve of Afridi's second outing and mentioning to the owner, Abdul, that 'Boom Boom' was playing up the road the next day. "The whole shop stopped what they were doing. Everyone was very excited. I told Abdul I would get him a signed photo, as I had a friend playing for Little Stoke. He gave me the biggest smile and, as I came to pay for my kebab, said: 'On me, my friend'."

After his exploits at Checkley, *The Independent* dispatched a reporter to the Potteries in anticipation of another firework display. "The motto on Little Stoke's crest, *Non progredi est regredi* ('Not to advance is to go back'), seemed made for Afridi. Chauffeured by a local balti magnate, he arrived at Longton in a red cricket shirt bearing the badge of the Non-Descript Club, which contains an overflowing pint of ale. The previous day he had played for them in a benefit match at Finchley, and legend already claimed he had placed his sixes between parked cars."

After a pair of tentative prods at Longton's South African pro, a single took Afridi down to face Staffordshire opening bowler David Edwards, who ran Stoke City's community football scheme: "He hit my first ball on the pavilion roof, defended the second, hit the third *over* the pavilion, and fourth ball I bowled a back-of-the-hand slower ball. He tried to belt it and it lobbed up to point." He had made 13 from seven balls in a total of 132 – quintessential Afridi, you might say – then went without joy in a seven-wicket defeat, 15-year-old Pete Wilshaw batting through for an unbeaten 67. Little Stoke's chairman, Barry Roden, mused that a longer stay at the crease might have seen an already sizeable crowd swollen even further as word spread among the city's many Pakistani taxi drivers. Those that had turned up left as soon as Afridi was dismissed.

Meanwhile, Connolly had forgotten all about his signed picture. Not wishing to preclude himself from the best chicken tikka in town, he had a local printer procure "a professional-looking picture of Afridi. Then a Pakistani lad from our fourth team did a very passable forgery of Afridi's signature, adding the words 'to all my friends at Kebab King' – written in Urdu for maximum effect. Abdul nearly cried when I gave it to him, and couldn't thank me enough. My chicken tikka kebab was bursting at the seams and, of course, I didn't have to pay. The next time I went in, the Afridi picture was in a frame and proudly mounted on the wall. For a good five years after that, I could jump any queue with just a shout of 'Boom Boom!'"

Edwards' slower ball may not have been quite as brilliant a heist as this, yet it had been the decisive moment in a comprehensive victory that was a major feather in Longton's cap. Nevertheless, it was doubtless still something of an unwelcome surprise for them to see Afridi striding across the outfield the following week – two cricket bags in tow, each carried by a flunky – when they arrived for their game at Leek. With Kemp back at Little Stoke and Leek's regular pro Albie Morkel nursing an injury, the Moorlanders had been quick to swoop.

This time, Longton declared at a respectable 226/7, skipper Richard Harvey top-scoring with 83 as Afridi snared the top three and briefly threatened to blow them away with his fizzing top-spinners, vicious drift and 80mph bouncers, which Leek's unhelmeted 41-year-old keeper Brian Mellor would eventually learn to pick. "The secret was his arm started lower, between his knees, although he did almost hit me on the crust a couple of times!" (By the time my team played Leek I was waiting for this ball and, to the eternal tedium of future teammates, pulled him for six on to the car park.) At 40/2 in reply, Afridi joined ex-Derbyshire man Tim Tweats. Edwards was again bowling, and again tried an early slower ball: "He defended it and, smiling, said 'Not this time!'"

From here, Longton moved briskly through Plans B, C and D. As the partnership developed, and with their main spinner finding some grip, Harvey decided to dust off his own seldom-used left-arm twirlers – a brave (or perhaps foolish) move on a club ground to one of the world's most celebrated six-smiters. "It seemed Afridi had been waiting for this moment to unleash the carnage," Harvey recalls, "and he struck five consecutive sixes off the first five balls of my second over. From memory, a couple didn't clear the boundary by much – in fact, in my defence, one of them was caught at long-off, but he was a yard the wrong side of the line!"

Palms now sweating, Harvey decided to go over the wicket for the final delivery and fire in a legside yorker: "Easier said than done when you're at best a part-timer. Anyway, that was the plan. The reality was a knee-high full-toss that should have been dispatched into Leek town centre, but he must have taken his eye off it at the critical time and thankfully toe-ended it down to deep mid-wicket for one!" While Harvey counted his blessings, Edwards duly bagged his famous scalp for the second game running, this time for a whirlwind 81: "Caught at long on, six anywhere apart from Leek, although the game was gone. He was nice to me in the bar after, too, saying 'well bowled' and signing an autograph."

It was one of the few occasions Afridi did stay behind, recalls teammate David Fairbanks. "He didn't interact with the team at all. He'd sit padded up with his family, or his driver. He didn't really engage in any chat between overs either. I was struggling in a Talbot Cup semi-final, batting second, with pressure mounting and wanting reassurance. Zilch. He ended up tossing it off and putting me under even more pressure. He was very standoffish and unapproachable. I got the impression that it was all a chore for him, that he thought he was bigger than the club."

Longton would go on to win the title, but playing back-to-back matches against a game-wrecking megastar, whatever his level of commitment, was clearly unfair and brought on a bout of head-scratching among the NSSCL's bigwigs. Eventually they would rule that a sub-pro could only play for one club per season, subsequently making the search for adequate deputies in an ever-diminishing pool as tricky as bowling a maiden to Afridi, particularly with stringent post-9/11 UK Border Authority controls.

('The Afridi Rule' certainly caused my club, Moddershall, much angst. In 2008, we had to find subs for Imran Tahir on a number of occasions. The following year Rangana Herath was spirited away mid-season to play against Pakistan after Murali suffered a shoulder injury, prompting 11 weeks of sub-pro scouring. So, for 2010 we decided we needed someone with zero chance of higher honours, and in October signed a Pakistani left-arm pace bowler with just two first-class appearances to his name. He was seven feet tall, from Gaggu Mandi, and the prospect of him bowling on league decks dilated our sadism glands. Unfortunately – and perhaps unsurprisingly at that altitude – Mohammad Irfan was unable to remain under the radar for long. First it was PCB training camps, by the summer the ODI squad touring England. We waited half a season for his replacement, Asad Ali's visa to clear, scraping the fast-evaporating talent pool for subs. One week we got a tubby 38-year-old offie who played in silver trainers and a NY Yankees baseball cap. Worn backwards.)

A couple of weeks after the Longton double-header, Afridi turned out against his former teammates at Little Stoke, skipper Nick Bratt having him caught behind for 47 before Kemp's 87* secured a tepid draw. Either side of that reunion, Afridi was outperformed by a pair of Lahore-born leg-spinning Imrans. First he was out-batted by Tahir – then with his previous club, reigning champions Norton-in-Hales – who made 93* in a 20-over romp past Leek's 125, having earlier had Afridi *caught at long-off for a single.* Then he was out-bowled by Farhat, whose contribution to Porthill Park's win was 5/20 and 32 to Afridi's 2/52 and 18.

"Afridi hadn't even arrived when we went out to field," recalls Porthill batter David Griffiths. "He turned up about six overs in and tried to come in at No.3, but it looked like he was persuaded to take five rather than rush out. We got them three down unusually early, then out comes Shahid. From the car. We proceeded to put everyone on the boundary. Literally everyone. He wasn't deterred. He plinked one short of long-off, got a few streaky boundaries away, then hit one straight to Immy at deep-square. Cheers, youth! We were all pissing ourselves. Instead of returning to the dressing room, he headed straight back to his mate in the car and sat there in his pads for the rest of the innings. I'd be surprised if he won their Clubman of the Year award. I hit him for a four later on and he called me a 'c**t', which was nice."

Afridi, of course, was always a cricketer adored and derided in equal measure by his compatriots, for whom he was either *pathan* daredevil or out-and-out idiot (with or without the *savant*), and for the exact same reasons. A man who brought a sword to a pillow fight. The sword that he lived by. Leek were only receiving a crash course in what a great many captains and coaches had or would discover: namely, that this was not a man around whom you could throw a paternal arm, riffing earnestly on the notion of 'employee responsibility' while pointing at a copy of the league table. It was a theme park ride to which you either signed up or you didn't. Leek's ticket was yet to expire, and the next three matches duly saw 'Boom Boom' reel off a triptych of berserker half-centuries.

He was stumped for 58 against Caverswall in the first of them, charge-slog-sweeping opening bowler Simon Davies. In the third, he made 78 against Barlaston, clearing its mighty oak tree a couple of times while batting in a back brace and later sending down a volley of bouncers. Between times, there was an almighty pro-on-pro ding-dong with Tejinder Pal Singh, who made 126 in Audley's sizeable 260/3 declared.

"It was the worst sledging I've ever heard on a cricket pitch," recalls Audley opener Dan O'Callaghan, a 6'5" slab busy making 86 while Singh smoked Afridi's increasingly irate bumpers everywhere. "I didn't understand most of it, but their dislike for each other was pretty apparent. Afridi ended up offering 'Tidger' out on to the car park at tea. So, at the end of one over he asked me whether I'd go with him as back up! Afridi's attitude wasn't great in general. At drinks, four or five kids who'd obviously turned up especially to watch him ran on asking for an autograph. He refused, and gave them a bit of a mouthful as he waved them away."

When Leek came to bat, off-spinner Andrew Johnson followed the Porthill model and stationed all nine fielders on the boundary – a boundary that Leek had even brought in by 10 yards, just in case – on the basis that it was absolutely no deterrent whatsoever. "The first ball gripped and he sand-wedged it over long-on for four, who may have snuck in a bit," Johnson recalls. "He hit the next ball over the massive tree at mid-wicket. The ball after that, he top-edged into his throat, sweeping, and said 'Well bowled, Murali'."

It was indeed coming out quite well for Johnson. Seven days later, he would bag what remains the NSSCL top-flight record figures of 10/32. Before then, though, he had a hand in Afridi's demise. "I caught him at long-on for 50-odd and I don't think he stuck around to see the next wicket fall. He was probably home for *You've Been Framed*."

For the keen amateurs of north Staffordshire, the sight of that familiarly bustling, bow-legged walk to the crease – the gait of a rodeo rider, someone who indeed saw his job as the brief surfing of some energetic explosion – was a decidedly uncanny experience. It was odd, too, witnessing that bouncing, balletic run-up, curtain fringe flapping away like an oil-covered seagull that cannot quite achieve take-off. In fact, playing a club match against arguably the world's most singular and surreal cricketer was so absurd that by the time we got around to facing Leek in what turned out to be his last meaningful match for the Moorlanders, I spontaneously intercepted Afridi en route to the crease to ask, in the voice of 'Michael Jackson' from cult UK comedy show *Bo Selecta!*, and apropos of nothing: "Hey Shah-HEED, where the muthaf****n' llam-AZE at, shamone?" Cool as ever – he had looked fairly relaxed while his chauffer smoked something pungent behind the pavilion at tea – he replied: "What is 'llamaze'?" (They were llamas.)

Earlier, we had been frolicking in the sunlit uplands of 78/1 when I feathered an Afridi leg-break to fall for 36 (did I mention I had put him 20 metres up the car park?) and only Iain Carr's defiant 70 got us up to 172 as Shah-HEED bagged what turned out to be a NSSCL best of 4/67. Two early wickets were then nipped out by our West Indian pro, Adam Sanford – whose Test victims at that stage included Tendulkar, Dravid, Ganguly and Laxman, but who was also only a few months from having Boycott certify him as slower in pace than a couple of generations of his female ancestors – and at 18/2, with the ball still new, we had a sniff.

Afridi took 25 balls to make his first 20 – hinting, perhaps, at the Leek committee's recent devising of an ad hoc win-bonus – only then to have a wild yahoo at Sanford, the ball nipping back and missing the leg bail by a fag paper. (This narrow escape induced a weirdly ambivalent feeling: part of you wanted to see him make 30- or 40-odd, with a couple of mammoth blows, but not to go *too* crazy and ruin the game.) Thereafter, he smeared, swooshed and swiped his way to 105* from 56 balls, sealing both the win and his century with an eleventh Cape Canaveral-launched maximum. "I see them mind games backfired," quipped a home supporter as I trudged off. A grizzled veteran in our ranks thought the innings "disrespectful" but it was entirely consistent with how he would play in just about any situation, for any team. Foot to the floor. Be damned, speed cameras.

Despite Afridi's efforts, this was just Leek's second win with him in the ranks. Two weeks later, still not mathematically safe from relegation after an abandonment at Betley, they flew Morkel in from South Africa for the final game at a cost of £1,000. It was extravagant in 2003, and would be even more so after the 'Afridi Rule' was established.

Even so, Afridi's north Staffs sojourn was not quite done yet. A year later, in high summer, with Little Stoke's new pro Dinesh Mongia having been commandeered in mid-season by Lancashire for their T20 campaign and Afridi roaming the shires, playing a week for Kent then two for Lashings, the maverick's maverick came once more through the gates at the Sid Jenkins Ground for two final NSSCL appearances. Boom Boom was back in the rooms. Or the car. Whatever.

Such was the Afridi box-office appeal that even seasoned Pakistani pros at other clubs were keen to see him do his thing. Tanvir Ahmed would go on to play six Test matches for his country, counting Jacques Kallis, AB de Villiers and Kane Williamson among his victims, but in 2004 he was an unheralded 26-year-old yeoman turning out for Newcastle & Hartshill in the NSSCL's third tier. Ahead of their game at Eccleshall, knowing Afridi was back at Little Stoke for the afternoon, Tanvir gave skipper Martyn Elliott specific instructions for the toss.

"He told me I *had* to bowl first," Elliott recalls. "He will bowl them out, he said, and he will then open the batting and knock them off. 'Okay, let's see how it goes', I say, and go out to toss. Normally he's nowhere to be seen, but he rushes on to find out the outcome. I'd won it. He was delighted, and set about demolishing Eccleshall. At one point, we had eight in the slip cordon. We bowled them out for 56 in 19 overs. He took 8/28, along with breaking someone's nose who was batting without a lid. When we bat, he opens and smacks a quick 30-odd off 15 balls, dispatching the new ball into the cemetery as people visiting graves ran for cover. We knocked them off in under nine overs and Tanvir was up at Little Stoke for four o'clock to watch Afridi. If only he'd done that every bloody week!"

It was good timing, too, because Little Stoke were just wrapping up Porthill's innings for 199 ahead of the main attraction. Warm-up acts Haydon, who would bat through for 42*, and Dave Leese, who made a breezy 33, then juiced the crowd. "We were going nicely but steadily," recalls Haydon. "I was faffing about with Webster, the off-spinner, who wasn't a bad bowler. Afridi came in and I explained what he bowled, that his arm-ball swung, and he just laughed and ran at him. Poor Matt, a nice lad, absolutely crumbled to pieces and could barely let it go. We put about 70 on. He made 64."

"The ball kept disappearing into the houses over the road, over and over again," adds Griffiths. "We had a poor attack that day, the pro wasn't fit to bowl, and I remember thinking 'carry on, youth' as it was hot, we were definitely losing, and there were ales to be drunk."

Afridi was unavailable the following Saturday – not terrible news for relegation-threatened Knypersley, who had managed to avoid him the year before as well – but a week after that he was back at Little Stoke for the derby game with Stone, third plays second, the final show of the Pakistani's wild 13-leg tour of north Staffordshire; intimate venues, massive rig, lunatic stagediving, blown amps, smashed guitars, avid groupies, lavish riders, bum notes, improv psychedelic jams and full-throated balls-to-the-wall anthems. And the best was yet to come. For the finale, Shahid would go full Afridi.

Counter-intuitively, Little Stoke had prepared a nibbly green seamer, inviting their neighbours to have first use. Afridi would not bowl, however, as 43-year-old uber-dobber Steve Colclough's unchanged 25-15-25-3 locked down one end and Stone were slowly throttled for 120, pro Mohammad Hussain top-scoring with 44 and only one other batter making double-figures.

Known by all as Mo or 'Reggie' (a nickname that stuck after a committee member at his first club, Porthill, forgot his not so unusual moniker), Hussain would become a cult figure across his dozen highly productive spin-bowling seasons in Staffordshire. With a monobrow that looked like a child's charcoal drawing of a bird, a paunch that belied his birth certificate, and pigeon legs invariably slipped into plastic sandals, he cut an instantly recognisable figure, and certainly stood out from the hot-faced ravers at Golden nightclub, where he would sometimes find himself dancing on the bass bins late on Saturday nights. Throwing himself into the local culture, Reggie enjoyed a pint and a fag (some more exotic than others), and occasionally offered his after-match cooking services. "One day he said he'd do a barbecue," recalls Stone skipper, Adrian Butters. "He brought chicken marinating in grout buckets, and we finished late so he cooked in darkness. Needless to say, it was undercooked and a couple of lads had to have a week off work."

Michelin stars he may not have had, but Reggie could certainly bowl. Good enough to dismiss Michael Slater and Darren Lehmann in his two Test appearances, his NSSCL career eventually yielded

841 league wickets at 14.56 from a hefty 5314.5 overs, no fewer than 1,905 of which were maidens – four times he bowled upwards of 200 in a season – which is more dots than the Braille version of *War and Peace*. Stone's plan was therefore centred on his left-arm parsimonious, says Butters. "We thought: 'If we get Afridi out, 120 isn't a bad score'. It was seaming about. We'd played him at Leek in the Talbot Cup and had a theory that Mo should bowl one end and we'd rotate at the other, so he didn't get used to anyone. It worked there and he never got set, being stumped for 20-odd. Mistake was getting Rob Haydon out in Wiffa's [Andrew Winfield] first over!"

Afridi bound out at 1/1, and decided to have a look-see. "He had a lot of respect for Mo," says Leese. "As we got together between overs, he was chatty. He would say to me, 'I will get a single off Mo, you take the rest of the over and I'll hit the other end!'" (Afridi's respect for Hussain meant the latter got away with an economy rate of 4.87, possibly the highest of his NSSCL career.)

Before that hitting eased into its most violent gears, however, Winfield came off after five relatively tidy overs, costing 23. Johnathan McCredie then disappeared for 27 off two, and Little Stoke were 91/1 off 15 – Afridi on 77 from 45 balls – the goose as good as cooked. Perhaps reckoning that a man who had played 766 games of professional football at centre-half was the best recipient of a hospital pass, Butters then turned to Chris Banks's off-breaks, the short straight boundary to his back.

"The skipper looked around and saw everyone with their hands in their pockets, so I offered my services," Banks clarifies. "First ball, he had a massive swipe at a good length ball, which lobbed over extra cover for two off a leading edge. I called him an 'effin' jammy bastard' as he turned for the second. I believe that was my mistake!" The next ball sailed out of the ground. And the next. Enormous hits. The one after that went for four. Afridi was up to 95. Little Stoke to 109.

"We paid him decent money, obviously," says Colclough, "but there was also a bonus for him making a hundred. At tea, after we'd bowled them out for 120, I remember Barry Roden saying to me, 'Well, at least we'll save a few quid on the bonus today!'"

"The strange thing was," adds Leese, "despite hitting these massive sixes, he kept saying his side was hurting and that he couldn't continue. I remember telling him, 'We've not far to go. Carry on and you can have some treatment when the game is won'." That moment was now knocking loudly at the door. And Shahid was definitely *the one who knocks*. He *was* the danger.

Banks's fifth ball was launched for another towering six – described in the fisherman's style as having reached the railway crossing down the hill or even the petrol station at its bottom, not far short of halfway back to Stone CC – and with it Afridi had broken the league record for the fastest top-flight hundred: 50 balls, 45 minutes of carnage. "By this stage, even my own teammates were sniggering," adds Banks. "I was pretty pissed off. And angry. So I bowled a beamer straight at his head, which he swatted nonchalantly over square leg into the farmer's field to win the game!" If consolation was thin on the ground for Banks, at least his 1-0-30-0 wasn't the most expensive NSSCL over sent into Afridi's deranged hitting arc. Positives have to be taken where they can.

With the derby match thus settled by the most savage flourish imaginable, Leese and his extremely *pianissimo* second fiddle walked off unbeaten on 11, into the beaming faces. Afridi was not remotely interested in soaking up any small-stage acclaim, however – nor in any treatment for his side, it turned out – and was already off in the opposite direction, making a bandy-legged beeline from crease to scorebox. "He collected his cash from Barry Roden, who was scoring," says Leese, "then walked back to the dressing room, handed back his Little Stoke shirt, picked up his kit and, with two or three of his entourage, got in the car and left. We never saw him again."

And that was it: the air had ceased vibrating, Storm Shahid had passed through. Well, not quite. On his way out, he tossed a used nappy out of his car and was chased off the ground by a fist-waving Little Stoke stalwart – the gunslinger skipping town in a cloud of dust with his fistful of twenties, a league record that still stands, and not too many new Facebook friends.

In his 13 NSSCL games, Afridi had smote 763 runs at 76.3, while returning an unspectacular combined analysis of 147-31-470-18 – numbers that might surprise those accustomed to his prodigality with the bat and streetwise tightness with the ball. A week later, Mongia was back in situ for the run-in, during which, Little Stoke will have felt relieved to know, they definitely would not be facing Afridi themselves.

8

Kapil Dev
at Nelson CC

For the cricketers of the Lancashire League – its clubs clustered tightly in the M65 corridor that runs from Blackburn up to Burnley and a little beyond, extending across a smattering of small mill towns to the south – Saturday June 25, 1983 was a free afternoon, a legacy of the competition's emergence from the Victorian work regimes of the 1890s. Had any of them switched on BBC1 to catch the day's live cricket broadcast – the certainly more prestigious yet far less important matter, parochially speaking, of a World Cup final – they would have seen no fewer than five players who had appeared as professionals in the league two summers earlier. West Indies' quicks Andy Roberts and Michael Holding were the hired help at Haslingden and Rishton respectively, while the Indian trio of Madan Lal, Player of the Match Mohinder Amarnath and skipper Kapil Dev turned out for Enfield, Lowerhouse and Nelson.

The league's connection with the two line-ups didn't end there, either. Clive Lloyd (Haslingden) and Larry Gomes (Nelson) had enjoyed two dominant seasons apiece in east Lancashire; in 1978, his third and final year playing for Littleborough in the neighbouring Central Lancashire League, Joel Garner had a game as stand-in pro for Burnley, taking 8/37; Vivian Richards would later spend the 1987 season at Rishton, arriving for his debut in a helicopter; and less than 24 hours after Kapil lifted the trophy on the Lord's balcony, off-spinner Kirti Azad turned out in a derby game for Lowerhouse, picking up where he'd left things in early June.

The 1981 campaign wasn't Amarnath or Lal's first dip into Lancashire League waters. After a season with South Shields in the Durham Senior League, Mohinder signed for Lowerhouse in 1977, living with his brother Surinder, pro at their cross-town rivals, Burnley: th'Amarnath derby. The Lowerhouse skipper that year, Steve Gee, became close friends with 'Jimmy,' attending his wedding reception in Dewsbury after he had tied the knot with Inderjit, a doctor who would work six-month placements in the UK while her husband played club cricket, as well as for Durham in the Minor Counties competition.

The Amarnath boys were following their father's footsteps in east Lancashire, with Lala, India's first ever Test centurion, having spent the final two pre-war years at Nelson, helping them to a four-way joint-first finish in 1938 (they lost a semi-final playoff) and second place the year after. That was the closest an Indian professional had come to winning the Lancashire League title until the post-Independence cricketers of the 1950s began to make waves. Vijay Hazare's double of 1075 runs and 104 wickets saw Rawtenstall finish second in 1949, Dattu Phadkar's 100-wicket haul helped Nelson come second in 1951, while Polly Umrigar's Church side also finished runners-up in 1953, pipped to the title by Haslingden thanks to Vinoo Mankad's 88 wickets and 930 runs.

Mankad's ground-breaking success was followed a couple of years later by Subhash 'Fergie' Gupte, the mystery spinner's 136 league wickets leading Rishton to a league and cup double. In 104 Lancashire League games across four seasons, Gupte took an astonishing 53 five-wicket hauls, with a best of 9/10. In the cup – played as timeless single-innings games over consecutive weeknights – his best was 10/101. Neither Everton Weekes nor Clyde Walcott, the league's premier batters of the era, were able to pick him.

In 1976, Syed Abid Ali repeated Gupte's feat, helping Rawtenstall win a league and Worsley Cup double, while the following season, his first in the league, Madan Lal's 82 wickets and 726 runs brought Enfield the title. In 1980, Lal scored 1087 runs at 77.64 for Enfield, and his yearly batting average never fell below 42 – coincidentally, Amarnath's final Test batting average – while Amarnath's Lancashire League average, curiously, never made it into the forties.

By 1981, then, Lal and Mohinder were solid, reliable, occasionally devastating and relatively cheap club pros in their thirties who had already faced off in the Lancashire League on half a dozen occasions, and neither had played a Test in over a year. Conversely, Nelson's 22-year-old swing-bowling all-rounder was an emerging superstar of the game, with 32 Test appearances – including a hundred against the West Indies and eight five-wicket hauls – already under his belt.

He sat third in the ICC Test bowling rankings, and big things were expected of Kapil at the club whose 17 league titles – including seven in nine years between 1929 and 1937, with Learie Constantine as pro – made them the Lancashire League's most successful.

Kapil had put pen to paper at Nelson the previous August, while staying overnight with Gee in Burnley. They had become friendly a couple of years earlier, when Gee's week-long stay with the Amarnaths in Lancaster had coincided with Kapil turning up in the back of an MGB GT sports car, his leg in a brace following knee surgery, having escaped the boredom of hospital in Birmingham.

Kapil's brief pit stop in Burnley had reached enterprising officials from Limavady CC, near Derry in Northern Ireland, who flew a delegation across the Irish Sea to sign him up for their three-day North West Cup final against Sion Mills that weekend. After pyrotechnics in a Saturday afternoon practice session forced the club president to resituate his new black Mercedes, Kapil returned 3/63 from an unbroken 30-over spell the following day. Underdogs Limavady replied with 227, a lead of 35, Kapil scoring 85, before Sion reached 143/8 off 54 when play was ended by bad light. Rejecting a 2pm resumption on the Tuesday, Sion agreed to start at four o'clock, but in the end failed to show up. Limavady were nonetheless obliged to change into whites and send down a token delivery, the umpires declaring all remaining batsmen timed out before pronouncing the match forfeited. The winning team repaired to Limavady for the celebratory craic, Kapil enjoying a couple of wine miniatures and signing some pieces of kit before heading off, back toward the bright lights.

That winter, he played three Tests each in Australia and New Zealand, his 5/28 with a heavily strapped thigh at the MCG, as India defended 143, securing India's historic 1-1 result. Then, on May 6, he married Romi Bhatia, having proposed to her by suggesting they have a photo taken together in front of a billboard carrying one of Kapil's endorsements, "so that we have something to show the kids". All of which delayed his arrival in Lancashire until the middle of May. "We were aware of that before," says Nelson skipper, Chris Hartley. "It wasn't a case of him letting us down. He'd made it clear when he signed."

By then, Amarnath and Lal had already been through five rounds of matches, the second of which ought to have seen them play each other but was instead snowed off (although, less than 10 miles to the west in Blackburn, Andy Roberts' Haslingden shivered their way through a full game at East Lancs). Nelson, meanwhile, had two no-results and three wins – David 'Bumble' Lloyd deputising for Kapil in the first – leaving them in second place.

The pro's belated debut came at Ramsbottom, a nail-biting one-wicket win secured with a last-over six by Steve Calderbank, to which Kapil contributed 4/59 and a breezy 42. The following week, at home to high-fliers Rawtenstall, Kapil took 6/47 – his best figures of the season – off a full allotment of 17 eight-ball overs as the visitors mustered just 92 all out. It proved plenty, though, as Franklyn Stephenson's 5/20 hustled Nelson out for 52. It would be their only defeat in the first half of the campaign. The next outing saw Kapil contribute 27 and a decisive 5/48 in a tense two-run win over Church, the visitors collapsing from 109/4 to 125 all out as the pro snared the final wicket in his final over. In the post-match euphoria, hopes were raised of an 18th title.

They followed up with two abandonments, however, although not before Kapil had displayed the hitting prowess that would famously see him pass the follow-on target at Lord's with those four consecutive sixes off Eddie Hemmings, crashing a 48-ball 75 in the derby match with Colne that included a six that "cleared the bowling green, the house behind that – the first time it had ever been done – and ended up by the roundabout", recalls teammate Ian Clarkson. He followed this with 90, 12, then 68 and 69* in back-to-back victories over Accrington. With seven wins, one loss and five no-results from their opening 13 fixtures (it was four points for a win, one for bowling out the opposition, one for a cancelled game), Nelson were five points clear at the top at the halfway point of the season. Everything looked rosy. Well, almost.

"There were a few at Nelson disappointed that Kapil was only seen at the club at the weekend," reflects Hartley. "I used to say: will we see you for practice this week? It would occasionally happen, but not a lot. He spent some of his time going to Europe, as a sort of honeymoon. The thing was, pros could be useful at nets, but we didn't get anything out of him other than on match days. I don't want to be too critical. We got on well and he was a brilliant player, but you felt he was going at 80 or 90 per cent a lot of the time."

Some of Kapil's early-season absences had been spent at Northamptonshire, for whom he made a County Championship debut in June, followed by a couple more appearances in July, picking up only six wickets while averaging 35 with the bat – unspectacular stuff, perhaps, but ideal midweek practice, the Nelson members might have thought, for the serious stuff up in Lancashire.

Meanwhile, Amarnath's Lowerhouse – the only one of the league's 14 clubs never to have won it, which was not expected to change – found themselves one place below halfway in eighth at the mid-point of the campaign, while Lal's Enfield were tied for tenth, which perhaps accurately mapped their respective status in the Indian team. Lal had two half-centuries for the season – he would finish with nine, the most in the league – while Jimmy had not yet had occasion to raise his bat. He had bowled with customary economy on the damp early-season pitches, however, albeit only taking one five-bag: 7/60 in victory over eventual champions Rawtenstall. Nevertheless, Amarnath had edged the first duel with Lal, a two-wicket victory to which he contributed 4/40 (Lal making 43 out of 93 all out), before top-scoring in the chase (b Lal 33).

Amarnath's performance on that fabled Saturday at Lord's two years later would of course be deeply entwined with Michael Holding's – the latter castling him for a gritty 26, India's second top score, before he trapped Holding lbw to put the seal on India's coming-of-age victory – and Lowerhouse knew they would need Jimmy to stand up in their mid-season double-header against Holding's Rishton, which fell on the last two Saturdays in June. They were coming off a run of four straight no-results, indicative of the wet weather that formed part of a trifecta of vexation for the Jamaican. He had suffered the ignominy of being biffed (well, top-edged, duck-hooked and smeared) for four sixes by IT engineer Ian Osborne of Church, and was using his weekly column in the *Lancashire Telegraph* to grouse about damp wicket ends – some unavoidable, some tactical – and the lack of 'walkers' among the local batters (who, you may have thought, would be highly motivated to get the hell out of Dodge).

"In the game at our place, he hit me on the chin and first slip caught it," recalls Lowerhouse's current chairman and then their No.3 batter, Stan Heaton, who was working as a gravedigger before joining the police. "Obviously, I didn't walk, because I hadn't hit it. He started to have a pop at me, but then stopped when he could see the blood trickling down my chin." Heaton was eventually run out for 25, while Amarnath was bowled by Blackburn Rovers centre back John Waddington for 15. However, thanks to Pankaj Tripathi's 47, Lowerhouse scrapped their way to 134/9 and Rishton fell five short.

Heading into the return game, Holding had heard that a bullish Tripathi – rather foolishly, some might argue – had questioned the Jamaican's speed-gun credentials. Suffice to say, it wasn't a brainiac move. Lowerhouse were blitzed for 67, with Holding's figures – and remember, these are eight-ball overs – a death-whispering 13.2-6-13-9. Seven were bowled, two caught behind. Tripathi was hit in the face second ball and retired hurt with a broken nose, resuming to have his castle demolished for just three, Mikey toying with him as a cat would a songbird. To his credit, Amarnath stood firm with 43*, two thirds of the total and, at that stage, his highest score of the season.

Amarnath was of course famed for his courage, a helmetless 'happy hooker' who was knocked unconscious by Imran Khan, had his skull fractured by Richard Hadlee, his teeth dislodged by Malcolm Marshall, his jaw cracked by Jeff Thomson, and was sent to hospital by Michael Holding, requiring stitches in his head. "What separated Jimmy was his ability to withstand pain," remarked Holding. "A fast bowler knows when a batsman is in pain, but Jimmy would stand up and continue." Amarnath would go on to tangle with Mikey a lot over the next two years, not just at Lord's. He amassed 598 runs at 66.44 in a brutal series in the Caribbean immediately prior to the 1983 World Cup (including 60 out of 97 all out in Jamaica as India called off their innings with five men unable or unwilling to bat), then scored one run in six knocks at home against West Indies four months later, forcing Kapil and the selectors to cut him loose.

Kapil had spent a lot of time with Amarnath during that summer of 1981. Initially, Nelson had billeted him and his new wife in a modest two-up, two-down Victorian terraced house in the town, but it wasn't entirely to his satisfaction so he and Romi relocated to the Amarnaths' more salubrious lodgings in Lancaster, which came with Inderjit's placement at the local hospital. Clarkson regularly borrowed his father's car to drive him the 40 or so miles north when it wasn't possible for Kapil to rendezvous with Amarnath for a lift home.

"We had a gatekeeper at Lowerhouse at the time," recalls Heaton, "a chap called Frank Holmes: salt of the earth, long gone, didn't know an awful lot about cricket. Nelson had rolled someone over one afternoon so Kapil turns up at our place. He got dropped off on the main road in his whites, bag over his shoulder. He walked up the drive and Frank says, 'How've you gone on?' Kapil says, '75 and 5/30' or whatever it was. So Frank says, 'Well done, lad. Keep that up and you'll soon be in the first team!'"

Nelson had begun the second half of the season with a four-wicket loss in a rescheduled fixture at Burnley, which drew their opponents to within a point. Next came what would prove, one way or another, the decisive bloc of six fixtures: home and away against Haslingden – who were one point behind Burnley – Rishton and Bacup, each with their West Indian quick bowling pros: AME Roberts, MA Holding, and Ray 'Spray' Wynter, a Jamaican journeyman and later West Indies rebel.

The game at Haslingden brought a first team debut for young Nelson keeper Michael Bradley, on the eve of his 18th birthday, standing in for his 48-year-old (and still sprightly) future father-in-law Alan Haigh. Bradley entered at a somewhat perilous 33/8, with Roberts having taken six cheap wickets, including Kapil lbw for 11. The youngster ground out an unbeaten 19, helping No.3 Milton Lord – who "was black and blue where Andy Roberts had bounced him," recalls Bradley, "with red marks on his shirt where the ball had hit him in the chest" – take the score to 72, Roberts finishing with 7/38.

Kapil then knocked over four early wickets to leave the hosts wobbling at 29/4, but a brisk 31 from Roberts settled the game, while opener Bryan Knowles batted through for an unbeaten 26. In fact, Knowles was on his way to 1050 runs for the season – more than the Indian trio, more than Todmorden's Mohsin Khan, who made a double-hundred at Lord's a year later – the first amateur to reach four figures for 62 years, the first to top the averages for 24 years. Not bad for someone who sold towels and bedding on Ormskirk market.

Nelson exacted a measure of revenge in the return game, compiling 168/5 with the pro again trapped lbw by Roberts, this time for 32.

Opener Clarkson, an insurance salesman who finished with 823 league runs to Kapil's 880, top-scored with 77, drawing Roberts' fury after failing to walk for an edge to the keeper ("I was batting with him," says Hartley, "and he knocked the cover off it"). In reply, Kapil took out Knowles, Roberts and Mike Ingham – the league's all-time highest run-scorer when he retired – as well as three lesser lights in the middle order, to finish with 6/57 as Haslingden closed on 123/8. Nelson picking up four points for the win but were denied the bowling bonus point. For Kapil, it was honours even with Roberts across the two games, a win apiece: 43 runs and 10/94 plays the Antiguan's 41 and 11/110.

Those Haslingden encounters were each followed by games against bottom-placed Bacup, who would lose all 13 games after the turn of the season. The hapless visitors were dispatched by 10 wickets at home, Kapil taking 5/46, yet put up much more resistance in the return, fiercely defending their modest total of 126/9. Kapil came in at 52/3 and departed at 82/4, caught on the boundary having clubbed 27. "He absolutely hammered this ball," recalls the left-arm spinner who claimed the prize scalp, Keith Roscoe. "I don't think it went above five or six feet high, then smacked long-on in the chest, who managed to hang onto it after being poleaxed. I think he's still got the bruise." It took another tenth-wicket partnership to get Nelson over the line and keep their faltering title challenge from folding completely.

The two games against Rishton went somewhat less well. The first, a ten-wicket loss, saw Nelson bulldozed for just 54, of which Kapil made a third, dismissed by Waddington's left-arm swingers. Holding took 7/16. The home game wasn't going much better when it was terminated by heavy rain, Nelson having staggered to 45/9 – a two-game total of 99/19 – with Waddington again snaring Kapil, whose highest score in seven knocks since the turn of the season was just 32. With six games left Nelson were off the pace, and there were mutterings about the pro bowling with the handbrake on, perhaps saving his exertions for bigger (international) battles ahead.

The one time he truly bent his back was against Todmorden, four weeks from the end of the season. Kapil clubbed 75 out of Nelson's 143, and the home team had reached 50/1 in reply when "a lad called Philip Morgan hit him for four", recalls Hartley, "then said something like, 'You never could bowl'. Kapil suddenly said, 'Right, wicketkeeper, back you go'. They all went back three or four yards. He then put his back into it and ripped them out for 107 [taking 6/53]. You felt he could have done that more."

Finally, in mid-August, Kapil squared off against the two men he would soon be leading to World Cup glory, a mini round-robin for dressing-room banter supremacy, beginning with his housemate. Amarnath came into the game with scores of 62, 91*, 50, 2, 58, 79*, 0 and 67 since his joust with Holding, yet failed to trouble the scorers as Lowerhouse battled to 162/9. His first consolation for the drive home was that he wasn't among Kapil's 5/72. The second was that, although Kapil crashed 60, Nelson could only muster, well, Nelson: 111 all out, Amarnath's canny military mediums taking 4/36. Personal bragging rights for Kapil, maybe, but also defeat, and what turned out to be the decisive blow to their title hopes.

Still, the following weekend's double-header delivered Kapil a win over both his compatriots, first scoring an even 50 in a 56-run romp against Lal's Enfield. The next day brought a 22-run win over Lowerhouse in which the gods of the drive home decreed that both Kapil and Amarnath should score 39, with the former bagging 5/36, the latter 5/38. An honourable draw.

The final game of August saw Kapil's 79 – including a huge six onto the speedway track adjacent to Nelson's Seedhill ground – anchor another win over Todmorden, which left just one last short shuttle down the M65 for the return game with Enfield. Well, that and a midweek trip to New York with Romi, from which they hadn't yet returned as Saturday ticked around.

"The chairman got a phone call from Kapil saying, 'I am going to be a bit late for the game because I'm stuck at Heathrow'," recalls Bradley. "He got Kapil on a flight up to Manchester and then by taxi to Enfield, but he turned up at the ground with no kit whatsoever. So he went to the Enfield dressing room and knocked on the door and said: 'Lal, Lal, I need some kit'. Madan Lal found him some kit, but Kapil was a lot taller than Lal, so he ripped all the turn-ups off and turned them down."

He had missed the first six overs of the game, but his 2/50 – bringing his season's haul to 67 (at 14.77), seventh in the list – helped restrict the hosts to 175/9, with Lal making 52. In reply, Kapil managed 23, bowled by the owner of the trousers he was wearing. However, skipper Hartley's 52* steered Nelson to a six-wicket win and a final league position of fourth. Champions Rawtenstall owed a large debt to Franklyn Stephenson's 105 wickets at 9.26, while Roberts' 82 wickets at 13.2 translated to joint-second place for Haslingden. Holding's 86 at 10.74 left Rishton in sixth, one spot below Lowerhouse and four above Enfield.

Lal finished the season with 897 runs at 47.21 – a higher aggregate and a better average than both India's No.3 in that World Cup final (Amarnath finishing with 765 runs at 38.25) and their No.6 (Kapil's 880 coming at an average of 44) – which perhaps goes to show that India's 43-run win might have been even more emphatic had Kapil got the batting order right.

Two months after facing each other in the Lancashire valleys, Lal (5/23) and Kapil (5/70) were skittling the England of Gooch, Gower, Boycott and Botham for 102 in Mumbai, Kapil going on to win Player of the Series. Nelson did not try to re-engage him for 1982, however, although in any case he would end up signing for Northamptonshire. And that was Kapil done with club cricket.

Two summers' later, as the Lancashire League stalwarts flicked on to BBC, they would have seen the trio at the heart of India's greatest ever win. They would have seen Madan Lal enter at 130/7 and chisel out 17 priceless runs, then take the three prize top-order wickets of Desmond Haynes, Vivian Richards and Larry Gomes. They would have seen Kapil Dev send down 11-4-21-1 and cling on to the steepling catch that the mighty Viv sent into that north London sky. And they would have seen Mohinder Amarnath – in many ways the quintessential league dobber, bowling to ring fields with the keeper up – finish a decisive spell of 7-0-12-3 by trapping Holding lbw to send his nation into raptures. Some of them might even have been impressed. Stan Heaton certainly was. "I consider myself, an ordinary Joe Soap, very lucky to have played with and against some of the greatest cricketers in the world," he says. "One tries to be modest, but if I can get it into a conversation that I made my maiden Lancashire League fifty against Kapil Dev, I'll do what I can to throw it in there."

9

Allan Donald
at Rishton CC

Friday night, eve of the match, end of the working week. You're down the local, as you often are before a big league game, only this time, instead of a couple of steady, relaxing beers ("one's not enough, two's too many, three's just right" as the old adage has it) and the usual chit-chat with the pub's cricketing infidels – people who don't know their trigger movement from their trigonometry and couldn't care less whether you're going to shorten your backlift tomorrow – you've lost your beverage-discipline and are ordering chasers with each pint, soon foregoing the beers altogether while vaguely justifying it to yourself as an occasional pre-match ritual of Garry Sobers. Instead of winding down, you're getting wound up. And with justifiable reason, too, for tomorrow's new-ball spell, away at Rishton in the Lancashire League, is going to be brought to you by Allan Donald. *White Lightning*. You pop to the offie on the way home. For White Lightning.

The year was 1996 and the 29-year-old Donald was still very much in his pomp, still two years out from his iconic Trent Bridge tussle with Michael Atherton, at which point he sat directly above Ambrose, McGrath, Muralitharan and Warne at the top of the ICC bowling rankings. He had been Player of the Match in his most recent outing, against England in Cape Town, and would record figures of 42-17-69-7 in his next, on a featherbed in Ahmedabad.

The previous summer, he had topped the County Championship bowling averages (88 at 15.48) as Warwickshire hoisted the pennant. However, the Bears had already pre-signed Brian Lara for the 1996 campaign, although he later pulled out of the deal, citing "exhaustion" (before attempting a U-turn), and it was Shaun Pollock, not AD, who stepped into the breach at Edgbaston. Donald was already set on his sabbatical season, working as Warwickshire's fitness coach during the week while testing his newly learned stretching regimen on the soft outfields of east Lancashire each weekend.

Donald wasn't the first big name to have been lured to Blackburn Road by the chutzpah of Rishton's cheeky-chappy chairman, Wilf Woodhouse: Michael Holding had pro'd in 1981, Viv Richards in 1987, and Mohammad Azharuddin the year after that. But still, this was *Allan Donald*, the quickest bowler on the international circuit, a man who put the willies up the best of the best. Awesome as he was, Isaac Vivian Alexander Richards wasn't necessarily someone who'd have you necking pints of Anxiety Quencher on a Friday night amid feverish dreams of ambulances and A&E. Announcing the South African's signature the previous November certainly gave the top-order teachers, taxi drivers, tree surgeons and travel agents of the Lancashire League plenty of notice to book their holidays at a different time of year than usual.

The season at Rishton would not be Donald's only spell of league cricket. Six years later, by then a Worcestershire player, he signed for Knowle & Dorridge of the Birmingham League, a 35-year-old warrior with an eye on a last hurrah at the winter's World Cup in South Africa, having played his final Test in February. Donald's body was feeling the unsentimental squeeze of Father Time after 15 thrilling years bowling like the wind, and there would be just eight BDCL appearances to add to those he made back in the late-1980s, when Warwickshire IIs used to enter a team. His second debut brought 3/36 from 15 lively overs in defeat to reigning champions Stratford, and teammate Daniel Dalton recalls someone who was still plenty sharp – a few weeks later, one opposition batter would walk off for a caught behind that he was "nowhere near" touching – even if those hypersonic levels were no longer available to him.

Nevertheless, the old fires still burned fierce bright, as Dalton found out when refusing a run chase at Moseley. K&D had fielded with nine men for much of the innings, after a sliding Jamie Spires had his cheekbone broken by the knee of a leaping Calver Wright, both of them taken to hospital after a 20-minute stoppage. Moseley racked up 225/4, with current ICC general manager Wasim Khan making 98 and his opening partner Ian Stokes an unbeaten 76, after which K&D's No.3 Dalton unilaterally decided to shut up shop, the visitors crawling to 87/2 from 40 overs before blinding sunshine over the sightscreen stopped play 10 overs early. "Allan was livid,"

Dalton recalls. "He said, 'I haven't come here for this. I'm here to compete. I'm here to win.' The message was pretty clear."

Donald would finish with 22 wickets at 16.73, his best figures of 4/46 – which came on the day he heard of his great friend Hansie Cronje's death – ensuring Coventry & North Warwicks fell two runs short of their target and dragging K&D off the foot of the table. However, says Dalton, his most ferocious spell was the 11.3-5-12-3 at Aston Unity, although he had to limp out of the game with an ankle injury. This, then, was still very much someone to bring out the cold sweats in your average club player, even in a strong league, as Dalton suggests was the case when they visited top-of-the-table Himley and found "a waterlogged pitch in the middle of a heatwave. Their guys were saying the covers had leaked after a localised storm, a tall story if ever there were one. AD looked at the pitch and said, 'I'm not bowling on that, I'll kill someone'."

Nevertheless, the skippers decided to give it a go, with K&D agreeing to bat first. "Allan told me to go down if any ball hit me," continues Dalton. "First ball, off Tim Heap, a good bowler but with no pace by this stage, hit me on the gloves and we stopped for about 10 minutes. Next ball hit me on the helmet off a length and all the Himley players just walked off. 'Yep, seen enough.' We went to the pub down the road for three hours and Allan shared a load of stories from his international career." It confirmed the impression of a warm, approachable icon of the sport whose ego-free competitiveness and professionalism was never more manifest than in his fielding. "He was probably the most enthusiastic fielder in the side," says Dalton, "chasing everything, full-length sliding stops, just a great example."

Rewind six years to peak AD and Rishton opening batter Craig Smith's first impressions of the new pro when he arrived for his debut at home to Ramsbottom were that "he probably didn't realise what he was coming to, because he turned up with a briefcase of multi-coloured Oakley sunglasses. There must have been 10 or 15 pairs. I don't know when he intended to wear them."

The visiting skipper, Jack Simpson, the man who would face Donald's first ball in Lancashire League cricket, remembers there being "about three or four thousand people on the ground. You couldn't move. Sky Sports were also there – I used to have the DVD of this – and as me and Ian Bell [not that one] came down the steel staircase from the dressing rooms to begin our chase [of 146], Rob McCaffrey collared us and said, 'So what's it like going out to face the world's quickest bowler?' Instinctively, I said, as a bit of a joke: 'Well, he' – meaning Belly – 'is absolutely shitting himself'. McCaffrey said, 'Cut, cut; we can't have that' and had to ask me something else."

Simpson, father of Middlesex keeper John, would hook the first ball for four and go on to make 44, while sub-pro Meyrick Pringle, Donald's new-ball partner in the 1992 World Cup, also made a nuisance of himself. "He'd been picked up at Preston station with just a bag for his boots and whites," recalls Simpson. "When I was batting, unbeknown to me, he'd been in the Rishton changing room, got Donald's gear and walked out to bat in it. As Donald came in to bowl he pulled up, realising his gear was being used. There was a mighty altercation in Afrikaans, which went on for a couple of minutes. I asked Pringle what was going on and he told me Donald has gone berserk because the gear was so new even *he* hadn't used it."

Rishton went on to win by 30 runs, following up with victory over Rawtenstall, but then lost three of their next four games, starting with Burnley – by which stage, perhaps appositely, Donald's wicket haul was four, four, two. After a one-wicket loss to Nelson, whose No.11 hung on for nine balls, the quirks of the fixtures threw up back-to-back games against Todmorden, the first of which saw Rishton skittled for 97 on a wicket that Craig Smith considers the quickest he ever played on at Blackburn Road.

"Before starting to chase our target," recalls Todmorden opening batsman Brian Heywood, "our lads were terrified. I knew they were terrified and I had no confidence we were going to do anything against him at all. I'd always felt it was the short straw, playing them early: if he was ever going to throttle back, he wasn't going to toss it off in the first half-dozen games. Maybe later, but not in May. But I told the lads, 'We just have to sell our wickets dearly. Make him work for every one and we'll get 'em.' The pitch was flat."

Todmorden started well, largely because Donald, says Heywood, "bowled from the wrong end, up the bank. He bowled me a bouncer and I hooked him for four. He gave me a little clap but I thought, 'That's all well and good but it wasn't your proper bouncer. I'm not doing it again because the next one will be!'"

After reaching 35 without loss from seven overs, Heywood's partner Stuart Priestley ran himself out, and Tod duly subsided to 70 all out, Donald snaring 8/38 – although not Heywood, who finished unbeaten on 29 from 82 balls, with negligible support from the middle order. "Heath Kennedy turned his back on his first ball and was hit up the backside, while Dave Whitehead, usually a pugnacious cricketer, couldn't have stood further toward square leg if he'd tried. Donald came round the wicket and throated Dave about a yard outside leg stump and the ball ricocheted onto the stumps. Mind you, one lad, Mohammad Saleem, came out to bat without a thigh pad…"

Nevertheless, Todmorden exacted revenge the following Saturday, chasing down a rain-adjusted target for the loss of just one wicket – Priestley was again run out, although this time for 55, one of only four amateurs to take a half-century off Rishton all season – with Heywood making an unbeaten 44 and AD going wicketless.

Having won a first league title for 40 years the previous summer – with a little help from Phil Simmons – Rishton needed to get their act together and promptly won the next seven games, a run that began with the return Nelson fixture, the only match Donald missed all year. This was followed by a three-run victory over Enfield, then revenge against Burnley, for whom a 16-year-old Michael Brown – later of Middlesex, Hampshire and Surrey – opened the batting with his father, Phil. "Second ball of the innings, Dad lost his off stump, having played a textbook forward defence. Unfortunately it was at least a second, maybe two, too late. My second ball, I also played a forward defence, which went for four between the keeper and first slip off the toe of the bat. I just thought: 'Wow, this is rapid! How are you meant to score runs against this?'" It was indeed a problem: Donald returned figures of 16.5-9-14-6.

Next up came back-to-back wins over Lowerhouse, for whom Chris Bleazard made 60 (out of 131) and 58 (of 136), the two highest amateur innings against Rishton all summer. Colne's Gary Hunt, these days presenting a cricket show on BBC Radio Lancashire, became the third local half-centurion the following Saturday, scoring a 42-ball 54 as Donald finished with 1/93, giving him 46 wickets at the halfway point, while the four points pocketed for winning – not accompanied, for once, by a bonus point for bowling the opposition out – left Rishton 11 points clear at the top of the table. On the final day of June, however, the winning streak was brought to a halt by East Lancs, who would emerge as Rishton's chief rivals over the second part of the campaign.

The July sun brought harder pitches and more supple muscles, and Donald duly eased into that familiar, menacing stride, like Concorde coming into land at JFK. Indeed, the visit of Haslingden, champions in seven of the previous 11 years, produced what Donald considered his best display of the campaign: 7/18, all clean bowled, as the visitors were routed for 31 in just 12.3 overs to lose by 133 runs.

After that they travelled to Roger Harper's Bacup, where Rishton's destructive top-order batter Russell Whalley – the son of Eric Whalley, a cardboard box tycoon with a lounge named in his honour at the club who the previous winter had bought a controlling stake in Accrington Stanley FC – remembers Donald's finely-tuned fast-bowling machinery not being best pleased with the conditions. "It was a fine day, cracking flags, and Allan put his feet down where he was going to bowl and it was piss wet through. They'd watered the ends, hadn't they. They said they hadn't, but at the end of the day we didn't give a toss 'cos we bowled 'em out for 42 and won the game. They pissed him right off and it backfired on 'em, big time." Figures of 7/22 would bear the analysis out.

A five-wicket win over Accrington – AD chipping in with 8/47 – was followed by a return trip to Haslingden and one of the most extraordinary games in the history of the Lancashire League. The home team scrambled to 104 all out, with Mike Ingham, the league's all-time leading run-scorer, top-scoring. "I remember hitting Donald on the up over cover for four," he recalls. "I thought, 'What have you done?' He gave me two quick bouncers, one past my nose, and then went round the wicket for what I thought would be a big inswinging yorker, so was back and across waiting, but it wasn't. Next thing I know, I was waking up with a crowd around me. It took him three goes, but he got me in the end."

The run-chase had reached 92/2 when Whalley, having flayed 56 from 50 balls, was bowled by New South Welshman, Brad McNamara. A mini-wobble ensued, Rishton slipping to 94/5, but they made it to 103 without further loss, leaving them needing two runs from 14 overs – at which point came the mother and father of all chokes, the kind that ought to have girded Donald for the next phase of South African cricket: the Heimlich Manoeuvre Years. In the sort of passage of play for which the cliché "you couldn't have scripted this" might genuinely apply, Rishton saw five wickets fall for no runs in 18 balls – starting with a hat-trick by left-arm spinner Alan 'Dick' Tracey – to lose by one run.

Next up was Bacup, eager to erase their earlier, soggy-ended humiliation. On a quickish surface, Roger Harper threw some Caribbean shapes to the barrage of chin music, blazing 161* from 103 balls as Donald travelled to the tune of 2/119 from 21 unchanged overs, although rain had the final say. Not to worry, though: the following Saturday, after sending his first ball over the keeper's head for four byes (which may not have entirely helped settle the home dressing room), AD went on to return figures of 7-4-3-7 as Accrington were filleted for just 18, nine of which were extras.

Entering the final straight, AD recorded only his second wicketless innings in the victory over Rawtenstall, after which came a two-run loss to Ramsbottom (Ian Bell, evidently not shitting himself, making 50), victory over Church, and a memorable encounter with West Indian paceman Franklyn Rose at Enfield. Donald took 6/25, all clean bowled, as the home team fell for 70, the 10th time that year Rishton had knocked sides over for under three figures. But Enfield's Jamaican, a few months away from winning Player of the Match on Test debut, wasn't really one to meekly accept second-fiddle status and Rishton themselves soon subsided to 39/6, Rose bagging all six, with keeper Andy Bartley – advised by teammates it was safe to go helmetless – retiring hurt after being struck in the face first ball, the middle part of a *de facto* hat-trick. However, Craig Smith's unbeaten 31 saw Rishton over the line without further damage and another big step toward glory had been taken.

The penultimate game was a top-of-the-table showdown with East Lancs – Donald taking 5/49 to pass the 100-wicket mark for the campaign – which ultimately succumbed to inclement weather. Two points apiece meant Rishton required just one more from the final game to guarantee the league title.

The curtain-closer came up at Colne, whose pro, Brad Johnson, was en route to a season's aggregate of 1,718 runs, which to this day remains the highest in the league's 131-year history. AD's final job, then, was to take Johnson out. The South Australian was duly nicked off for 26, Donald signing off with 5/58 – an eighth five-for in 13 outings over the second half of the season – as Colne were rolled for 134 with 12 overs unused. A demob happy run chase then saw Rishton skittled for 74, but East Lancs – who won one more game than the champions yet failed to bowl sides out anywhere near as often – had been pipped by a single point and so the day's only real dampener was provided by the celebratory drinks.

"My dad was happy we lost," quips Whalley, "because I found out years later, just before he died, that he was paying Donald a £100 win bonus out of his own pocket. I think he were on 20 grand overall."

The cash prize for winning the league was, of course, minuscule by comparison, but that's scarcely the point in such matters of parochial braggadocio. And with 106 wickets at 10.74, top on both counts, White Lightning could scarcely have done more. Indeed, despite the limitations of his batting, he even put together a mid-season sequence of 37*, 32*, 30, 40, 31*, 0, 22*, 20, 69*, 33 and 22*, testament to someone who, despite driving up from Birmingham on the morning of games and leaving shortly after stumps, took all facets of his job extremely seriously once he crossed the line, giving every drop of sweat to the Rishton cause.

"He absolutely gave it 100 percent," reflects Brian Heywood. "He must have done for Rishton to win the league, because they were nowhere near as good as in 1995. And he played with great honour and dignity, too, competing fiercely, but a great sportsman at the same time."

You suspect that no one who played with him – much less those who had the dubious pleasure of facing him – will forget the year Allan Donald roared into bowl in the shadow of the east Lancashire moorlands.

10

Curtly Ambrose

at Chester Boughton Hall CC and Heywood CC

Long before he became a dreadlock-ponytailed plucker of bass guitar and jovial occasional member of the commentary box, Curtly Elconn Lynwall Ambrose established himself a permanent, *primo* pitch in the English cricketing psychodrama of the 1990s, a gangling, bristling, haunting figure, all pumping knees and elbows, galloping in to dispense, at best, a brand of splice-hitting strangulation or, at worst, wrecking-ball devastation, a figure straight out of a Stephen King novel – specifically, the one with the black truck in the desert – as adapted for the screen by Kubrick or Cronenberg. If he wasn't sending the first ball of an Edgbaston Test trampolining straight over both Michael Atherton and wicketkeeper's heads for four byes (England were blitzed out for 147 and 89, Robin Smith and his masochistic streak contributing 46 and 41), he was making it scuttle along the Trinidad deck as England were routed for 46. You may also have seen him in such movies as *Seven for One in 32* and *Horror at Sabina Park*. That Curtly.

England's first glimpse of 'Ambi' had been on the West Indies' 1988 tour when, as a change-bowling three-Test greenhorn, he picked up 22 wickets at 20.22 with an economy rate of 2.19 as their hosts went through four captains in losing 4-0 to the Caribbean steamroller. Well, not quite the first glimpse, for two years earlier he was playing for Chester Boughton Hall of the Liverpool & District Cricket Competition. For free. As in: unpaid. Without remuneration. *Sans salaire.* A 22-year-old Curtly Ambrose, gratis. Taking the new rock for your club team. Or *their* team.

Precisely two years before winning the first of his 14 Test Player of the Match awards – that's one every seven games, a rate bettered only by Steve Smith and Wasim Akram of those with more than five – Mr Ambrose was taking 7/42 at home to Formby, six clean bowled and one caught behind. All in, he bagged 84 LDCC wickets at 9.8 – some 61 of which involved a radical *feng shui* rethink of the stumps' traditional arrangement, while only one was trapped lbw. Which is half as many people as he dismissed hit wicket. That 61/1 disparity might suggest that the majority of batters were – how to put this – primarily looking to score through the off-side.

His Chester debut had come in the away fixture with Formby, a well-to-do commuter town separated from the Irish Sea by the sort of spectacular sand dunes that lend themselves to the area's three Open-hosting links golf courses. Ambrose scored a season's best 50* yet returned figures of 0/28 on a drizzly north-west afternoon. "It was wet underfoot," recalls teammate Brian Gresty, "and Curtly didn't have any spikes. He was slipping and sliding all over the place, both bowling and batting. No one had any boots his size to lend him, as you can imagine. But I had a sports shop in Whitchurch [in Shropshire], so I took Curtly down and sorted him out with some bowling boots. Size 16, they were. I also measured him for some trousers and I think his inside-leg measurement was 41 inches."

Ambrose had just one first-class appearance under his belt at this stage, and had come over on a Vivian Richards Cricket Scholarship arranged through the Chester-based travel agent Geoff Moss, whose company, Caribbean Connections, covered his airfare and living expenses. Sadly, Gresty's recollection that Boughton Hall's free-of-charge future fast-bowling great "spent the week working in a travel agent" has been anecdotally alchemised over time, says Moss. "No, he didn't work for me. He just strolled around, listened to music, strummed his guitar and occasionally went to practice. He lived in a house near the club with Sam Skeete [a Desmond Haynes Scholar, who was playing at Oxton] and wasn't expensive to keep. He basically lived on cornflakes and cheese sandwiches."

Curtly's co-recipient of the Viv Scholarship was George Codrington, a Barbadian all-rounder whose professional career never took off but who would later end up playing for Canada against England in the 2007 World Cup as a rotund 40-year-old off-spinner, returning figures of 10-0-70-1. "We didn't want two overseas players," recalls Moss, "so I offered George Codrington to Whitchurch, but they didn't want him. So then we offered him to Birkenhead Park, who took him. It was our captain who decided to keep Curtly."

The previous season's Viv Richards Scholarship recipient – that is, Chester Boughton Hall's overseas amateur – had been Winston Benjamin, who hailed from All Saints in central Antigua, a dusty mile up the road from Ambrose's village, Swetes. Benjamin's skiddy pace and appetite for chin music had brought 106 wickets at 7.57, with a best of 8/20 – 48 more scalps than anyone else in the division and, unsurprisingly, top of the LDCC charts on both counts – while the lusty batting that saw him make a Test best of 85 yielded 503 runs at 35.92, fourth in the averages. It was a hefty contribution to Chester winning the LDCC title. All of which was good enough to earn him a deal at Leicestershire for the 1986 season, doubtless to the relief of Merseyside's club batters. Until they saw the replacement.

"After Curtly's first game," recalls Chester's skipper, Robin Jones, "we got back to the club and they all asked me, 'What's this fellow Ambrose like?' I said, 'Well, he's not the bowler Winston was, but I think he's going to be a reasonable batsman'."

Ambrose had a lot to live up to, then, and followed his wicketless bow at Formby with a wicketless home debut for the champions, returning 20-10-34-0 against Sefton, at which point one or two at Boughton Hall might well have wondered whether Birkenhead Park had had rather the better of the arrangement. On the other hand, the figures did highlight his ability to – as they say on Merseyside – not bowl much shit. Over the next five weeks, the big Antiguan found his radar, taking 7/30, 5/30 (also making a second 50*), 1/35, 9/58 and 8/50 against Neston, the last five men all clean bowled, for 0, 1, 2, 1, 0. Areas, Curtly.

After that flurry, Ambrose again suffered back-to-back wicketless outings, the second coming in a draw at Ormskirk whose No.3 batter, John Davies, a 27-year-old engineer, became the only man to score a hundred against Chester that summer. "When I came in there was a pool of blood on the wicket," he recalls, "after Colin Mitchell had been floored by Curtly."

"Colin was a good player," adds Jones, "who played for the league representative XI. At the end of the first over, I walked past him as he was tapping down the pitch and he said, 'He's not so quick, Jonesy,' which wasn't a good idea. Curtly heard him, see. Next over, he bowled him a short ball, which he went to hook, and it hit him straight between the eyes, fracturing his forehead like a burst orange. He was poleaxed on the pitch and within five minutes or so an ambulance was there on the outfield. Curtly was quite shaken up for a while and didn't want to bowl."

"I didn't have a helmet on either," continues Davies, who finished unbeaten on 101, "although, to be fair, Curtly pitched it up after that. Well, he did until one of our lads came back from the local sports shop having bought a couple of helmets, which we all shared between us. He started bowling bouncers again after that!"

This wasn't Ambrose's only act of GBH for CBH, with Hightown's NL Gwyther – the only batter not to be Curtlied in that 9/58 – also being retired hurt by a man with a good memory for adversaries who perhaps thought they had his measure. John Davies can attest to this himself. In the return fixture, the last match of the season, he was bowled by Ambrose for a single, a brief stay yet long enough to have his hand broken by the Antiguan. "We declared on 71 for nine," chuckles Davies, "because our No.11, Dave Brighouse, totally refused to bat. By then I was on my way to hospital for an x-ray, so I didn't see them knock the runs off." Nobody here was objecting to Curtly's sweatbands.

Somewhat incongruously, however, Ambrose only had one wicket at home by mid-June (Warwickshire coach Alan Oakman had even been to scout him, concluding that he wasn't up to scratch). This anomaly was rectified with 4/39 against Liverpool, albeit in an eighth draw in 10 unbeaten games, the visitors ambling to 85/4 in reply to 179/4 declared, which showed that the format of timed games, with cagey, sometimes spiteful declarations, did not particularly lend itself to cavalier cricket.

There may have been a subtext, muses Gresty. "The year before Winston, we had a Barbadian spinner called Alan Rogers, who I think was the first ever overseas player in the Liverpool Competition. There were no professionals allowed. Then came Benji, who knocked sides over one after the other. We regularly bowled teams out for double-figure scores [96, 74, 58, 58, 58, 49 and 42]. The other teams resented it, so when we turned up with another West Indian quick the following year they took umbrage. They went to any lengths to try and stop us winning."

Nevertheless, Ambrose's 6/46 helped beat eventual runners-up St Helen's Recreation in their next jaunt north of the Mersey, trips fondly recalled by Jones, whose job it was to ferry his West Indian warhead about. "I'd given him a red cap, a club cap, which he wore all the time. So when he sat in my car, which had an open-topped roof, with him being six-foot eight, you'd see this red cap sticking through the roof, which was probably quite a sight going through the Mersey Tunnel."

Ambrose neither drove nor drank, "but he'd be perfectly happy for me to spend an hour or so socialising after an away game," adds Jones. "He would potter about looking at old photographs on the clubhouse wall. But once or twice in the season he did come up to me and say, 'I want to go now, man'. So we did."

Perhaps put off by an early-season net session at which he discovered the hard way what stinging nettles were, Ambi wasn't exactly an avid trainer, recalls Jones. Not that too many of his colleagues were unduly vexed about this. "The club has great net facilities now – Lancashire sometimes train there – but at that time they weren't the sort that you'd want to have faced Curtly in."

Unbeaten until the final week of June, yet drawing too many games, Chester suffered a four-game mini-slump of two defeats and a draw that dealt a fatal blow to their hopes of retaining the title. First, they were bowled out for 84 by Southport & Birkdale to lose by 92, then travelled to Huyton in the middle of a heatwave to find the square flooded. "The game was almost called off, it was that bad," recalls Gresty, and Ambrose went wicketless for the fifth time in 13 outings.

Next, it was Northern, whose openers added 30-odd untroubled runs as Ambrose struggled with footholes. Winston Benjamin then dropped in unannounced and, says Jones, the sight of his sponsored car emblazoned with 'Leicestershire CCC' was "like flicking a switch" in his fellow Antiguan, who finished with 7/32 in a straightforward win. After this came a trip up the Wirral to Birkenhead Park – the 15th and final opponent of the first run of fixtures – and a clash with the overseas player that Chester had passed over.

Park made 193/4, Codrington dismissed by the man who had taken his position at Chester, but the visitors were then hustled out for 180, Ambrose chipping in with 45, the last wicket falling to a 49-year-old Tony Shillinglaw, the man who later decoded Don Bradman's 'rotary' batting technique. The victory would propel Park to the title – perhaps Chester *did* have the wrong man – and leave CBH off the pace with a nine-match home stretch left to play, two of which would be lost to the weather.

In those final seven outings, four wins and three draws, Ambrose's returns were that 7/42 against Formby, 5/41, 6/39 (all bowled), 1/27, 2/39, 6/54 (five bowled) and 5/38. One more win would have seen them finish third rather than sixth, yet his colleagues were in no doubt about the Antiguan's quality. It had been amply demonstrated in a tight Liverpool Echo Knockout final, played over two innings of 20 overs, when Bootle had needed 10 off two overs with all 10 wickets intact and Curtly defended three in the final over with a series of laser-guided yorkers.

Warwickshire's Alan Oakman may not have been sufficiently impressed by the Antiguan tyro, yet toward the back end of the season a two-man delegation from Central Lancashire League side Heywood had come to run the rule over Ambrose, with a view to signing him the following year. Bob Cross and John Rhodes, now club president and chairman, were those tasked with the scouting duties, and legend has it that after two balls of his spell Cross turned to Rhodes and said: "I've seen enough, we're having him." They did, but not for free.

Although now defunct, the CLL had a long history of stellar West Indian pros – Garry Sobers and Frank Worrell at Radcliffe, Rohan Kanhai and Sonny Ramadhin at Crompton, Colin Croft, Larry Gomes, Learie Constantine, the ferocious Roy Gilchrist at Middleton – and Ambrose would find a clutch of familiar Caribbean faces throughout the opposition ranks. Unlike the Liverpool Competition, the CLL saw a full home-and-away programme of 48-over matches, 30 fixtures requiring several Sunday and bank holiday appointments. Its 16 clubs were clustered tightly around the northern and eastern fringes of Greater Manchester, and 10 of them had West Indian pros in 1987, including the likes of leg-spinning Jamaican all-rounder Robert Haynes, Joel Garner, Vanburn Holder, Ezra Moseley, and two of Ambrose's fellow Test tourists the following summer, Gus Logie and Carl Hooper. The makings of a steady league rep' team. Certainly something for local batters to ponder.

After the traditional pre-season friendly at Colne had been snowed off, first up in the league was Rochdale, who had the West Indian 'rebel' quick Hartley Alleyne as stand-in pro. The visitors made a good start, adding 87 for the first wicket and reaching 107/1 in the 34th over, with Ambrose's figures, either side of a change of ends, an underwhelming 0/44 off 14. Some of the longer-toothed, I've-seen-'em-all sages that chunter from the sidelines of northern club cricket have been known to reach their final verdict by that stage.

"I asked him what field he wanted," recalls his skipper David Fare, then a veteran 38-year-old left-arm spinner. "He said: 'You de captain, man. You set de field.' He was a man of few words, was Curtly." Indeed he was, and he was also prone to use those few words to talk about how he was a man of few words, usually while referring to himself in the third person. Thus the famous follow-up to a reporter who he'd advised to "ask Curtly if you want to know about Curtly": *Curtly talk to no man.*

Similarly, when Curtly was minded to communicate with Fare, he referred to him not by name, or even by his nickname 'Shag', says Colin Wroe, Heywood's diminutive opening batter and short-leg fielder. "He always called him 'the Heywood captain', even in the bar. 'Ask the Heywood captain.' Or: 'Heywood captain, what number am I batting?' And we didn't know him as 'Ambi', either. He called himself 'CB', which stood for 'Curtly Bouncer'."

This verbal minimalism only added to his on-field aura, notes the Heywood captain, an observation that was also made by Steve Waugh about the man he considered his toughest adversary. "He always made a big thing of going down to the batsman's end before he'd bowled a ball," says Fare, "basically to look at where he wanted to pitch it. Which was fair enough, and he said as much to Wardy [Ian Ward] in an interview on Sky Sports. What he didn't say was that it was also about intimidation. As well as looking at the pitch, he also had a bit of a glare at the batsman. Which at our level you'd probably find quite worrying."

Not that it was working too well on debut. However, after having his end switched by the Heywood captain, Ambrose turned things around reasonably well with a spell of 7.2-3-10-8, finishing with 8/54 as Rochdale were bowled out for 131, which did not prove enough. Indeed, Heywood won three and drew one of the first four games – Ambrose taking 4/67 at Crompton amid sleety conditions, 7/47 against Norden, including the wicket of Logie for 51, and 5/71 against Stockport – but it would prove something of a false dawn as they embarked on an 11-game, 71-day stretch without another league victory.

The first game of this drought exemplified the team's issues. Ambrose chipped in with 9/42 as Littleborough were hustled out for 102, which seemed eminently attainable as Heywood reached a solid 19/0 in reply. This turned out to be half their final total, however, as Ezra Moseley bagged 5/21 and Brian Clarke returned 13-8-15-5. Heywood's batting woes were such that there was only one 60-plus score all season, just four half-centuries, and Curtly, despite telling 'the Heywood captain' he was "a No.3 or No.4", only twice reached 20. ("Curtly had his big pads, but no other gear," recalls Wroe. "He didn't bat in a thigh pad. He had his big bat with five grips and I think he thought he was Clive Lloyd. But it took about one match – a couple of those big lunges – for 'Shag' to realise he wasn't a No.3.")

One of these batting bounties came in the next game of the win-drought, against Ashton. Chasing the visitors' total of 168, Heywood had reached 167/8 – Ambrose on 45* but at the non-striker's end – when Ashton skipper Dave Mellor clean bowled No.10 Vinny Ball, then had No.11 Bob Yardley, son of former England skipper Norman, caught behind without scoring. Mellor finished with career-best figures of 8/43 as Ashton completed a one-run heist, leaving Curtly bewildered and helpless. "He didn't say anything," observes Mellor, "but then the only time he spoke on the field was when he appealed."

The day after the Ashton game, Dipak Patel – who made his Test debut for New Zealand that year, batting at a giddy No.5 – stroked a chanceless, untroubled 103 as sub-pro for Royton. A fortnight later, completing a run of four draws that saw Heywood lose touch with the leaders, Castleton Moor opener John Stapleton, a dustman and semi-pro rugby league player with Rochdale and Swinton, made the same score: 103 out of 176/7. "He hit me flush on the arm second or third ball, which hurt a lot," recalls Stapleton, "but I just got stuck in."

Although Ambrose had not added to his solitary first-class appearance over the preceding winter, he was evidently a high-grade operator. However, a combination of deathly slow pitches and marathon spells meant he was rarely at full tilt. He sent down a whopping 525.2 CLL overs in total. Assuming he had never been taken off or switched ends, the maximum possible amount it could have been was 551.3. With Ambrose's package around £2,500 plus air fare and accommodation, about £4,000 all in (over £11k in today's money), Heywood were keen to get full value. The workload may have blunted his edge, but in any case, says Wroe, the league's history of big-name and/or slippery pros meant that local batters weren't easily spooked, even by the Alpine trajectory of Ambrose. "I could be fitting a clutch at work in the morning, then facing Joel Garner in the afternoon," he says, which indeed he was on the final day of May, with the visit of Oldham.

Garner had had three seasons at Littleborough in the late-70s and was now back in the CLL having been sacked by Somerset (as had Vivian Richards, of course, who was playing 25 miles north, at Rishton of the Lancashire League). In the end, Garner's showdown with the man who would fill the tall-and-parsimonious niche in the West Indies team that he had vacated in March that year failed to catch fire. Ambrose took 3/64 as the visitors made 225/8, which was always going to prove a stiff ask (that 167 against Ashton would be Heywood's highest total of the season), and they stumbled to 122/8, despite Garner only being able to bowl a single spell of 8-4-7-1. Still, 'Big Bird' would go on to top the CLL averages, with 90 wickets at 9.59 (which included two 9/37s, an 8/14 and an 8/15), just pipping Ezra Moseley, whose 119 wickets cost him 9.84 apiece.

The 11th round of matches brought a battle over who would do the week's washing up – Curtly facing off with his flatmate, George Codrington, who had followed his mate over the Pennines and was now pro at Walsden, where the pair of them lodged. Ambrose still had no driver's licence by this stage, so would often catch the bus from Walsden down through Rochdale to Heywood, or the train into Manchester Victoria before connecting over to Chester, where he often passed his weekdays staying with Jenson Joseph, fellow Antiguan and that year's Viv Richards Scholar. Meanwhile, it was down to Wroe and Yardley to ferry Ambi back home to Walsden after matches. "We usually stopped off for KFC," Wroe recalls. "But he'd always say: 'No wings, man!' He used to come and have tea with me and the wife, too, then I'd take him home, or over to Rochdale to get the bus. He'd leave his bag outside the front door.

I'd say, 'Why are you doing that?' He said, 'Well who's going to pinch it?' Life was a bit different in Antigua."

The Walsden game saw Heywood bowl first for an 11th straight league game, Codrington top-scoring with 31 on a damp day as Ambrose's relatively expensive figures of 5/61 helped dismiss their hosts for 97. In reply, Heywood nudged to 63/3, before a remarkable spell of 9-7-6-5 from Chris Barker bundled them out for 85. Calamitous it may have been, but at least Ambrose didn't need a lift home to make a start on those dishes.

The following weekend, he took 6/71 and 7/47 in a pair of defeats – Middleton's Trinidadian pro Kelvin Williams making 99* out of 162/7 in the first, Heywood 55 all out chasing 145 in the second – before the final Saturday in June saw a trip to Werneth, one of the CLL's smaller grounds, and a toe-to-toe with Carl Hooper. The game started two hours late, and was reduced to 29 overs each. It was a no-contest.

Hooper, a man who once took off his thigh pad against Lancashire at Old Trafford because his gloves were catching on it when dealing with Wasim Akram's nip-backers, smashed eight sixes and five fours in a 62-ball hundred, finishing with 101* as Ambrose travelled to the tune of 15-0-91-0. "Carl just kept depositing Curtly into the school yard over the leg-side boundary," observes Fare. The ball wasn't the only thing that went to school that afternoon.

Chastened he may have been, but figures of 4/54 against Hyde gave Ambrose 74 league wickets at the halfway point of the marathon campaign. The second half of the season saw only nine games survive the rheumy Pennine weather, however, with six cancellations denying Ambrose the chance to achieve something very special, perhaps approaching what Roy Gilchrist had done, with 137 and 145 wickets in back-to-back seasons for Middleton. As it turned out, his mauling by Hooper kicked off a six-game streak without a five-for, during which his best figures, 4/42 against Littleborough, were again put in the shade by Ezra Moseley, who took 7/40.

Ambrose's batting had also fallen off a cliff by this stage – there was only one score over 10 in 17 innings after that 45* at Ashton – but amid the late-August rains he picked up 6/55, 4/56 and 6/58, piquing interest at Northamptonshire, who invited him down to trial in the lead-up week to their NatWest Trophy final against

Nottinghamshire, which started on a drizzly Saturday and finished on a Monday, with a Sunday League game in between.

"He was over in Chester visiting Jenson Joseph," recalls Moss, "when I get a call from Steve Coverdale at Northants. He said, 'We're very interested in Ambrose' and asked him down to bowl a few overs so they could have a look at him. I called Curtly and said, 'Good news: Northants are interested. Come down to the office.' He said 'I'm busy, man.' I said, 'What's wrong with you? Do you want to be a cricketer or not?' He said, 'I'm busy, man,' which meant he had a girl round there.

"Anyway, he came over and I told him Northants were going to offer him £4,000 a year, which wasn't a lot, and he said, 'I don't know'. I said, 'I'm going out of the room for five minutes and when I get back you can tell me whether you want to be a cricketer or not'. He said he'd go, then I said he had to go smart: 'We'll go to Marks & Spencer and get you a shirt, tie and jacket'. He says, 'No, I'm not doing that'. After a bit of negotiation, we settled on a sweater rather than a jacket, with a shirt and tie, and that's how he went.

"He missed the train, but eventually got there. Next day, Steve Coverdale rings me up and says, 'Oh my god, he nearly knocked Allan Lamb's head off. We had to tell him to calm down because we had the NatWest final the next day.' They offered him just short of £4,000, sent the contract to me, but by that stage he'd gone back to Antigua."

Back in Lancashire, the cancelled games meant no return encounters with Hooper or Logie – whose 1,342 runs at 63.90 for champions Norden were top on both accounts – but the feelgood vibes of the Northants trial fed directly into a devastating spell of 16-8-21-8 at Hyde in what turned out to be his final gallop at Heywood's Crimble ground.

If Hyde was the best of Ambrose, his last appearance in English club cricket was more Dr Jekyll. Perhaps having mentally clocked off – it was also the day before his birthday – he was carted all round Rochdale by Robert Haynes, who made 71 in a chase of 109 as Ambrose disappeared for 8-0-51-0. Not the ideal way to sign off. Heywood had finished a disappointing 11th, although Ambrose's 109 league wickets at 12.48 – higher than his batting average, denying him his coveted all-rounder status – was a substantial return. Now

24, with an enormous volume of club-cricket overs under his belt, he was ready for take-off.

"At the end of November," continues Moss, "Coverdale rang me, saying Curtly hadn't sent the contract back yet. By the end of February, he'd broken the Red Stripe Cup record for most wickets, but still hadn't sent the contract through. Steve rang again to say he was doubling the money, at which point Curtly signed it and sent it over."

By April, he was debuting against Pakistan, and by June he was touring England, where colleagues from both clubs caught up with their former spearhead at the Old Trafford Test. Ambrose also brought the West Indies squad down to Chester Boughton Hall for a social game, with Desmond captaining and Viv looking on, but by that stage the 22-year-old who'd turned up on a scholarship, slipping and sliding like Bambi through his opening spell on English soil, had turned into the real-deal terminator, albeit still one with whom communication could be challenging, as Colin Wroe discovered.

"I caught up with him at one of the Tests and told him I was going to write him a letter and asked for an address. He said, 'Send it to "Curtly Ambrose, Swetes Village, Antigua". It *will* find me'."

11

Imran Tahir
at Moddershall CC

It is difficult to say with complete certainty, but as far as I am aware the question "Name something associated with the cricketer Imran Tahir" is yet to have featured on *Family Fortunes*. However, if it did, chances are that the top two answers would concern his inimitably demented wicket celebrations – not everyone's cup of tea, true, with grumblings about it being over-the-top to the point of contrivance – and, in second place, to win a state-of-the-art vegetable dicer, the enormous pile of teams he has managed to rack up: 31 professional sides, a multitude of invitational and international teams, a handful of English clubs.

In among that list, while Imran was still navigating the uncertain waters of his pre-international years, came a two-part stint at my own club, Moddershall of the North Staffordshire & South Cheshire League, during which time, despite us playing in front of three men and their dogs, we were occasional witnesses to the full unencumbered iteration of that celebration, and can thus vouch not only for its spontaneity and authenticity but also Imran's humility and all-in dedication to our cause. So much so, in fact, that one frenzied sprint into the outfield hinterlands – the kind of moment that comes only from a place of total commitment, with a dash of the irrepressible inner child's undimmed love of the game – kept me psychologically nourished for several months during one of the most difficult periods of my life. Indeed, it left a lifelong mark on everyone who was part of it.

Before all that, though, his first club cricket port-of-call was Kidsgrove of the NSSCL's second tier, arriving in 1999 just a few weeks after his 20th birthday for what turned out to be a three-year spell. "At first, the club put him in a house in Shelton [in Stoke]," recalls Mandy Green. "Two or three weeks into the season, I dropped him off after the game. The place was a dump, so I told him he had to come and live with me. Richard [her son] moved into my room and Immy took Richard's."

Aside from bowling all day in the back garden at her then 10-year-old boy (and future Moddershall teammate), Green's lodger is chiefly remembered for "making curries at very strange times of day and having the heating on full-blast in the middle of summer", as well as throwing some enthusiastic shapes at club socials whenever the summer's hit *Cotton Eye Joe* was played, dance moves that were soon dubbed "The Immy Shimmy". At the end of that first year, having heard that Imran's agent had been withholding part of his wages, the club held an impromptu fundraiser, raising £600 to cover any losses and ensure he felt properly looked after.

For the next two years, he lodged with Dave and Dawn Rigby, who took him into their family to such an extent that, over 20 years later, Imran still calls Dawn his "second Mum". The Rigbys kept him occupied, starting with what was supposed to be a leisurely early-season walking tour of the Lake District that Atlantic weather systems soon turned into an arduous yomp up several rain-lashed hills. Dave also took Imran ten-pin bowling and to the snooker hall, and was more than a little surprised when he knocked in a 37 break on his first visit to the table. "I said, 'You've played this before, haven't you?' and he just smiled." However, while this domestic stability gave Imran the best platform on which to perform, it was Dave's VHS collection that would have the biggest effect on things, short and long term. "I had the Richie Benaud leg-spin video," he recalls, "which showed Terry Jenner demonstrating how to bowl a flipper, flicking this ball off his fingers. Immy watched this and within a couple of hours he had it perfected. Probably just as well, given how many catches we dropped off him!"

Despite the clumsy fielding, Imran's stay at Kidsgrove brought respectable hauls of 75 and 70 wickets in his first two years and a stellar 95 in his third – 240 at 13.63 all in – but it wasn't enough to bootstrap them into the top flight, and for the 2002 season he was snapped up by Norton-in-Hales, a village just over the Shropshire border about to embark upon a maiden Premier League campaign. It went quite well: 'The Tractor Boys' became only the second newly promoted team to win the title – replicating Moddershall's achievement of five years earlier – with Imran taking a league-record 104 wickets at 10.45, eclipsing Garry Sobers' 97 in 1964.

By then, Imran was back living among the student housing in Shelton's tight grid of terraced streets, although he had become fast friends with his new teammate Ramzan Mohammed, who he accompanied on delivery runs for the latter's fledgling takeaway firm, knocking on doors with bags of spicy food then heading back to base camp for "burnt roti, burnt naan, or burnt pitta; he always had to have it burnt". To kill time between his weekend five-fors, Imran would spend hours watching Pakistani movies in the upstairs office at Rendezvous Fast Food, which also became an informal English Language School, with Ramzan formulating sentences in Urdu then having the gaggle of Pakistani pros translate them back to him. Practical stuff. Like, "Which stump is that missing, umpire?"

Imran added a further 74 wickets in 2003, again finishing as the division's top wicket-taker, albeit with the team slipping back to third. At which point, Moddershall decided to swoop, a somewhat counter-intuitive move given that we had beaten them in all four league encounters, taking 95 points from three bat-first wins and a chase – yours truly with 47* in the latter, an innings in which Immy would probably have burned all the three reviews as I padded up to wrong'uns, the umpire playing a *blinder.* Imran collected just seven wickets as we swept and slog-swept him to distraction, a tactic admittedly borne of not being able to pick him. Bamboozlement is the mother of necessity, and we all know whose mum that is.

With Immy on board, the local paper immediately installed us as joint-favourites for the 2004 title alongside champions Longton, with whom we'd been dancing an eight-year vendetta ever since our star 21-year-old batter Richard Harvey had signed for them. We had been through a few years of transition after the successes of the late-1990s – that 1997 title, backed up with a league and couple double in 1999 – and were emerging again as genuine challengers, finishing fourth in 2003 with West Indies Test quick Adam Sanford as pro, as well as making the final of the Staffordshire Cup (I won Player of the Match in defeat, a proud moment for my mother as she handed me £20 and an invitation to have a drink on her; she was somewhat less proud 15 hours later, when I shambled out of Longton police station wearing an unrippable, anti-suicide jumpsuit with sick-covered clothes in a carrier bag, no phone or money, having essentially forgotten to eat any food for a day, passing out in a pub car park and, apparently, flailing semi-consciously at some paramedics). *The Sentinel*'s prediction very much didn't pan out, however, with the new pro's settling-in period probably not helped by the club's decision to have a pig roast on the opening day of the season, the coals fired up and carcass mounted before the start of play. Something of a cultural oversight.

The first four league games brought two defeats, a draw and an abandonment, enough time for our greenhorn new captain to alienate several senior players, especially sidelined bowlers. With the dressing room on the cusp of mutiny, the skipper jumped ship, leaving the club altogether, and I was asked to step in. Notionally in the writing-up year of my PhD, I knew I wasn't going to finish on time, so accepted. It had been a rocky start – six winless games in, Immy's combined figures stood at 10/319 – but we stabilised in the league, losing only once more, Imran eventually pushing himself up to second in the divisional wicket charts, although a slew of draws ultimately resulted in a disappointing eighth-place finish.

If Saturdays were a grind that first year, Sundays were a different matter. We won the club's sole Staffordshire Cup and, before that, reached the final of the Talbot Cup, losing at Audley, a day when I had to stand in as wicketkeeper – a job I didn't enjoy at the best of times, even more so after spending the previous day getting sizably oiled at a close friend's wedding in Cambridgeshire, which meant a four-hour, thick-headed trek across the country and a T-20 minutes arrival time, not ideal for a cup final. I dropped my kit in the dressing room and, still in my civvies, walked out to lose the toss. Audley batted and soon got ahead of the game, at which point I reached for the Immy button in an attempt to take out their pro.

A sylph-like left-hander later branded a cheat by the High Court judge who ruled in the Chris Cairns vs Lalit Modi match-fixing libel trial, TP Singh was among the few South Asians batters unable to pick Immy. The problem was, neither could I. Another problem was that Imran kept forgetting to give me the signal for his googly – previously a tug on his shirt or jumper but recently changed in a moment of McCarthyite paranoia to a quick scratch of his bowling mark – and so when Singh skipped down the pitch to assert himself on things, the ball beat both stranded batter's outside edge and reluctant, fuzzy-headed wicketkeeper's gloves and skipped away for four byes. Next over from Immy, same thing: TP down the pitch to an unsignalled googly, missed stumping, four byes. It was a sultry August day, the air was fast coming out of our tyres and my chill-o-meter was now at volcano. "Immy, for f**k's sake, I told you: *I need the signal for the googly!*" "Sorry, skipper. Next time." "Just do it subtly. I'll be watching you like a hawk." Third ball of his next over, TP back on strike, Imran was stood at the top of his run, scratching his mark like a cartoon bull about to charge, eyes glaring straight down the pitch at me. Oh, Immy.

Imran had by then become fully integrated into the club, beavering away in the kitchen one night to heat up two large vats of curry he'd made, and, at the end-of-season do – after I'd petitioned the DJ to cut through the mainstream musical offerings with a wonky underground house cut that briefly threatened to empty the dancefloor – throwing some fierce (and, for me, face-saving) shapes that soon had the more adventurous souls bouncing around him. The track was 'Mars' by Tiefschwarz, and Immy insisted I had it played again later, around midnight, by which time his English teammates had quaffed just about enough Inhibition Reducer to bust out their own moves. Out of the trophy cabinet and into this throbbing delirium came the Staffs Cup, Immy taking it on a sassy little strut around the dancefloor. A beautiful moment.

Buoyed by the two cup runs, we were ready to hurl ourselves into a proper title challenge in 2005, this time winning three of the first four with Imran taking 5/29, 3/11, and 7/63 against Betley, in which he snared the final wicket from the penultimate ball of the match, a stiff-backed poke to gully from ex-England man Rob Bailey's brother, before setting off on a sprint out toward a distant postcode at deep cover, which did not go down well with the opposition, one of whom grabbed me round the throat as we left the field.

Our arch-rivals Longton – coming off back-to-back titles and having strengthened their team with an eighth Minor Counties player and Alfonso Thomas as overseas pro – remained the team to beat. By the time we played them at our place in the ninth round of matches – a game watched, bizarrely, by Pakistan head coach Bob Woolmer, there to scout Immy, who at that stage still hoped to play for the land of his birth – we were joint leaders on 121 points.

The game ebbed and flowed. We had them in trouble at 128/7, but I was later talked into taking the new ball at 55 overs, a tactical error. They recovered to 216. We lost early wickets, then Iain Carr and I took it from 20/3 to 99 without further loss, at which point – amidst a bumper barrage from Alfonso, Iain hooking, me ducking – I declined an offer of bad light, something I would regret when we found ourselves eight down with six overs left and two teenagers at the crease (one of them Mandy Green's son). But we survived. And by the time we met them again for the third-last game, Imran's final outing of the season before heading back to Pakistan, we held a 17-point lead (which would have been 34 but for a bungled home defeat to eventually relegated Betley), having picked up seven wins from 10 games, Immy contributing a steady 8/56, 4/64, 7/42, 7/68, 6/33, 4/15 and 7/67 to those victories. It was the moment of truth. Could we hold off one of the NSSCL's strongest ever teams and deliver a third title?

They had prepared a hard, green, Immy-proof pitch. For the second straight season at Longton, I faced a dilemma at the toss. A year earlier, out of the title race but with the not-negligible incentive of throwing a spanner in their works, I had put the decision to a vote for the only time in what would be nine years of captaincy. The sweltering July heat said bat, the pitch said bowl. The vote went 7/3 in favour of batting, so I popped next door to inform them we would have a bowl, then publicly told the team's three pro-bowl 'emotional thermostats' – Iain, his brother Darren and John Myatt, 60 per cent of our bowling resources – that if it went tits-up it was on them. Immy was duly neutralised by the surface, but Iain bowled like a man possessed – swing, bounce, decent pace – to take 9/51, although eight or nine overs in, with five for spit and a face like a grilled tomato, he was trying to get himself taken off. "Mate, you're beating the bat three times an over, I can't do that."

Chasing 115, we fell to 25/5, but got over the line thanks to an unbeaten 47 from a not very pretty but extremely gritty second-teamer who had come off at tea, after 40 minutes of having his technique brutally deconstructed, saying "there's no way these c***s are winning this". A great day. We may even have phoned the bar from our dressing room, pretending to be the Pakistani pro of their main rivals, curious and then flabbergasted about the result. Twelve months later would not be quite so tip-top.

The dilemma at the toss in 2005 was this: if we batted first, thereby restricting them to a maximum 20 points, we would need to pick up four points to ensure still being top of the table when we started the car to leave (although pragmatic, this felt a little too much like accepting the likelihood of defeat). If we bowled first (opening up the 25-point win for them) and lost, we would need nine points to remain masters of our destiny, which was quite a lot considering there were only 10 bonus points available. In the end, perusing the grassy surface and unable or unwilling to strategise around an 'acceptable' defeat, I made the 'safe' or perhaps macho call – either way, wrong – and put them in, gambling on another heroic bowling performance from our seamers and/or our ability to bat out for a draw. They made 191/9 (Immy 23-7-67-1) and blitzed us out for 55 – itself something of a recovery from 21/8 – emerging from the game with a four-point lead, which they maintained for the final two games to complete the NSSCL three-peat. It was, by a considerable distance, my worst day as a cricketer. And when Imran compounded the misery by fulfilling a promise to a friend known as 'Tango' to sign for our nearest neighbours Meir Heath (Everton to our Liverpool, with Longton as Manchester United), it looked like being his final act in a Moddershall shirt. A story of what might have been.

The emotional toll of it all was one of the main factors in me playing the next two years in Nottingham, where I was living. But there were also the difficulties I was having with my PhD, which I already knew – long before that evisceration at Longton – was going to run into a second extension (which is to say, a second blagged depression diagnosis, although perhaps at some stage life did begin to imitate art). The reasons for my tardiness? The Spanish language component of my teaching commitments, which induced acute imposter syndrome; taking a year to come up with an object of study, Peronist Argentina, then biting off an initially unchewable morsel of esoteric French philosophy and pursuing it across the oceans like Moby Dick until I could properly grasp it; undiagnosed (and unrecognised) Attention Deficit Disorder, along with the various coping mechanisms, the amateur self-medications; low self-esteem from not being able to push forward, along with a generalised anxiety shading into occasional panic attacks and guilt about not turning over work to my supervisor; and, I suppose, a reluctance to forego the time-consuming escape valve of cricket, even at the cost of building an academic career.

Things were going pretty badly, and in June 2006 they got a whole lot worse. I was burgled. While I was in the house. They took my laptop, which just so happened to have all the very recently backed-up copies of my thesis attached to it. I lost 15 months' work: 65,000 words (let's not dwell on the fact that this was still just the theory chapter, which I was doing first, against all received wisdom, and which should have been about one sixth of the strict 100,000 total word count, not 65 per cent). It was utterly devastating. I felt numb with shock. I didn't even tell my supervisor. I just sat and watched the World Cup. Then I had an enormous stroke of luck.

My best mate had just started a sales job, flogging advertising space on the website of Real Estate TV to property companies. These were the bounteous, pre-Crash years, money being flung about. I tagged along with him to Turkey and, despite knowing nothing about property and having no sales experience, made £3,750 in commissions in 10 days, significantly more than the £60-a-week Jobseeker's Allowance I'd been claiming. So I told my supervisor I was deferring my third extension by a year and went gallivanting around the Mediterranean and Caribbean – work to which I was probably better suited, neurologically speaking, than academic research – before it became apparent that the guy selling the service to RETV was a spiv and things began to peter out. Late summer 2007, motivation low, I turned back to the thesis, and early the next year took a call from 'Mr Moddershall' Andy Hawkins, a long-time teammate. "Dog, would you fancy coming back as captain? Oh, we've signed Immy again."

There was a catch, however. I had to attend practice and selection, to be hands-on after a difficult couple of seasons. This meant leaving Nottingham. It also meant leaving Wollaton CC after two hugely enjoyable years there. It was a wrench, but I had a think, fixed up a place to live, and agreed. Then the room fell through, which meant moving back in with my folks at 35 years old. These were not my happiest days. I would have to pour everything into the cricket.

But there was more bad news: four important first-teamers were no longer going to be available, players responsible for 60 per cent of the overs bowled by amateurs the previous year, including both off-spinners, an all-rounder who scored 575 runs (Richard Holloway, Mandy Green's son), and the team's best player and outgoing skipper, Iain, who disagreed in principle with me coming straight back in as captain and, worse, had read a recent email exchange between Hawk and myself containing some moderate criticisms of his tactical acumen. The net result was the considerable thinning-out of a team that had finished one place above the relegation trapdoor in 2007.

* * *

This, then, was the situation that Immy had rejoined. A dressing room still scarred by that humiliation on the home turf of our biggest rivals, still haunted by the narrow failure to take down the best side we would ever play against. A team that was, on paper, a pale imitation of the one that had pushed Longton so hard in 2005, the team that had won the Staffs Cup in 2004. A captain who was using cricket to stave off the circling misery that came with spending hundreds of hours doing something very difficult that wasn't leading to anything tangible. Welcome back, Immy *bhai*.

I was not optimistic about things, although we did have Imran, who was if anything even more hawkishly motivated to get the most out of his career following some profound changes in his life. Late in 2006, after his 76 wickets had kept Meir Heath in the top division and two games into the Patron's Trophy campaign for PIA, he lost his father, whose dream it had been to see his boy play for Pakistan. He never appeared in another first-class match there. Heartbroken, he headed to Stoke to spend some time with Ramzan, then flew to Durban and married Sumayya Dildar, a recently rekindled old flame first lit during the 1998 under-19 World Cup in South Africa. He spent the following summer pro-ing at Marton in Durham before that winter setting out on the road to Proteas qualification, playing for Titans under the captaincy of Martin van Jaarsveld, who was not averse to whipping him out of the attack if he overdid his variations. Noted, although never exercised.

So, we were four players down, but we still had Imran. There were also a couple of last-minute signings: Ali Whiston, a 22-year-old wicketkeeper who, mercifully, was able to pick Imran's variations without sub-KGB jumper-tugs, and Amer Siddique, a top-order batter whose younger brother Hamza, on a summer contract at Derbyshire, had been the original target (two years later, I would visit the family's swanky rasoi restaurant on this very mission, albeit having picked up the norovirus on a hospital visit that afternoon, which meant spending the whole meeting running to the toilet and unable to take a single bite of the excellent food). Amer was a confident boy. He came to our indoor nets before having put ink to transfer forms and announced that he was "the best looking Asian in Britain". Not too long after this, our sole surviving experienced first-team bowler, Shaun 'Moose' Brian, not necessarily thinking big-picture, scudded a bouncer into his grille, potentially jeopardising everything. Sake, Moose.

It was at this same pre-season net session that I had something of an epiphany, telling our 45-year-old opening bat, Roger Shaw – who was coming off a hip operation that had forced him to miss a season and stand down from his role as wicketkeeper – that his rolled-out, barely turning, yet unfailingly accurate offies could do a job, despite him never before having bowled a ball in first XI cricket. It was a punt, but then he wasn't one of life's great worriers and our pantry was bare. Two new faces; still a little rag-tag; but we did have Immy. Not for the first game, though.

In his absence, we drafted in a 40-year-old Chris Lewis as sub-pro, six years after his retirement, eight months before he was arrested at Gatwick for attempting to smuggle 3.37kg of liquid cocaine into the country. He had also just been snapped up by Surrey on a pay-as-you-play T20 contract, and so it was that on a freezing cold day at our exposed, hilltop ground, with the opposition tumbling to 24/4 and me suggesting to him that one more wicket would break them open, Lewis threw himself into a 30-over spell (2/43) in several sweaters and brown Surrey beanie, that beautiful action as liquid as ever. At tea, he picked up a message from the Surrey coach telling him there had been an outbreak of food poisoning in the camp and he was needed for their Friends Provident derby game against Middlesex the next day at The Oval, in which he sent down 6-0-51-0, with Cricinfo reporting that he "looked decidedly rusty". Erm.

After tea, as we huddled in the dressing room from the knifing winds outside, and Hawk and Rog laid a solid 57-run foundation to our pursuit of 155, Chris was amiable and extremely garrulous company, curious about our league and mentioning apropos that one or two of the pros we were due to face had dabbled with the old Colombian marching powder. He disappeared to his car, from where he had to be fetched as wickets tumbled and 57/0 became 59/4 in 11 balls, Lewis the fourth of them, heading into the Patagonia outside still velcroing down various pads after a panicked rummage through his kit, then somewhat scattily chipping his second ball to mid-on for a duck. Nevertheless, Amer and I took it to 127 without further alarm, at which point Porthill started grousing about the gloom and a particularly self-important umpire produced the first ever light meter I had seen in a club game and promptly marched us off, leading the usually placid Hawk to angrily confront the officious gizmo-wielder. His outburst was the first sign of just how much of a struggle the last couple of years had been.

* * *

Thankfully, Immy had arrived in time for the next game, at Longton, scene of his most recent appearance, the ghosts still hovering. Once again, he found a green, nibbly surface – fine: we hadn't expected them to roll out a straw carpet – and he finished with a third straight one-for (1/89) down there. Rog nipped in with 2/14, his first senior wickets, but with our one experienced seamer, Moose, a skiddy swing bowler unsuited to the conditions, and the rest of the attack too callow and inconsistent to build pressure – albeit, Rob Bagnall did nip out their pro, Nathan Astle, for 28 – Longton posted 238/8 from 56 overs, leaving us 54 to chase against a decent six-man seam attack. I felt it was too much and, swerving the proto-Bazball approach, instructed the team to bat for the 175 (a maximum five batting points), building confidence for another day. We finished on 195/7, Britain's Best Looking Asian with 68.

After the match, the captains met to mark the umpires. Unusually, they were party to our deliberations, a new gimmick designed to promote greater harmony between players and officials but in the end only really serving to suppress genuine honesty. Astle told me he was "surprised [we] didn't take the chase on". I told him I was surprised he didn't declare earlier, that I felt he batted on two or three overs too long, suggesting this was because he didn't really know the strength of our team – although he may have remembered Moose from the beamer a year earlier that trapped his fingers against the bat handle – or the state of our collective confidence. He then told me he thought we were "a bit negative" and that we should have "gone hard up front, maybe for a couple of wickets, then re-assessed". I told him I was surprised that, with 238 on the board, he had moved his second slip out after our very first scoring shot, a push through extra cover for two. The conversation had by this point hit something of a cul-de-sac, so we signed the forms, shook hands, and went our separate ways. I popped into the bar and had a beer with a couple of old adversaries from the 2005 shellacking, telling them I was worried about relegation. "Nah, you'll be fine," they said. "Immy'll win you a couple of games."

Not the next game, however, when we went down to Leek by 166 runs, with a couple of hundred people braving the brisk winds at Moddershall to witness the debut of their new pro, Tino la Bertram Best, four years on from a ferocious spell in Jamaica that Mark Butcher would later describe as being "as quick as anything I faced in Test cricket". I won the toss, an opportunity to defer the realisation of my fever-dreams by a few hours, and Leek were given a rollocking start by openers Tim Tweats, co-holder of Derbyshire's record partnership for any wicket, and Rob King, a buccaneering Staffs player and postman who later had the misfortune of winning just £10 on the gameshow *Deal or No Deal*.

In an effort to give our amateur bowlers a little help, I asked Immy to bowl into the wind. He wasn't happy about this and, after serving up a pair of shin-high full-tosses to Worcestershire staffer Dave Wheeldon, snatched his sweater from the umpire and rasped: "I'm not a f***ing league bowler, man", a response that was both sub-optimal and a complete surprise, the only peep of anything other than total commitment in three seasons. I replaced him at that end with my rarely-seen ultra-medoes, burgled a caught-and-bowled, and generally ghosted a profusely apologetic Immy for half an hour before explaining to him that, while with us, a league bowler is precisely what he was. He came back on and finished with 2/83 from 17 overs, taking a little bit of late tap from Tino – who had launched his very first ball, from Moose, miles over the pavilion, a shot which, disappointingly if understandably, had elicited precisely zero "mind the windows" quips. Leek declared on 255/4 with 15 overs unused. Oof.

It was the longest tea, through which I mainly smoked. I did find time to suggest to Rog, a compulsive hooker, that although the pitch was sluggish it might be an idea to have a look at one before taking it on, which he completely ignored, getting off the mark with a hook for four. Barrelling in downwind, Tino soon burst one through his defences, as he did to Hawk and Amer, and we were 39/4 when I trudged out past a grinning Tweatsie at second slip, an old pal from imaginary Test matches and sweet-shop missions back when our fathers played together. "He's f***ing quick, mucker," Tim helpfully observed, wild eyed and almost cackling with glee. Given that he was fielding closer to the boundary than the wicket, this had not escaped me. Tino was indeed getting it from A to B at haste.

Shortening my backlift to around 5:27pm, I managed three scoring shots off him in 20-odd balls of reflex-bothering rearguardery: a jabbed two to long leg from a bumper that only made it to chest high, the second run more or less obliged by Kingy's bottle-querying shout of "one's the call, steady one" from mid-off; an inadvertent Natmeg for two from a yorker dug out to deep square-leg, just about averting several broken pinkies; and finally, becoming more accustomed to the sci-fi velocity I was being asked to operate at, a bunted cover drive for four that drew non-sarcastic applause from a bowler who had hitherto been exhorting me to "play some shots, Geoffrey, the crowd come to see it". (I flashed back, "Well, if you slip me a full toss to get me going, that would help," forgetting the possible height range for that type of delivery.) By then, Immy had holed out in the deep off a spinner, a pretty standard dismissal of his, and at 89/7 – a total to which we would add no further runs – I got myself stumped for 27, with Rog's 10 the only other double-figure score. An absolute todgering. Three miserable points. Renewed thoughts of relegation.

We would fail to win either of the next two games, although did score 245/8 against a Knypersley side featuring future Protea Lonwabo Tsotsobe and former England batter Kim Barnett, with the bulk of the runs made by spin twins Rog (87) and Imran (73). Knypersley finished on 166/9, Immy's figures on an unresponsive

262

pitch a disappointing 1/64. Rog, meanwhile, just lobbed it on the spot and snared a career-best 4/34, giving him season's figures of 7/73 to Imran's 4/236. We weren't quite at the stage where Rog would be getting choice of end, but his strike-rate at this point was 18.86 while the future T20 and ODI world No.1 bowler's sat at a flabby and concerning 102. Immy did then pick up 4/33 against Stone, a rain-reduced game in which, crucial toss lost, we were unable to force a victory, and so five winless games in we had just 42 points, 60 fewer than Burslem, who had won all five, the most recent against Leek, for whom Tino was beginning to lose the plot.

Our next outing, a trip to promoted Stafford, already felt like a must-win, although this outcome didn't seem likely at 65/4 on a hard and bouncy shirt-fronter. Nevertheless, in one of the season's crucial turning points, myself and Simon Hemmings, a free-spirited 20-year-old shot-maker, added 133, the pair of us benefiting from a bespoke session of sweeping practice at training as the former Sri Lankan Test spinner Niroshan Bandaratilleke took 1/100 from 27 overs of toil. Shemm fell for 80, Immy came in and pongoed a 19-ball unbeaten 40, the skipper made 67* and we declared at 250/5. Immy then asked for the new ball, and bowled unchanged to take 6/66, Rog also nipping in with 2/15 to break some late resistance. We had 25 points. More importantly, we had a template for winning. This was laid out by Andy Hawkins, a *Dragons' Den* pitch to which I offered the full amount without asking for any more equity. "I'm in."

* * *

With both our openers the wrong side of 40 and high summer approaching, it made little sense for them to field for three-and-a-half hours before batting. Moreover, the middle order were 23, 15 and 20 years old, and setting targets was less psychologically taxing than chasing them. The plan, then, devilishly simple, was that we would bat first – 25 points for a win, as opposed to 20 chasing – exploiting the potential 60-50 split in overs if we needed to, and ideally asking the opposition to chase north of 200 with Imran bowling half our overs (the fact that they could take our new ball at 55 overs and try and damage it as much as possible, standard practice, only helped us in this approach). Furthermore, at home, Imran's bowling would be on pitches giving him the maximum possible assistance, without completely taking the piss. (I say 'pitches': actually, until August 9, it was *pitch*, singular.) I would not over-attack to begin with, only encircling the batters once we had pushed the required rate above 4.5 per over. With Immy unlikely to go at over threes in most conditions, that meant the motley crew of part-timers and non-bankers at the other end just had to keep it to below sixes and the opposition couldn't win. That was the theory, anyway.

Next game, against leaders Burslem, we declared at 250/5 and knocked them over for 139, Immy taking 6/62. A week later, at third-bottom Barlaston, we fought our way to 205 all out, our 20-year-old No.10 Martin Weston flaying 30, then rolled them for 106 in response, Immy bagging 6/27 to make it 75 points from three games as we moved into fourth place, eight points off top. *Hello.*

More good news followed when we heard that Leek had sacked Tino Best after just six weeks, attempting to get out in front of a near-certain ban from the league (which they nevertheless contested when it came, allowing them to play a sub-pro until the appeal was heard). The first cracks had appeared in defeat at Burslem, when a ragged opening over went for 17 and later, after hitting their skipper on the forearm with a bumper, followed up with "I hope I f***ing broke it", he was roundly booed from the field. A couple of weeks later, against Audley, he bowled a deliberate beamer at a batter who, distracted by kids running in front of the screen, had had the temerity to pull away as Best was approaching delivery stride. Finally, at Longton, he accused an umpire of being racist for turning down lbw appeals. He then refused to bowl, telling his skipper "the black man always has to do the white man's work", eventually returning to the attack, being smashed by Astle, whereupon he began whistling slave songs and bowling off-spin.

Our next outing, game nine, on a hot day at Moddershall against champions Audley – the afternoon when The Pitch really started to turn crusty – was almost the quintessential performance for a team without prime-age top-rank league players. We posted a solid 219, with four batters making between 35 and 40, plus a cameo 23 from England under-15s player Sam Kelsall, who smoked four boundaries in one over from another future Protea, 'Rusty' Theron, who wasn't bowling slowly. We then reduced them to 8/3, and things seemed to be following the familiar pattern, yet the next pair munched 180 balls between them to slow the stampede. Nevertheless, we took the ninth wicket with three overs left, Immy whirling away for 5/48 from 26 overs, but the last pair negotiated a few vociferous appeals to prevent us making it 100 points from four.

Meanwhile, with appeal pending and sub-pro on board, Leek won, as they would a week later when, fortuitously, everyone else was rained off. Tino's ban was finally enforced ahead of the last match of the outward leg of the season, which Leek nevertheless won at a canter against bottom side Barlaston. We stayed in touch by picking up 25 at Little Stoke, veterans Hawk (98) and Rog (63) laying a foundation for Immy to move up to first-drop and tee-off (he never needed much encouragement). He smote three enormous sixes in a 16-ball 31, following up with 5/66 in a 62-run win that still needed a crucial 3/13 from veteran novice Rog as the draw loomed into view. At halfway, we were 31 points behind Leek in third, Immy having sent down 135.2-42-322-32 in the seven games since that sticky start. Ominous form.

The first game of the homeward leg saw my sole departure from the bat-first template, with the combination of a grassy surface at Porthill and a week of Imran hyping their pro, Fazl-e-Akbar, as the most skilful seamer in Pakistan leading me to insert. Anticipating it to nip around, I even declined to give Immy the new ball – a regular occurrence in his first two years but almost inconceivable under current circumstances. When he did come on, 12 overs in, he sent down a mindbending 16.4-8-8-5, all eight runs coming behind square. It was a phenomenal display, leaving us a chase of 105, which wasn't necessarily going to be a stroll, given Akbar's pedigree. He had shared the new ball with Waqar Younis on Test debut 10 years earlier, picking up Gary Kirsten as a first international wicket, and the first ball of our innings, pitching back-of-a-length outside the left-handed Hawk's leg stump, seamed straight to first slip with the keeper heading down the leg-side. *Okay then.* However, amid a lot of play-and-missing, we scampered home, four down (entering with 20 needed, I went full McCullum and charged at my first two balls from Fazl, both of which were sent flying over second slip for four), before the heavy black storm clouds could do their worst.

Next up was the visit of Longton, by which time The Pitch, lovingly patched up and thrown back into action, was close to its phase-transition from *crusty* to *crumbly*. Astle didn't look overly impressed with it at the toss – wiping dust from the coin, I told him we would bat – but any embarrassment I might have felt about such flagrant advantage-seeking evaporated at the merest thought of the three green flyers that had greeted us, and Immy, at Longton. The trauma was still alive, alright. Okay, perhaps there was a momentary pang when their opening bowler, Dave Edwards, one of the prime architects of that trauma, felt forced to come around the wicket due to the lunar footholes, but he still took 6/40 as we hustled to 185 all out from 59 overs, Kelsall top-scoring with a grafter's 44. They would have 51 overs to get them.

Reader, it ragged square. At drinks, they were 44/2 from 26 overs. And they had batted well. Mike Longmore, a professional fruit machine player, used those deft hands of his to great effect, eventually making 41 from 104 balls, but Imran's googly was repeatedly thudding into Astle's chest. He may have wondered why one of them elicited cat sounds from around the bat. (The explanation was that, one rainy day, sat around the dressing room, Immy had shown us his repertoire, adding in sound effects. The leggie was a *ftrrr*, the flipper a *woosh*. For some unfathomable reason, the noise for his googly was *miaow*. It stuck. He never needed prompting to send down a *miaow*, but occasionally we would salute a good one in *katzensprache*.)

Last over before the drinks break, with the required rate approaching sixes and me reasoning that two skilful batters blocking the next eight overs would effectively kill the game – also mindful, however, that the man with the fastest double-hundred in Test history (TMWTFDHITH) was still at the crease and could push the button at any moment – I had brought on Roger Shaw, hitherto the bowler of 39 overs in his entire life, who as usual shuffled up in his carpet slippers and dropped it on the spot, albeit not exactly imparting monster revs (each ball was like a carcass in the hyena enclosure: nowt on it). To my astonishment, Astle – a man who, 10 weeks earlier, had advocated us "going hard up front" in conditions tailor-made for his attack – played out a maiden, showing all the sprightly intent of a student stoner deep into the second week of the World Snooker Championships. It was especially baffling given that the only man fully back on the boundary for TMWTFDHITH was on the sweep, while both long-on and deep cow were hanging 10 yards off the edge – something of a concession on a club-sized ground for a man who smote *eleven* huge sixes that day in Christchurch. Off Flintoff and Caddick. What gives, MWTFDHITH?

During the drinks break, I started to bristle at what I considered the rank hypocrisy of it all, particularly as his dealings with the local paper had seen him regularly bemoan the "negative cricket" being played. So, I told Mick 'No way these c***s are winning this' Astley, a thick-skinned son of Burnley who was in for his first game of the season, to go in at short-leg for Rog and start chirping Astle, a job he positively threw himself into. Rog, still some way off perfecting his *doosra* by this stage, rolled out his next over – more *merrily* than Murali – and once again TMWTFDHITH played him from the crease, patting back four dots before punching a single to long-on. Briefly and sheepishly, I started to slow handclap. "Really bringing the crowds back, this…" Didn't go down well.

Anyway, having first made sure he shut us out of the game, TMWTFDHITH went up a couple of gears, smearing a straight six off Immy before skying to mid-off for 43, attempting the same shot. Longmore fell in the same over – at which stage they needed 68 off eight, us six wickets – and they ended up 27 short, six down. We took the winning draw, scoring at 3.12 runs per over to their 3.10 – a handy two points, it would turn out – and as I walked toward Astle for the customary post-match handshake, he said: "Don't ever f***ing bag me out on the field again, mate". Marking the umpires was going to be fun.

We had a quick team de-brief, then I went inside to pick up the conversation, only to be told by one of the umpires, the NSSCL chairman no less, that Astle had already filled out his bit. Oh. He was by now having a beer and holding court with his troops, back to the room. I walked over. "Excuse me, Nathan." Thinking perhaps he hadn't heard me in the hugger-mugger, I tapped him on the shoulder, first offering to buy him another beer. He declined, turning his back. After a moment to weigh up whether to pursue things, I said: "Nathan, I'm not being funny, but what exactly was the difference between what we did at your place, when you said we should have 'gone hard up front, then reassessed' and what you did today?" He told me, curtly, that we had a world-class spinner playing (I assumed he wasn't referring to Rog, who finished with an average of 13.86 that season, at a superior strike-rate to Immy) and refused to discuss it any further, again turning his back.

* * *

Nine points apiece helped neither side in their pursuit of Leek, on a five-match post-Tino winning streak when we travelled there for the next game. On a slow, grey pitch, Immy sent down a typically excellent 25-12-34-5 but they snuck up to 151, after which, with seven overs lost to a tea-time shower and two players on holiday, we ebbed from a promising 57/1 to finish on 113/7, all the while being goaded as "Immershall" by their young opening bowler, Ed Jones. A gap that had been eight points five weeks earlier was now 49. With our always unlikely title pursuit floundering, we then suffered two hammer blows in a week.

First, a one-tonne electronic control panel fell on Moose at work, snapping his femur. With Martin Weston, second change in that 2004 Staffs Cup final, having left us for Cannock & Rugeley three weeks earlier (women and work, rather than over-allocation umbrage), we were now only able to call on the bowlers responsible for 5.37 per cent of the previous season's amateur overs. Our stocks were looking as bounteous as that student stoner's fridge.

Secondly, and more terminally it seemed, Imran was signed by Hampshire following a successful trial game. We were offered a derisory £1,000 in compensation – a fee that Hampshire claimed had been verbally agreed between the agent and our chairman – about which we were extremely unhappy on a number of levels, feelings we conveyed in a fraught correspondence with Hampshire chairman Tim Tremlett as we scrambled to line up a replacement, Mohammad Hafeez and Malinga Bandara among the names mentioned. My involvement in this back-and-forth – along with the weekly email debriefs and opposition dossiers I was compiling each week in a retrospectively transparent ruse of uber-procrastination – meant that even less progress was being made with *Capturing the Imagination: Peronism and the Micropolitics of Desire.*

We were well aware that county cricket was one of Immy's major ambitions – he had played three games for Middlesex in May 2003 and one for Yorkshire in September 2007, without much success, a record he was keen to set right – but we nevertheless had to remind Hampshire that we held Imran's work permit and unless we received fair dues then we could not agree to release him from his contract. It was a game of chicken. We were never going to stand in his way, but our gambit meant we couldn't loop Imran into the charade lest he show our hand, all of which caused him some anguish. In the end, the deadlock was broken by an increased offer and Immy studying the Hampshire fixtures and telling us that we should forget about a permanent replacement: he would be available for four of the last eight games, and would commute from Southampton to Stoke-on-Trent to see the job through. All's well that ends well.

He made his Championship bow for Hampshire that week, taking a county record debut haul of 12/189 in victory at Old Trafford, including 7/66 in the second innings, a nice warm-up for the more important business at Moddershall on Saturday, where Knypersley were the visitors and The Pitch was given its final airing, Kim Barnett requiring a two-second glance when the covers were removed before marching off shaking his head. I won the toss, Shemm's 70 and 49 from the skipper steered us away from a wobbly 75/4, and we declared at 55 overs on 209/8. After two early wickets, Kim then chiselled out a 100-ball 49 and with Staffs vice-captain Paul Goodwin sweeping his way boldly to 55, things were in the balance. Once again, however, Immy broke the game open – he probably should have played in a UPS uniform, so often did he deliver – before laying siege to the rest of the order, finishing with 8/74 as we won by 31 runs, 25 valuable points banked with him unavailable for the next two games.

For the following week's trip to Stone – traditionally a spinner's pitch – we roped in Asad Ali, a lively 19-year-old swing bowler who would go on to play a few ODIs for Pakistan (and who was, coincidentally, Imran's final first-class victim in Pakistan). Asad took 1/60, bowling with great heart and good pace on a featherbed, but he was not Immy.

Another absentee at Stone was Amer, who cried off the night before, telling me he had retreated to Leeds after a row with his father. Unfortunately for this story, one of his friends tagged him in a Facebook photo at the Emirates Stadium, where Arsenal were playing a glorified pre-season friendly against Juventus. Not cool. Nevertheless, a title chase is not the time for po-faced morality to trump more pragmatic concerns, so I quickly PR-ed the situation. After a hasty de-tag and letter of apology – penned by yours truly, which he emailed 'voluntarily' – the water started to flow under the bridge for those who felt we should have cut him loose.

A day later, Thursday afternoon of what would prove a pivotal week, day two of Hampshire's game with Yorkshire, Imran called Hawk and told him not to get a sub-pro as the game wouldn't go into the fourth day. This was the moment it became crystal clear that Immy had not left us fallen soldiers behind on the battlefield, that he was genuinely invested in our 'meaningless' little club cricket story, rather than simply offering a compromise to secure his release to play for Hampshire. He finished with match figures of 5/67 in a 10-wicket win at the Rose Bowl, then headed north, arriving at a mizzly Moddershall in his swanky sponsored Mondeo, something of an upgrade on the rickety white Honda Civic he had trundled around in as a "f***ing league player".

We went into the game in fourth place, five points behind Longton, 10 behind Audley and 27 behind Leek. Opponents Stafford were battling for their lives at the other end of the table. It was not a game you want rained off at that stage of the season, but up at Barnfields we often found ourselves among the water droplets when it was fine elsewhere (I once had a discussion with an umpire on this very point, unsuccessfully trying to convince him that the airborne moisture he could feel wasn't *rain* per se but in fact low cloud, and thus, technically, it was permissible to start play).

For once, the weather was kind to us (eventually), allowing us to get on earlier than anywhere else, albeit with the game reduced to a 36/28-over split, heavily favouring the chasing side's chances of outright victory. It was a big toss to win – becoming even more so when a further seven overs were trimmed off our innings by another brief shower – and Immy bowled incredibly well in the Hebridean conditions to snare 7/41 as we restricted them to 125/9. With Bandaratilleke likely to bowl 11 of our 21 overs, I chucked Immy in as a pinch-hitter. He smeared 48 and we won with a couple of overs to spare. Meanwhile, Audley, Longton and Leek failed to make it to the second innings of their games, leaving us 12 points off top in second. Well well well.

Alas, the karmic tables were turned the following week somewhat, when Audley were the only side to pick up a victory, pushing them back above us into second place. Our game at Burslem had ended at tea with us on 164/8 from 57 overs, a WinViz 52-48 sort of score, even with Imran in the ranks before scooting off to Taunton for the week.

He returned north for our home encounter with bottom side Barlaston, a game we were expected to win at a canter. Roger, Amer and Ali were on holiday, however, stretching already thin resources to graphene levels. From out of the bare cupboard we pulled a once brilliant 44-year-old keeper from the second team, Phil Hawkins, while retaining our 42-year-old coach, Chris Kelsall, whose five years of retirement showed. We had four 'frontline' bowlers, two of whom were 17-year-old first-team freshers with 66 overs between them in their two and five Premier League appearances. Our main seamer, Rob Bagnall, could lay claim to a grand career total of 25 Premier League wickets at 32.3, only once taking more than two in a game. The previous year, he failed to take a wicket in the 17 overs he was given. This season, he had eight at 41 apiece. But we still had Immy, and where there's an emerging world-class leggie, there's hope, even on the sort of glue-pot wicket that greeted us (The Pitch was now a distant memory, on the slow journey to wormfood), hardly an ideal surface for a wrist-spinner. Despite all this, by the evening, this creaking, bedraggled bandwagon would have hauled itself to the top of the North Staffordshire & South Cheshire League for the first time that season.

Not that this felt remotely likely as I was trudging off at 34/7, having been caught at short-leg off a firm leg-side clip, my decision to take first use less a reflection on conditions than the imperative to pick up 25 points. Just as all seemed lost, Immy – whose batting was less terrible than you might imagine (he once made 93 against Shahid Afridi for Norton-in-Hales), but who you knew was never very far from a massive hoy – grafted out a crucial 21, with one of the 17-year-old newbies, Dom Wright, making 13. We crawled up to 78 all out from almost 40 overs.

The mood at tea was not great. Surely, we'd blown it. All those journeys up from Southampton for 78 all out against the wooden-spoonists, a team whose sixth-youngest player was 44 years old. I told the boys that we had a 25 per cent chance of winning (which I probably thought was closer to 10 per cent) and that the plan was to bowl dots and prolong the game, giving Imran the maximum amount of deliveries to do damage. For his part, Immy gave the new/old wicketkeeper a physical demonstration of how he was expected to appeal (essentially: frantically attracting the attention of an air ambulance from the forest below).

The School of Imran paid early dividends when the other 17-year-old, left-arm spinner Matt Stupples, won a caught-behind decision that appeared a little forearm-y (sorry, Tate). A 48-year-old pinch-hitter then ran himself out going for the third, at which point Immy got to work and The Carpenters' *Close to You* started playing on our collective mental jukebox (birds indeed suddenly appeared every time he was near). Barlaston had subsided to 37/9 from 18 overs.

Just as the fat lady was loosening her vocal chords for a duet, the 50-year-old Phil Taylor – father of Northamptonshire's Tom and Surrey's James, not the 16-time world darts champion – smeared two big sixes over cow off Immy and suddenly they were up to 62. Bums were getting squeakier. Thankfully, Baggers snuck one through Taylor to finish with a career-best 3/11 from 10, while Immy took 5/35 as a huge 25 points were secured. My get-out-of-jail celebrations were of such wildness that I forgot to shake the umpires' hands, which they reminded me about when informing me I'd only scored 4/5 on the deportment marks. They upped this to 5/5 after a quid pro quo.

Immy buzzed off to Lord's, we got stuck into some beers, and news drifted in that Leek had lost to Longton, while Burslem had the better of a rain-affected draw against Audley, our next opponents. With three games left, the standings were: Moddershall 270, Leek 261, Audley 257, Longton 254. It was an opportune time to emerge, however shakily, from the slipstream. The bad news was that Immy was only available for the final one of those three games. Or so we thought.

* * *

Hampshire had started a four-day game against Durham at Basingstoke on Wednesday. By close of play that night, they were 65/6 in reply to Durham's 156 and Imran was again on the phone to Hawk asking if we had lined up a sub-pro (we hadn't), again telling him we didn't need to because "the pitch is really doing a lot" and he was "500 per cent certain" the game would be done inside three days. Notwithstanding the likelihood that Immy's calculations had failed to include meteorological factors, once again the mere fact that he was petitioning us was, all told, phenomenal devotion to the cause. It would have been incredibly easy to pull a sicknote, to head back to his Southampton apartment with "a minor niggle" backed up with "the physio says…" But no. He was all-in. And you can imagine how delighted we were to have him for the last push.

The second day's play at May's Bounty positively belted forward (and no disrespect, lads, we weren't too fussed which way it went; we just needed it to be over on Friday): Hampshire fell for 96, knocked over Durham for 179, and by stumps had reached 108/5 in pursuit of 240. At which point all eyes turned to the Met Office and/or sky gods, dependent as to one's view of things metaphysical. Not a great night's kip.

Here we were, 24 hours out from a season-defining game against the reigning champions, and we didn't have a sub-pro lined up – not an easy thing to find at the best of times, even more so at the back end of the season, especially one with Imran's cutting edge and ability to cover the paucity of our bowling resources. I was not relaxed about it all. Given first-class cricket's much higher bar for playable conditions, it felt like something of a high-wire act. Our eggs were tightly nestled together in one collective basket case. Thankfully, the elements obliged in Basingstoke, where shortly after lunch Imran entered at 216/8, game on the line, and, armed with the confidence from back-to-back top-scoring performances for Moddershall, made 8* as Hampshire squeaked home. Immy and his 7/58 match figures then wended their way up to his Potteries digs for the big one.

The pitch at Audley was predictably verdant. They had the 36-year-old-looking-24-year-old Azharullah as sub-pro, about to become a T20 legend for Northamptonshire, and before the match we sat on the outfield discussing whether we should stick to Plan A. In the end, it was redundant; I lost just a third toss in 12 games. Surprisingly, they chose to bat, which could have been Imranophobia, an attempt to disrupt our gameplan, or simply because they felt 25 points were essential. Either way, the nibbly surface blunted some of Imran's edge: he was denied a 12th consecutive five-for and had to settle for a relatively meagre 23-7-42-4, with Baggers, visibly growing into his role, picking up a third career three-for, although Audley recovered from 89/9 to make 130. An eminently f***upable chase.

At tea, I got to (over)thinking. Since the new ball was the chief danger – Azharullah had taken 5/39 against Burslem the previous week – I would protect some of our resources. With Rog still away, Ali Whiston went up to open, while Kelsall Senior slid in at three. Suffice to say it didn't work. Ali nicked Azharullah to slip, Chris had his poles obliterated first ball and we were in a pickle at 40/5 when I entered, the plan to see off the new ball some way from being completed. However long it took, this was the most pressing task. Azharullah was lively and hooping it, but only in one direction. I eschewed all interest in scoring runs, minimising the backlift, crabbing across the crease, blocking half-volleys, and by the time Immy came in at 71/6, I'd dug myself into something of a shotless bunker. Thankfully, he had his mojo and counter-attacked his way to 44 – three top-scoring performances in a row! – in a 53-run partnership that took us to the brink of victory. I walked off with 16 of the ugliest runs imaginable out of the 94 scored while I was at the crease, but it was 20 precious points and mission accomplished.

The post-match refreshments tasted even better when news bubbled through that none of our rivals had won, giving us a 21-point lead over Leek with two to play. On the flipside, they would face the bottom two sides and have Kiwi Test seamer Iain O'Brien to lead their attack. Theoretically, we needed 30 points to seal it, a tricky number inasmuch as one 20-point win and a dominant draw still might not be enough. However, the weather gods did us a hefty favour when the penultimate round of matches – for us, a trip to Wood Lane to face their lager-loving former Windies leggie Mahendra Nagamootoo – were claimed by a week of heavy rain and a showery Saturday. We had Zimbabwean medium-pacer Gary Brent as sub-pro, whose final international appearances had come that year. He came, he hung around looking at a patently unplayable swamp of an outfield until I was sure all other games were off, and he took just £50 of his £250 fee, to cover his petrol. Eight days later, he would email to ask whether we had finished the job.

We therefore headed into the final Saturday needing 'just' five points to wrap it up – assuming Leek picked up 25 against already-relegated Barlaston, who it was rumoured had some kvetch to scratch and might bat first if they won the toss, thus handing us the title before a ball was bowled.

The equation for us had evidently been made much easier by the washout, but it was still far from a done deal, something I had to point out to the reporter who rang me for some pre-match comments and offered wholly premature congratulations. The doomsday scenario was quite clear to me: more rain, a wet pitch, a lost toss, and us getting knocked over cheaply. We were, after all, a team that had been 25/4, 34/7 and 40/5 in our last three innings, a team with one wheel held on by gaffer tape. Not so much a no-fear captain, I was more a 'realistic fear' type. And sure enough, the doomsday played out almost to the letter.

* * *

Instead of raining all week and continuing to tip it down through the weekend – an anticlimactic way to win a title, sure, but preferable, on balance, to *not* winning the title – it rained a lot until Friday morning and then decided, coquettishly, to stop. Friday evening saw some Canutian mopping up, and I arrived at the ground just before 8am on Saturday to find the hardcore back at it. It was a 12 noon start, and the outfield was totally saturated, which it remained after a couple of hours' worth of forlorn forking and sponging and bow-drying. At which point, I had a flash of inspiration and went off in search of a league handbook to find out the minimum permissible boundary distance, which turned out to be 45 yards from the middle of the pitch. We measured this out with a rope – immediately placing a 15m² puddle beyond the new boundary – and refocussed our efforts. (It only occurred to me some weeks later that this is what we ought to have done in these circumstances *regardless* of the weather, since with five points required it would evidently have made run-scoring easier – for the opposition as well, of course, but the result was immaterial – while having only a negligible effect on our ability to take wickets. Immy didn't get too many caught on the fence. Serendipity moves in mysterious ways.)

Players started to dribble in. Every pitchfork, hessian sack and squeegee was in use – even Imran put in a shift on the sponges – but the watery autumn sun and half-hearted winds weren't pulling their weight. It ticked past noon, and news came in that Leek were starting at half-past and would be batting, increasing my fretfulness and the urgency of my solicitations toward the umpires. In all honesty, it wasn't fit – the Hampshire hierarchy would not have been thrilled to see Imran padding about on such sodden turf – but the umpires probably intuited that they would not have made it off the ground alive had they not got the game on – probably intuited that things might have got a little hill-billy – and so a 1:10 start was agreed, with a 49/41 split on overs. I headed for the toilet, where I bumped into Little Stoke's opening bowler, Nick Bratt, to whom I made a proposal: if they gave us this toss, they could have both next season. He relayed it to the skipper, Gaz Morris, part of the Longton team that had mauled us three years earlier and not particularly close to my Christmas card list. He declined, not unreasonably citing the integrity of the competition, and so, Machiavellianism scotched, I went out to toss. Up it went – *please, just give us this one* – and down it came on the wrong side. He grinned like a crocodile. I did my best not to grimace.

The usual (pre-Bazball) reminders about digging in and selling wickets dearly were issued, and off we set on the final leg of this most unexpected journey, five points needed. Unsurprisingly, the wicket was an unadulterated snakepit, with two or three balls an over spitting from the surface like hot oil, and Rog, who hadn't batted for 28 days, soon prodded one to gully. We scrapped to 22/1, whereupon I decided to take a lap of the weirdly contracted field (mirroring a few sphincters, no doubt), keeping to its traditional boundary where some spectators had inched onto *terra* previously *incognita* for a close-up look-see and now appeared to be floating in curious half-and-half fielding positions in the outfield.

I had not made it far when Hawk bunted a long-hop straight to square-leg, and 22/2 became 22/3 when Sam was bowled in the same over. I wandered back to pad up. For tactical reasons, I had switched places with Immy, thinking he might exploit the short boundaries and accelerate the game (which is to say, get the torture over with), but I was too discombobulated to abort the plan before Shemm was sawn off by a rough lbw decision. Imran marched out whirling his bat with intent, then tried to turn his first ball off a length through the leg-side and was caught at point: 22/5.

Four wickets for no runs in 14 balls was not what you would call ideal. Things were not going well. The first batting point was still a distant 53 runs off, five months' hard yakka looked as though it was unspooling like a smashed Richie Benaud leg-spin video, and yet, as I walked out into the swelling catastrophe, I felt remarkably calm. The great enemy for people with attentional issues is an open reality, limitless possibilities, constant decisions. This was a super-defined situation – a *Shawshank Redemption* crawl through 500 yards of shit-smelling foulness – and an entirely unwilled hyperfocus kicked in, helped perhaps by the presence in the opposition ranks of Morris and another alumnus of *The Longton Shellacking*, Richard Harvey, their skipper that day, now Little Stoke's professional and Staffordshire captain but once a Moddershall teammate – and still a friend – whose transfer to Longton had spawned that rivalry. Whenever I felt the forces of distraction impinging, the desire for a short-cut singing its siren song, there were both their faces to keep me on the straight and narrow. *This is not f***ing happening again.*

This is not f***ing happening again – one thing to think it, another to do it. Our immediate task was helped enormously by the ECB's fast-bowling directive forcing the removal from the attack of 19-year-old Dan Colclough, even then a cantankerous purveyor of 63mph dobber-voodoo who at that stage had figures of 7-5-6-5. This was another destiny-tweaking beat of the Japanese butterfly's wings. Without a serviceable third seamer, Coke was replaced by the division's leading amateur wicket-taker in Morris, whose left-arm spin was considerably easier to face on a sticky dog for a right-hander than the off-spin he might have turned to. Still, Morris was an enthusiastic sledger and, along with the equally adept Rob Haydon, they soon lured in Amer, who was chirped relentlessly about his bottom-handed preferences and, despite my repeated warnings to bat with his brain and not his ego, he was caught off the leading edge at extra cover. When Dom padded up to Morris in the next over, we were 45/7 and two punches from the canvas. In came Ali, who would soon be heading to Sandhurst, and he did not shrink before the task.

So far into the zone was I that I don't recall more than a handful of shots: back-to-back extra-cover drives off Morris into Lake Scorebox and, the ball after a vociferous lbw appeal from Bratty (nipped back, may have shaved the top of leg, but stays with umpire's call), an insouciant straight six that cleared the regular boundary and was caught in front of the garage by Hawk, who was fiddling with his mowers as a way of managing his anxieties. Never have 45-yard boundaries felt so welcome. Slowly, we inched up to 75, then 100. Two points. A subdued cheer. At 117, Ali edged Morris to slip. Five runs later, I ran out Baggers trying to farm the strike, bringing 'Monty' Stupples to the crease at a precarious 122/9. Making the next three runs seemed of cosmically vast importance, the difference between having to take an achievable four wickets or a tricky six, particularly on a pitch ill-suited to Immy's box of tricks. There was no more wriggle room.

Those tiny boundaries were now a temptress. I took a single, leaving only one ball of Leach/Stokes anguish before I was able to resume strike, then ran one through third man and scampered back for two to seal that golden third point, celebrating like David Warner reaching three figures at the SCG. *Going nuts, for the 125!* This time, the team's roar was not subdued. It felt pivotal. I was stumped next ball, trying to score 25 off the remaining five deliveries, and walked off with a 100-ball 71 (six fours, four sixes), the best innings I ever played. "Un-f***ing-believable knock, Doggy," said Immy during the interval, before promising he would take care of the rest. There was a sense of giddy jubilation, grizzled supporters struggling to keep a lend of themselves, but I was morally obliged to burst those tyres, to inject the constructive fear. There was a job to finish. Tits could still go up.

Immy nicked off Haydon early on, but Baggers didn't hit his lengths and they edged up to a worrying 42/1, at which point our bowling options were Dom, Rog, Stupps or Sam – a grand total of 146 career first XI overs between them. I opted for Sam, who took a wicket first ball thanks to a smart catch by Ali, standing up. The needle flickered round to 'cautious optimism'. Harvey then bunted a pair of sand-wedged sixes over the tiny boundaries off a couple of not remotely bad balls from a vexed-looking Immy – another 15 minutes of this and bums would not so much be squeaking as leaking – and they were up to 65/2, with Harv now on strike to Sam's ultra-low-trajectory wobblers for the first time and presumably lining him up. Here we were, finally: the endgame.

* * *

As with all stories, all histories, we had been swept along to this crucial juncture by a vast accumulation of details, events large and small, none of them without significance but some evidently more significant than others. This was something my research into Peronist Argentina made abundantly clear: histories are made of contingencies. Change one thing here or another there and it may all have panned out very differently (if, for example, Rosa Parks had given up her seat on that Alabama bus in 1955, or Mark Robins hadn't scored that FA Cup goal at Forest to save a still-trophyless Alex Ferguson's job…). Imran's wickets were of course the most substantial element in our story, but there was also, among other things: the fortuitousness of Tino's ban; Rog's reinvention and crucial early-season interventions with the ball; the usual array of umpiring decisions and catches snared and spilled; advantageous weather; important tosses; several gritty, backs-to-the-wall partnerships; Leek's tardy over-rate, which had cost them six points in deductions; the ECB fast-bowling directive, and so forth. Cricketers understand this contingency intuitively; they know that details matter, that you shape the macro through the micro. Which is a high-falutin' way of vindicating any captain's justifiable fastidiousness about having the right fielders in the right spots and at the correct angles. And so, as Harv looked to put his foot down – right on our throats – I had the wherewithal to heed those mysterious muses of the hunch, who were whispering to me to shift my best fielder, Shemm, from point to mid-off, having given Sam one simple instruction: just don't bowl short.

What followed was the type of moment for which life simply cannot prepare you, a moment of such explosive elation that you have no idea how to behave, no clue what to do or think other than somehow cling on to the delirious outward rush of emotional energy as best you can. It may have been two balls or three, but that same over Harv *screamed* a slap-drive, hard and flat, toward Simon – saving one, albeit five yards off the boundary – who chose this moment of all moments to pull off the best catch of his life and one of the best three, maybe two, that I have ever witnessed: a full-length dive to his right, body three feet off the ground and perfectly horizontal, clutching the vaporising ball one-handed and at full-stretch, Superman-like, to more or less clinch a league title that was, half a second earlier, just as likely not to happen as happen. At which point everyone lost their minds.

This was the point at which the team truly felt that, just maybe, glory was within our grasp. But we hadn't won it yet. And so, as everyone clambered off the impromptu pile-on and tried to find their way back to sobriety, I reminded them that one more wicket was needed. We certainly had the man for the job. Over to you, pro.

Next over, everyone still giddy as kids who had strawpedo'd a week's worth of the fizzy, Immy stood at the end of his run, tossing the ball, blowing warm breath into his hands, eyes like a shark. It took four deliveries, a perfectly pitched googly – *miiaaaoooow* – Dan Hancock groping to find it, ball sidling in through the gate and into the top of middle stump. And then he was off – off out toward deep cover, out beyond the shrunken field of play, into the Outback, the Dreamtime, 10 of us in pursuit, a man on a mission – a mission now completed – a man who refused to leave us behind, refused to let our small dreams die as his big dreams took on ever more solid form. There he now was, screaming, as were we all.

Imran was already on the radar of Cricket South Africa, already an established county cricketer, already in one sense out of the room as a "f***ing league player". But on this day and over the weeks preceding it, he could not have been more in the room, more determined to see things through, to keep coming back with his special leg-spin sauce, his heart and soul, to provide a team (and indeed a whole club) with arguably its greatest triumph. Winning it as a newly promoted team 11 years earlier was incredible, but that was a team stacked with potential game-breakers. This was Leicester City.

Yet still, technically, we hadn't won it: there was the (admittedly remote) possibility of a points deduction for slow over-rate, so we scooted giddily through the remaining overs – Little Stoke knocking off, seven down, just our second defeat – with Imran picking up his mandatory five-for to bring his tally to 80 wickets at 11.13 from 17 innings, the sixth time in his final seven NSSCL seasons he had finished top of the pile. Setting aside that ropey start, he had taken 76 wickets at 8.62, with a dozen five-fors in 14 innings, 4/33 and 4/42 in the other two. Quite the cutting edge, but the "Immershall" tag, although clever, was misplaced. This was no one-man effort. Between Simon's 451 and Sam's 337, our top seven batters amassed 2,760 runs. Only one team got within 10 per cent of that. We stumbled into a gameplan, we exploited the playing conditions, and we gave Imran the platform to do his thing. And sure, those contingencies smoothed our passage. Things fell into place – had Nathan Astle bunted two singles from those 10 scoreless balls off Rog, we'd have finished level with Leek, who would thereby have claimed the crown on number of wins; had Longton taken those two winning-draw points, plus 25 rather than eight at their place should we have crashed and burnt *going hard up front*, they would themselves have been champions by a point, which shows that maybe our strategy wasn't so crazy – but it was far from a perfect storm. We lost our best two players before the season, plus two other quality cricketers. We didn't win for five weeks. We lost our best amateur bowler for the last eight games. Our pro was signed by Hampshire. But we held on. We held on. We went from 10th in 2007 to champions in 2008, an improvement of 118 points. The NSSCL umpires – God bless 'em – voted Chris Lowndes as Captain of the Year, who had taken Burslem from fourth to fourth, with an improvement of 20 points, which I suppose tells its own story.

Emotions roiling, we left the field to a throng of rapturous faces, Immy involved in more hugs than Jürgen Klopp on Champions League night, and one hardcore supporter of the glass-half-empty variety, certainly not one usually given to rhapsodic displays of affection, was on the point of tears when he told me, in a voice gravellier than Sean Dyche after a night on the lash, what he thought of my innings. The feels. We all crave the feels. And this was Cloud 10.

We milled a little, got beers, had some team photos taken, soaked it up, then reconvened in the dressing room for an unscripted 45-minute debrief in which I went round the room, one by one, outlining their input to the season, their role in the story, and thanking them for it. There were tears from the vice-captain, Hawk. And then I got to Immy, who we all wanted to thank from the bottom of our hearts for his brilliance but more so his dedication. In mid-July, still trying to find his place in the professional game, he had refused to accept the either/or between his personal goals and our collective goals. For this, we saluted him. Some lips may have trembled. He told us how happy he was that we finished the job and, after saying his goodbyes, he was gone – back to Southampton, then South Africa and several places beyond, surviving a chastening 23-0-180-0 mauling on Test debut to arrive in England for the 2017 Champions Trophy as the ICC's No.1 ranked ODI and T20 bowler. Simultaneously. A white-ball great.

He has not been a stranger to the club in the interim, dropping in unannounced a handful of times – on one occasion we staged a photo of him signing a fake contract and chucked it on Facebook – his outfits getting jazzier as his hair grows greyer, the twinkle in the eyes as bright as ever. "Every time he's over," says Ramzan, with whom he remains the closest of friends, "he says, 'I want to go to Moddershall' and 'I want to visit Dawn and Dave'. He doesn't forget where he came from." And in early 2022, 'Rambo' even persuaded him to sign a three-year deal with fourth-tier Wedgwood, hoping he might play seven or eight games, although in the end this was scuppered by his wildcard pick in The Hundred. The one match for which he was available, at Rode Park, was not assigned any ECB-qualified umpires, which invalidated his insurance and so his agent withdrew him from the game during the warm-up, 20 minutes before the start.

That Little Stoke match remains, at the time of writing, his most recent outing as a f***ing league player. I don't recall the exact words I said to him that September evening before he left, but the gist was this: "Imran, even if today had not gone how we wanted it to, none of us here would ever have forgotten your commitment to the cause, the effort you put in to help give our story a happy ending when you could easily have been putting your feet up in Southampton. In fact, you probably wanted to get on the road an hour ago! Thankfully, it all worked out well in the end. You will always hold a special place in our hearts and will forever be a legend at this club. Best of luck for the rest of your career."

A few days of Immy-assisted underdog afterglow later, I switched on the laptop and turned again to the piles of Xeroxed academic papers, those dark times now filled with a little more light.